THE BEST INTERESTS ASSESSOR PRACTICE HANDBOOK

Second edition

Rachel Hubbard and Kevin Stone

First edition published in Great Britain in 2018
Second edition published in Great Britain in 2022 by

Policy Press, an imprint of
Bristol University Press
1-9 Old Park Hill
Bristol
BS2 8BB
UK
t: +44 (0)117 374 6645
e: bup-info@bristol.ac.uk

Details of international sales and distribution partners are available at
policy.bristoluniversitypress.co.uk

British Library Cataloguing in Publication Data
A catalogue record for this book is available from the British Library

ISBN 978-1-4473-6818-2 paperback
ISBN 978-1-4473-6820-5 ePub
ISBN 978-1-4473-6819-9 ePdf

Cover design by Andrew Corbett
Front cover image: Alamy Stock Photo/Zoonar GmbH
Printed and bound by CPI Group (UK) Ltd, Croydon, CR0 4YY

Contents

About the authors

Rachel Hubbard is a qualified social worker and Best Interests Assessor (BIA) who is registered as both with Social Work England. She has over 30 years' practice experience in adult social care and mental health work for both the National Health Service (NHS) and local authorities. She had led learning and development for North Somerset Council on adult safeguarding, the Mental Capacity Act (MCA) 2005, the Deprivation of Liberty Safeguards (DoLS), the Care Act 2014, and social work continuing professional development (CPD), including the social work Assessed and Supported Year in Employment (ASYE) and post-qualifying training for social workers, Approved Mental Health Professionals (AMHPs) and BIAs. She has worked for Bristol City Council as a DoLS Coordinator and as a BIA for both Bristol and North Somerset supervisory bodies. She is now Senior Lecturer in Social Work at UWE, Bristol, where she teaches on their undergraduate and postgraduate qualifying and post-qualifying social work programmes. She is the BIA Module Leader and the social work CPD Programme Leader. She is a Doctorate in Social Work student at Cardiff University.

Kevin Stone is an Associate Professor of Social Work and lead social worker at the University of Plymouth. He has worked within health and social care for nearly 30 years. During this time, he has worked in both voluntary and statutory mental health agencies. He was an Approved Social Worker (ASW), converting to become an Approved Mental Health Professional (AMHP) when the former role was abolished, working as a mental health team manager and later as an emergency duty team officer. Following this, he trained as a BIA. Kevin has remained in practice as an AMHP working in the southwest of England. Kevin has published widely in the field of mental health law (domestic and international), focusing on the socio-legal impact of mental health legislation on families and carers, as well as considering mental health social work practice across Europe. He teaches law, social policy and mental health practice to undergraduate and Master's students and supervises doctoral students.

Acknowledgements

The authors would like to thank Isobel Bainton and all at Policy Press for their guidance, patience, understanding and hard work to get this second edition ready in time.

Thanks to all those who supported us with writing the first edition. We continue to be grateful to you all – Tammy Richards, Dameon Caddy, Julie Phillips, Don Jones, Jim Bagnall, Susannah Thomson, Fran Lawrence, Sam Baldwin, Jane Buswell, Sharron Price and Gary Underhill. For this edition, we are also grateful for the assistance of Lucy Series and Roger Laidlaw.

Rachel Hubbard would like to thank Ali, Austin and Floyd Hubbard again for their wisdom, patience, support, tolerance and sense of humour that helped sustain her through writing another edition.

Kevin Stone would like to thank his wife Helen for her understanding while this second edition was being written – everything for a time and a season. Kevin is also grateful to John, Mandi, Ewan, Alan, Corinne, Elsa and Callum with whom spending time is good for his mental wellbeing.

Kevin would also like to acknowledge his colleagues, who it is a pleasure to know and work with, and Rachel Hubbard in particular, for her support, motivation and literary abilities in bringing the book to completion.

Abbreviations and acronyms commonly used in BIA practice

ADASS	Association of Directors of Adult Social Services
AMCP	Approved Mental Capacity Professional
AMHP	Approved Mental Health Professional
BASW	British Association of Social Workers
BBR	British Bill of Rights (proposed replacement for Human Rights Act 1998)
BIA	Best Interests Assessor
BIAx	best interests assessment
BOAT/COT	British Association of Occupational Therapists/College of Occupational Therapists
CIW	Care Inspectorate Wales
CoP	Code of Practice (eg, MCA, DoLS or MHA)
COP	Court of Protection
CPD	continuing professional development
CQC	Care Quality Commission
CRPD	United Nations Convention on the Rights of Persons with Disabilities
CSSIW	Care and Social Services Inspectorate Wales
DHSC	Department of Health and Social Care (was Department of Health, DH)
dol	deprivation of liberty
DoLS	Deprivation of Liberty Safeguards
ECHR	European Convention on Human Rights
ECtHR	European Court of Human Rights
EPA	Enduring Power of Attorney
EU	European Union
HCPC	Health and Care Professions Council
HIW	Healthcare Inspectorate Wales
HRA	Human Rights Act 1998
HSCIC	Health and Social Care Information Centre
IMCA	Independent Mental Capacity Advocate
IMHA	Independent Mental Health Advocate
LGA	Local Government Association
LGO	Local Government Ombudsman
LHB	Local Health Board (NHS local health organisations in Wales)
LPA	Lasting Power of Attorney
LPS	Liberty Protection Safeguards
MA	managing authority

MCA	Mental Capacity Act 2005
MCAx	mental capacity assessment
MCAA	Mental Capacity (Amendment) Act 2019
MHA	Mental Health Act 1983 (2007)
MHAx	Mental Health Act assessment
NMC	Nursing and Midwifery Council
OPG	Office of the Public Guardian
OT	occupational therapist
P	person, or relevant person (ie, the person being assessed for DoLS)
paid RPR	paid Relevant Person's Representative (or paid rep)
RB	responsible body (LPS)
RCN	Royal College of Nursing
RPR	Relevant Person's Representative
SB	supervisory body (DoLS)
SCW	Social Care Wales (was Care Council for Wales)
SLT	speech and language therapist
SW	social worker
SWE	Social Work England
UDHR	Universal Declaration of Human Rights
UN	United Nations

DoLS mapping

The Deprivation of Liberty Safeguards (DoLS) contain prescribed safeguards to protect those who lack capacity. These are articulated throughout this book. The main safeguards in the legal framework are listed below, with page references for the main sections of the book where these safeguards are considered.

1

Introduction

> The world is full of obvious things which nobody by any chance ever observes. (Words spoken by Sherlock Holmes in Chapter 3 of *The Hound of the Baskervilles* by Arthur Conan Doyle, 1902)

Best Interests Assessors (BIAs) are experienced, knowledgeable health and social care professionals who investigate and explore people's lives and care and provide a snapshot of how their care is, or could be, the least restrictive possible. The independent, yet critical, observer role they play can be invaluable in bringing insight into ways to increase a person's ability to make choices about their life. Their ability to notice restrictive aspects of care that have been forgotten, or to identify paths for decision-making that have not yet been explored, is a vital element of their value. Like consulting detectives, BIAs are not there to carry out the functions of other professionals. They are required to observe, scrutinise and offer fresh perspectives on a known situation. They gather evidence by talking to the person themselves, analysing documents, consulting with people who know about the case, sifting through the evidence they find for meaning, and offering alternative solutions. Any actions as a result are handed back to those who have the continuing responsibility to make decisions about the person's care.

The BIA role is a challenging one, as it asks professionals to question the practice of their colleagues and suggest, at times, unpopular courses of action. This is vital or we risk the person continuing to be subject to 'poor care … [that] has infiltrated the culture of the organisation' (Graham and Cowley, 2015, p 24). BIAs can be the eyes that examine darkened corners 'in small places, close to home – so close and so small that they cannot be seen on any map of the world … the world of the individual person' (Roosevelt, 1958) – where Eleanor Roosevelt saw human rights as having their most profound meaning – and act to protect them. BIAs must also consider the power they have to remove these rights, perhaps by considering the five questions for people of power that Tony Benn (1993) asked:

> What power have you got? Where did you get it from? In whose interests do you use it? To whom are you accountable? How do we get rid of you? Anyone who cannot answer the last of those questions does not live in a democratic system.

In order to remain focused on the person and not the interests of those who decide on care arrangements, BIAs should ensure that they are fully aware of their power, accountability and the rights of others to challenge and question the decisions they make.

It is vitally important, then, that BIAs both understand the power they wield and value the role they play in giving voice to those restricted of their freedom to ensure that such restrictions only occur through necessity and that their impact is minimised. The BIA role is still relatively new, so our sense of identity remains fragile. We hope that this book will help to consolidate the BIA identity and explore the impact of how it will change in the future.

Terminology

In this book we use key terms in full at the first mention in each chapter followed by the abbreviation in brackets – for example, Best Interests Assessor (BIA) – and thereafter we use the abbreviation – BIA. A list of abbreviations used in the book and commonly in BIA practice appears at the start of the book.

We use the term 'the person' to mean the person who is being assessed under the Deprivation of Liberty Safeguards (DoLS), called 'the relevant person' in the legislation and Code of Practice. We note that there are different approaches to how language reflects the intersection between people and the disabilities they may experience. We recognise that there are powerful cases made for both 'disabled people' and 'people with disabilities', as examples of these descriptors and preferences regarding this are a personal matter. We have chosen to echo the language used in the Convention on the Rights of Persons with Disabilities (CRPD, 2006) and use the format 'persons with ...' throughout this handbook.

The Best Interests Assessor practice handbook, revised edition

This revised edition of the BIA handbook continues to be designed for qualified BIAs and BIA students as a practical and reflective guide to applying the role to practice. It does not replace the Mental Capacity Act (MCA) 2005 and the Deprivation of Liberty Safeguards (DoLS) 2007 statute or their Codes of Practice (DCA, 2007; Ministry of Justice, 2008) or Welsh Government guidance (Welsh Assembly Government, 2009a, 2009b). It should not be read instead of the increasing number of books on the law in this interesting area, such as Jones' *Mental Capacity Act Manual* (2018), Brown et al's *The Mental Capacity Act 2005: A Guide for Practice* (2015) or Mughal and Richards' *Deprivation of Liberty Safeguards (DoLS) Handbook* (2022). This handbook is designed to complement these law textbooks by offering a resource to explore the ethical and practical challenges of applying this law to practice as a BIA and to offer tools and ideas based on our years of teaching, advising and working as BIAs.

We have found from the first edition that the knowledge from this book is also invaluable for managers and staff in managing authorities, local authority supervisory bodies, including DoLS signatories, as well as health and social care professionals applying the MCA more widely and involved in supporting DoLS decision-making. This second edition is likely to be invaluable to those planning towards the implementation of the Liberty Protection Safeguards (LPS), including those newly taking on necessary and proportionate assessments and decision-making, new scrutiny roles as pre-authorisation reviewers and new responsible bodies, such as within the NHS.

This book does not cover the legal processes for deprivation of liberty outside the DoLS, for example in relation to those living restricted lives in supported living arrangements, extra care housing, Shared Lives schemes or their own homes, which require an application to the Court of Protection, as BIAs do not have a specific role to play in this process. We are aware, however, that the skills and knowledge of BIAs are invaluable to those who are involved in such applications, so this book should offer some guidance to those applying to the Court of Protection under Section 16 MCA. We also do not cover the inherent jurisdiction of the High Court.

This book has been mapped to the statutory requirements for the BIA role as laid out in the Mental Capacity (Deprivation of Liberty: Standard Authorisations, Assessments and Ordinary Residence) Regulations 2008, and the continuing professional development (CPD) curriculum for social workers on the application of the MCA (Beddow et al, 2015).

The book has been designed to consider some of the main practical elements of acting as a BIA, including the context for practice, the challenges of ethical decision-making and the necessity for ongoing learning in the role. We have included case studies, summaries of key information and wider reading as well as reflective questions to help you consider important issues and support your development as a practitioner.

The original *Best Interests Assessor Practice Handbook* was written in 2016–17 and published in 2018. Since then, significant changes in case law, professional regulation and a global pandemic have happened, many of which have directly impacted on BIA practice in England and Wales. The consultation on the draft Mental Capacity Act Code of Practice, Liberty Protection Safeguards (LPS) regulations and training plan became available in March 2022. So we decided that, in order to keep this handbook as relevant, up to date and valuable to practitioners as we have been told it has been, we would write a second edition. It is likely to be at least a year from the time of writing (April 2022) before the LPS are implemented – we have seen estimates of either October 2023 or April 2024 – and a lot of the valuable skills and knowledge we have gathered over the years will still be useful once the LPS are in place. We decided that there was enough new and revised material for a second edition of this handbook to be useful for practice.

So we have revised all the chapters for this second edition and added new case law, professional and practice guidance, reflective activities, research and statistical data as well as the impact of the COVID-19 pandemic. Chapter 10 has been completely rewritten in preparation for the implementation of the LPS and the variety of roles BIAs might play within this framework, including completing necessary and proportionate assessments, acting as pre-authorisation reviewers and the Approved Mental Capacity Professional (AMCP) role.

Structure of the book

The book is divided into three main sections with chapters exploring key elements of the BIA role.

Chapter 1: Introduction

This introductory chapter sets out the structure of the book and introduces some of the key ideas and themes, as well as setting out the main legal framework, case law and developments since the implementation of DoLS, including planned reform of human rights law in the UK.

Part 1: Context for practice

Chapter 2: The BIA role in practice

This chapter considers the BIA's duties, responsibilities and powers, how the role is regarded and the impact of significant case law since its implementation. It explores how assessors can maintain their independence and accountability in the range of contexts in which BIAs work, whether directly for local authorities or as independent practitioners, how to maintain their boundaries from the pressures of expectations in these contexts and the impact of COVID-19 on BIA practice.

Chapter 3: The multi-professional BIA role

This chapter explores the values and challenges of the BIA as a multi-professional identity as well as giving focus to the particular and complementary contributions made by social work, nursing and occupational therapy to the role. It explores reasons why psychologists appear less engaged in the role than other professions, the differences experienced by BIAs practising in Wales, and the contribution of other professional expertise, particularly the potential contribution of speech and language therapists to BIA skills and knowledge.

Chapter 4: Working with others

This chapter explores the practical skills and knowledge required for working with the person, their family, friends and carers as well as other roles relevant to the DoLS. These include advocacy and representative roles, powers of attorney given by the person, advance decisions or powers given by the Court of Protection as well as work alongside safeguarding processes. It considers consultation requirements with the Mental Health Assessor as well as managing authorities, supervisory bodies and professionals involved in ongoing decision-making with the person.

Part 2: Assessment: challenges and dilemmas

Chapter 5: Making Deprivation of Liberty Safeguards decisions

This chapter is structured around the six DoLS assessments and the other decisions that BIAs make during their assessment. It includes updated case law, scenarios and examples to help readers explore these decisions as well as common challenges and dilemmas.

Chapter 6: Evidence-informed practice

This chapter enables BIAs to explore the influences and context for their decisions, and offers tools and models to aid reflection and critical thinking with examples of BIA decision-making. It also offers theoretical and research contexts for commonly encountered conditions in BIA practice, such as dementia, learning disabilities, autism and acquired brain injury, and explores key challenges such as executive capacity.

Chapter 7: Ethical dilemmas in BIA practice

This chapter explores the role of the BIA to act ethically, the challenges of making decisions as a BIA when there are no clear 'right' answers, professional responsibilities towards professional practice and ethical models to assist with making difficult and complex decisions.

Chapter 8: BIA recording

This chapter focuses on the detail of how BIA assessments and decisions are recorded, including guidance on how to ensure that recording meets the highest standards of professional practice, requirements of case law and supervisory bodies. It includes areas where BIAs often seek advice, including getting the details right, writing the appropriate amount, recognising when the person is objecting, writing conditions and recommendations, and including other views.

Part 3: Developing good practice

Chapter 9: BIA continuing professional development

This chapter explains the qualifying requirements for BIAs, as well as their statutory and professional CPD requirements updated for new professional regulators, and offers suggestions for support and resources to achieve these.

Chapter 10: BIA futures

This chapter explains the current understanding of what the replacement for DoLS, the Liberty Protection Safeguards (LPS), will look like. It sets out the LPS as specified in Schedule AA1 MCA and the likely guidance for practice from the draft revised MCA Code and LPS implementation documents available for consultation in April 2022. It also considers the potential future roles for BIAs, whether as frontline health and social work professionals completing necessary and proportionate assessments, as those conducting pre-authorisation checks of LPS assessments or as AMCPs working with more complex assessments. The chapter considers the new learning that BIAs will need to ensure that they are ready for whatever the future holds for the role.

The rest of this chapter sets out the origins and requirements of the BIA role in the international, European, English and Welsh statutes, conventions and case law, including:

- Article 5 of the European Convention on Human Rights (ECHR)
- *HL v The United Kingdom* [2004]
- MCA
- MHA
- DoLS
- House of Lords post-implementation report on the MCA (House of Lords, 2014)
- *P v Cheshire West and Chester Council and another* and *P and Q v Surrey Council* [2014] Supreme Court judgment, referred to as the '*Cheshire West* judgment'
- UN Convention on the Rights of Persons with Disabilities (CRPD) (2006)

The origins of the BIA role

The BIA role was created with the DoLS amendment to the MCA. It was devised to carry out a specific function under this legal framework and is driven by social work and health professional values of ethical practice to promote a person-centred, rights-driven approach and demands defensible, evidence-informed decision-making from practitioners.

DoLS was enacted to fill what was called the 'Bournewood gap' – a gap in the mental health legislation in England and Wales relating to people who were unable to consent to their care in psychiatric hospitals and to whom the Mental Health Act (MHA) 1983 did not apply. The Bournewood gap was identified by the European Court of Human Rights (ECtHR) when judging whether the *HL v The United Kingdom* case had breached Article 5 of the European Convention on Human Rights (ECHR).

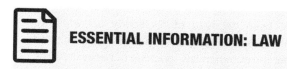

ESSENTIAL INFORMATION: LAW

Article 5 (ECHR)

Right to liberty and security

1. Everyone has the right to liberty and security of person. No one shall be deprived of his liberty save in the following cases and in accordance with a procedure prescribed by law: ...

   e) the lawful detention of persons ... of unsound mind ...

4. Everyone who is deprived of his liberty by arrest or detention shall be entitled to take proceedings by which the lawfulness of his detention shall be decided speedily by a court and his release ordered if the detention is not lawful.

European Court of Human Rights (2010)

ESSENTIAL INFORMATION: LAW

HL v The United Kingdom [2004]

HL was a man with a profound learning disability and autism who had been living with his carers, Mr and Mrs E, for three years following over 30 years as a resident of Bournewood Hospital in Surrey. While attending a day centre, HL became agitated and Mr and Mrs E, who were usually able to calm him, were not available. A doctor was called who administered sedation and HL was admitted to Bournewood Hospital where he became agitated again. Detention in the hospital under the MHA 1983 was considered but he was not detained as he appeared compliant and did not resist admission. He was admitted to the hospital as an informal patient. Mr and Mrs E asked for him to be discharged home to them but the consultant psychiatrist refused.

Mr and Mrs E started legal proceedings on the grounds that the detention was unlawful as the MHA was the only legal framework (at the time) that he could lawfully be detained under. The hospital claimed that the common law doctrine of necessity was enough to detain him lawfully. Mr and Mrs E took the case to the ECtHR after the House of Lords dismissed their claim in 1998.

The ECtHR found that HL had been deprived of his liberty unlawfully at Bournewood Hospital as the detention of a compliant, mentally incapacitated patient could not be justified under the common law 'doctrine of necessity'. The court noted that HL was deprived of his liberty as the professionals involved exercised complete control over his assessment, treatment, contacts, movement and residence and that he 'was under continuous supervision and control and was not free to leave'. The court also noted the lack of procedural safeguards under the common law 'doctrine of necessity' including his inability to consent to the arrangements as a result of his mental disorder and the lack of speedy access for him to appeal the decision to detain him.

Summarised from Jones (2016, pp 299–300)

 ESSENTIAL INFORMATION: LAW

The common law doctrine of necessity: a legal perspective

English law is uncompromising in its definition of necessity and considers that acts must meet a high threshold in order to be considered legally necessary, such as the person involved being at genuine immediate risk of harm. The principle has its basis in a Victorian case, *R v Dudley & Stephens* [1884], where two shipwrecked sailors killed their dying cabin boy and ate him. The court found them guilty of murder on the basis that there was not sufficient proof that it was essential to kill the boy; they were expected to hold out for rescue. Sympathy for their predicament translated into token sentences of six months' imprisonment in the place of the usual hanging. That sympathy may persist but the law has not lowered the bar perceptibly for the proof needed to prove that an act was undertaken by necessity.

The strict definition of necessity has been followed in more recent times where people have sought to prove that possession of illegal drugs has been necessary for the alleviation of medical conditions. In the case of a double amputee who was taking cannabis for pain relief, *R v Quayle and others* [2005], the court ruled that other (legal) medical alternatives were available. Statute takes precedence over case law and the defence of necessity is not available in these cases firstly (as the court in *Quayle* found) because Parliament had put a legislative scheme in place to deal with the supply of drugs, and chronic pain could not equate to the risk of serious injury that case law requires.

Necessity cannot be applied to deprivation of liberty because it circumvents the safeguarding regime in place under the MHA 1983. The leading case is *HL v The United Kingdom* [2004], where an autistic man was detained under the doctrine of necessity due to a crisis in his behaviour. Because he did not resist his detention in hospital, he was deemed compliant and recorded as a voluntary patient. Because of the absence of procedural safeguards and referral to court, the health authority was found to have breached Article 5 and deprived HL of his liberty unlawfully. The DoLS were implemented to ensure that the doctrine of necessity could no longer be used in circumstances where the MHA is not considered to apply.

Therefore, the only occasion when necessity can be used to treat a person who lacks mental capacity is when action is needed in an emergency. Imminent danger of death may be sufficient for necessity, for example where a patient is unconscious and requires lifesaving treatment in the absence of advance directives (for example, where a Do Not Attempt Cardiopulmonary Resuscitation (DNACPR) order is not in place). The doctrine of necessity for emergency medical treatment assumes consent where a patient would consent if they were able to do so – or at least there is no indication to the contrary. The decision-maker must still ensure that treatment is in the patient's best interests, whether or not a full capacity assessment is practical to undertake.

Emma Dmitriev, LLM (solicitor)

It is important to note that, when HL was detained at Bournewood Hospital, the MCA 2005 was not in effect and therefore there was no legally defined process other than the MHA 1983 available for the professionals making decisions about HL's care to follow, in the absence of his capacity to decide for himself. The MCA, and the DoLS amendment that followed, is the core legislation that the BIA applies in practice and BIAs must develop the skills and confidence to apply it consistently.

 ## ESSENTIAL INFORMATION: LAW

Mental Capacity Act 2005

Five principles of the Act (p 19)

1. A person must be assumed to have capacity unless it is established that they lack capacity.

2. A person is not to be treated as unable to make a decision unless all practicable steps to help them to do so have been taken without success.
3. A person is not to be treated as unable to make a decision merely because they make an unwise decision.
4. An act done, or decision made, under this Act for or on behalf of a person who lacks capacity must be done, or made, in their best interests.
5. Before the act is done, or the decision is made, regard must be had to whether the purpose for which it is needed can be as effectively achieved in a way that is less restrictive of the person's rights and freedom of action.

Two-stage test of mental capacity (p 42)

1. *Diagnostic test*. Does the person have an impairment of the mind or brain, or is there some sort of disturbance affecting the way their mind or brain works? (It doesn't matter whether the impairment or disturbance is temporary or permanent.)
2. *Functional test*. If so, does that impairment or disturbance mean that the person is unable to make the decision in question at the time it needs to be made?

The 'causative nexus' from case law, for example *PC v City of York Council* [2013], emphasises the need to establish that it is the mental impairment that is causing the inability to decide rather than anything else.

Functional capacity assessment (p 45, para 4.14)

A person is unable to make a decision if they cannot:

1. understand relevant information about the decision to be made
2. retain that information in their mind [long enough to decide]
3. use and weigh that information as part of the decision-making process, or
4. communicate their decision (by talking, using sign language or any other means).

Best interests checklist (pp 65–6)

If the person has been assessed to lack capacity to make the decision at the time, the following must be considered when making the decision on the person's behalf:

- encourage the person's participation in making the decision;
- identify all relevant circumstances;
- find out the person's views, past and present wishes and feelings, beliefs and values and any other factors the person themselves would have taken into account;
- avoid discrimination on the basis of the person's age, appearance, condition or behaviour;
- assess whether the person might regain capacity;

- if the decision concerns life-sustaining treatment, to not be motivated in any way by a desire to bring about the person's death;
- if it is practical and appropriate to do so, consult other people for their views about the person's best interests and to see if they have any information about the person's wishes and feelings, beliefs and values;
- avoid restricting the person's rights by considering less restrictive options;
- take all of this into account when deciding by weighing up all of these factors.

Summarised from the MCA 2005 Code of Practice (DCA, 2007)

It is important to note that the BIA role is specific to the requirements of the DoLS framework, as summarised below.

 ESSENTIAL INFORMATION: LAW

Deprivation of Liberty Safeguards 2007

History
The DoLS were brought into statute using the Mental Health Act reforms of 2007 and are detailed in Schedule A1 and 1A MCA. They came into effect on 1 April 2009. They are an amendment to the MCA 2005, with a supplementary Code of Practice (Ministry of Justice, 2008) to work alongside the main MCA Code of Practice (DCA, 2007), meaning that all the principles of assessment and decision-making included in the MCA are also embedded in the DoLS. The Care Quality Commission (CQC) and Care and Social Services Inspectorate Wales (CSSIW) were made responsible for monitoring the application of DoLS in England and Wales respectively.

Structure
The DoLS are designed to offer legal protection to those who may be deprived of their liberty in hospitals and care homes in England and Wales. A deprivation of liberty may be made legal by the following method:

- The managing authority can complete an *Urgent Authorisation* and send it to the supervisory body where the person meets the criteria for DoLS to legally deprive the person of their liberty for seven days, with the option to extend to 14 days in certain circumstances.
- The managing authority must also apply to the supervisory body for a *Standard Authorisation* at the same time in order for the six DoLS assessments to be carried out. This can be used to authorise a deprivation of liberty where the

person meets the criteria for up to 12 months. The authorisation can be reassessed and reauthorised for up to 12 months for as many times as the person remains eligible according to the six DoLS assessments.

- The person, their representative or the managing authority can ask the supervisory body during the time of the authorisation for any of the six DoLS assessments forming the DoLS authorisation to be *reviewed*.
- The person has the right to *appeal* against the DoLS authorisation in the Court of Protection under Section 21A MCA.
- Those who are deprived of their liberty under DoLS must have a *Relevant Person's Representative* (RPR), whether a family member or friend or a paid representative if there is no one else eligible to act. Both the person and the RPR have a right to the support of an *Independent Mental Capacity Advocate* (IMCA) under Section 39D MCA to enable them to exercise the person's rights.
- The person also has a right to support from an IMCA in other circumstances within the DoLS assessment and authorisation (see Chapter 4 for details of DoLS IMCA roles).

Six assessments

When a DoLS application has been made by the managing authority the supervisory body must commission the following six assessments to decide whether the person requires a DoLS authorisation or not:

1. *Age assessment* to confirm whether the relevant person is aged 18 or over.
   a. Completed by BIA.

2. *No refusals assessment* to establish whether an authorisation to deprive the relevant person of their liberty would conflict with other existing authority for decision-making for that person, for example, where an advance decision or someone with a health and welfare Lasting Power of Attorney or deputyship refuses to support the DoLS authorisation.
   a. Completed by the BIA.

3. *Mental capacity assessment* to establish whether the relevant person lacks capacity to decide whether or not they should be accommodated in the relevant hospital or care home to be given care or treatment.
   a. Can be completed by either the BIA or the Mental Health Assessor.

4. *Mental health assessment* to establish whether the relevant person has a mental disorder within the meaning of the Mental Health Act 1983. That means any disorder or disability of mind, apart from dependence on alcohol or drugs. It includes all learning disabilities.
   a. Must be completed by the Mental Health Assessor.

5. *Eligibility assessment* to establish whether the person is ineligible for DoLS because they are eligible for detention (or are already detained) under the Mental Health Act 1983 (2007) or there is a community section of the Mental Health Act 1983 (2007) in place which would conflict with the DoLS authorisation.

   a. Can be completed by the Mental Health Assessor or the BIA if they are also qualified as an AMHP under the Mental Health Act 1983 (2007).

   b. The Mental Health Act 1983 Code of Practice (DH, 2015a, paras 13.49–13.62) includes guidance on deciding whether admission to hospital under the Mental Health Act or DoLS is the preferred legal route.

6. *Best interests assessment* to establish whether deprivation of liberty is occurring or is going to occur and, if so, whether it is in the best interests of the relevant person to be deprived of their liberty, whether it is necessary for them to be deprived of liberty in order to prevent harm to themselves, and deprivation of liberty is a proportionate response to the likelihood of the relevant person suffering harm and the seriousness of that harm.

   a. Must be completed by the BIA.

If the person is assessed to not meet one or more of the six assessments, the DoLS cannot be authorised (pp 11–12).

Role of the supervisory body

The supervisory body is the local authority (or health board for hospitals in Wales) for the area where the person is ordinarily resident (under Care Act 2014 regulations in England or the Social Services and Well-being (Wales) Act 2014). It is the supervisory body's responsibility to:

- commission DoLS assessments from relevant assessors;
- scrutinise DoLS assessments;
- appoint RPRs and IMCAs;
- authorise DoLS applications, monitor the application of conditions and arrange reviews of DoLS authorisations.

When DoLS was first enacted, both local authorities and primary care trusts in England had this responsibility, which passed to local authorities solely when primary care trusts were abolished in March 2013.

Role of the managing authority

Managing authorities are the organisations responsible for the person's care at the time the DoLS application is made, for example, the care home or hospital where the person is currently residing. DoLS authorisations only apply in the place where the person currently lives, so if they leave that hospital or care home, the DoLS authorisation ceases and a new application will be required. Managing authorities are responsible for identifying who needs a DoLS application, providing information to assessors, ensuring that RPRs are in regular contact with the person, acting on conditions attached to authorisations, notifying the supervisory body of any changes in the person's care or level of restriction that might prompt a DoLS review and notifying the Care Quality Commission (CQC) or Care and Social Services Inspectorate Wales (CSSIW) of the outcome of the person's DoLS application.

Summarised from the DoLS Code of Practice (Ministry of Justice, 2008)

The BIA role and responsibilities

The BIA has a clearly defined role within the DoLS framework that is set out in the statute and DoLS Code of Practice (Ministry of Justice, 2008) as well as professional and qualifying training requirements (see Chapter 2 for more information).

 ESSENTIAL INFORMATION: LAW

Best Interests Assessor regulations

The BIA is expected to:

- communicate effectively with people who may lack capacity and with a range of communication issues;
- be experienced and knowledgeable in their area of health and social care;
- apply the legal framework applicable to the role effectively and with an understanding of the need to be responsive to changes as a result of legal decisions;
- be critically reflective and question the decisions of others with professionalism;
- write clear, well-evidenced assessments.

Summarised from Mental Capacity (Deprivation of Liberty: Standard Authorisations, Assessments and Ordinary Residence) Regulations 2008

Initially, the Secretary of State for Health maintained a list of English universities that were approved to offer BIA qualifying education. From 2016, the Department of Health began endorsing BIA qualifying courses (DH, 2016). Later that year, it was announced that social work registration in England was to be moved from the Health and Care Professions Council to a new body, Social Work England, which now includes BIAs as well as those maintaining an Approved Mental Health Practitioner (AMHP) qualification (SWE, 2019a). It also maintains the list of those universities offering BIA qualifying education (SWE, 2020a). In England, there is an expectation that qualifying BIAs successfully complete an academically accredited programme of study. This requirement was never brought in in Wales, although some Welsh BIAs have qualified via English universities. There is also a statutory requirement that BIAs complete learning relevant to the role every year after the year they qualify (see Chapter 9 for more information).

Critical voices on the Deprivation of Liberty Safeguards

It is fair to say that the DoLS have come in for a significant level of criticism since their implementation, whether about the complexity of the legal framework or patchy application of the law to practice (see Chapter 2 for details).

The House of Lords set up a select committee in May 2013 to look at the implementation of the MCA and DoLS. Its findings were published in March 2014, a week before the *Cheshire West* judgment, and praised the 'visionary' nature of the MCA and criticised the complexity of the DoLS. There were suggestions of ways to improve the patchy implementation of the MCA and a recommendation to scrap the DoLS and create a new framework 'with provisions that are compatible in style and ethos to the rest of the Mental Capacity Act' (House of Lords, 2014, p 7).

The CQC (2022a) has identified consistent concerns that had featured in its reporting since the implementation of DoLS in 2009, including:

- variation in knowledge and understanding of DoLS legislation, and in the quality of training;
- poor quality mental capacity assessments and best interests decision-making;
- delays and backlogs at a local authority level and providers not effectively escalating applications when needed.

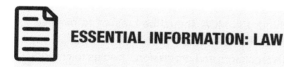

ESSENTIAL INFORMATION: LAW

House of Lords review of the MCA and DoLS

The House of Lords select committee on the implementation of the MCA and DoLS called for evidence on a range of questions in 2013 and heard evidence from a wide cross-section of those who use the MCA, for example organisations representing lawyers, doctors, social workers, local authorities, health agencies and so on, and those affected by the Act, for example, human rights charities, service user and carer organisations, and advocacy agencies, as well as individual practitioners, academics, service users and carers. It gathered evidence from these sources as well as hearing evidence in person at committee hearings. The final report was published on 13 March 2014. The findings are summarised as follows.

Mental Capacity Act

- In response to the question 'Is the Act working as intended?', the answer was: 'We acknowledge the widespread support which the Act enjoys among stakeholders. It is described in unusually enthusiastic language. It is disappointing therefore that the implementation of the Act has yet to receive the same acclaim' (House of Lords, 2014, p 8).

- The evidence suggested that 'the empowering ethos of the Act has not been widely implemented' as the five principles of the MCA were not being fully understood or implemented, often out of ignorance or risk aversion: 'The general lack of awareness of the provisions of the Act has allowed prevailing professional practices to continue unchallenged, and allowed decision-making to be dominated by professionals, without the required input from families and carers about P's wishes and feelings' (p 8).

- The key message from the report was that:

  The Act has suffered from a lack of awareness and a lack of understanding. For many who are expected to comply with the Act it appears to be an optional add-on, far from being central to their working lives. The evidence presented to us concerns the health and social care sectors principally. In those sectors the prevailing cultures of paternalism (in health) and risk-aversion (in social care) have prevented the Act from becoming widely known or embedded. (p 6)

The House of Lords recommended that, in addition to other measures:

- an independent oversight body for the MCA should be created to oversee and monitor the implementation of the Act;
- work should be undertaken with regulators and professional bodies to embed good practice in using the Act into training, standards and enforcement;
- public awareness of the Act should be improved.

Deprivation of Liberty Safeguards

- The evidence supported the purpose of the DoLS, to 'provide protection in law for individuals who were being deprived of their liberty for reasons of their own safety' (p 7), but the safeguards themselves were considered unhelpfully bureaucratic, confusing and alienating to those who were trying to use them in the interests of those they were designed to protect.

- At the time, there was significant concern that far fewer applications were being made than were seen as necessary – it was suggested that thousands or tens of thousands should receive the benefit of these safeguards. Since the *Cheshire West* judgment, this is no longer seen as an urgent issue.

- The committee stated that 'the only appropriate recommendation in the face of such criticism is to start again. We therefore recommend a comprehensive review of the Deprivation of Liberty Safeguards with a view to replacing them with provisions that are compatible in style and ethos to the rest of the Mental Capacity Act' (p 7).

- The Law Commission was subsequently given the task of drafting a replacement scheme, which will become the Liberty Protection Safeguards (LPS). (See Chapter 10 for details of the LPS and its requirements.)

Summarised from House of Lords (2014)

The following week, the Supreme Court published its judgment in the *Cheshire West* cases.

ESSENTIAL INFORMATION: LAW

Supreme Court judgment in the Cheshire West cases

On 19 March 2014, the Supreme Court issued its judgment in the *P v Cheshire West and Chester Council and another* and *P and Q v Surrey County Council* cases (the *Cheshire West* judgment). This judgment was to have a lasting impact on how the DoLS works in England and Wales and the practice of BIAs as a result.

The *Cheshire West* judgment actually concerned three individuals, all of whom had learning disabilities and two of whom were sisters (P and Q, also known as MIG and MEG) who had been subject to care orders prior to the age of 17 so the Court of Protection took over decision-making about their care. The third (known as P) lived where the DoLS did not apply, that is, they were not living in premises registered with the CQC as a hospital or care home so their deprivation of liberty needed to be authorised by the Court of Protection.

P and Q v Surrey County Council

MIG and MEG are sisters who first became the subject of care proceedings under the Children Act 1989 in 2007, when they were aged 16 and 15 respectively. MIG has a learning disability at the lower end of the moderate range or the upper end of the severe range. She also has problems with her sight and her hearing. She communicates with difficulty and has limited understanding, spending much of her time listening to music. She needs help crossing the road because she is unaware of danger. MEG has a learning disability at the upper end of the moderate range, bordering on the mild. Her communication skills are better than her sister's and her emotional understanding is quite sophisticated. Nevertheless, she may have autistic traits and she exhibits challenging behaviour. The sisters were placed in foster care because of concerns about their safety at home with their mother and stepfather.

MIG was placed in foster care where her foster mother provided her with intensive support in most aspects of daily living. She had never attempted to leave the home by herself and showed no wish to do so, but if she did, the foster mother would restrain her. She attended a further education unit daily during term time and was taken on trips and holidays by her foster mother. She was not on any medication.

MEG had originally been placed with a foster carer, who was unable to manage her severe aggressive outbursts, and so she was moved to an NHS facility for learning disabled adolescents with complex needs. She had occasional outbursts of challenging behaviour towards the other three residents and sometimes required physical restraint. She was also receiving tranquillising medication. Her care needs were met only as a result of continuous supervision and control. She showed no wish to go out on her own and so did not need to be prevented from doing so. She was accompanied by staff whenever she left the facility. She attended the same further education unit as MIG and had a much fuller social life than her sister.

The Court of Protection in 2010 decided the care arrangements were in the sisters' best interests and did not amount to a deprivation of liberty. The Court of Appeal in 2011 agreed and laid stress on the 'relative normality' of the sisters' lives, compared with the lives they might have at home with their family and their lack of objection to the arrangements.

P v Cheshire West and Chester Council and another

P was born with cerebral palsy and Down's syndrome and required 24-hour care to meet his personal care needs. Since November 2009, he had been living in

Z House, a spacious, cosy bungalow, with a pleasant atmosphere, close to P's family home, which he shared with two other residents. There were normally two staff present during the day and one 'waking' member of staff overnight. P received 98 hours' additional one-to-one support each week, to help him to leave the house whenever he chose to go to a day centre four days a week and a hydrotherapy pool on the fifth day. He also went out to a club, the pub and the shops, and saw his mother regularly at the house, the day centre and her home. He could walk short distances but needed a wheelchair to go further. He also required prompting and help with getting about, eating, personal hygiene, and continence. He wore continence pads. Because of his history of pulling at these and putting pieces in his mouth, he wore a 'bodysuit' that prevented him from getting at the pads. Intervention was also needed to cope with other challenging behaviours that he could exhibit, but he was not on any tranquillising medication.

At the Court of Protection in April 2011, Baker J held that P was completely under the control of the staff at Z House, that he could not 'go anywhere, or do anything, without their support and assistance' and 'the steps required to deal with his challenging behaviour lead to a clear conclusion that, looked at overall, P is being deprived of his liberty'. It was decided that it was in his best interests for those arrangements to continue. The Court of Appeal, later in 2011, held that his care did not amount to a deprivation of his liberty as, in Munby LJ's view, he 'considered it appropriate to compare P's life, not with that which he had enjoyed before when living with his mother, but with that which other people like him, with his disabilities and difficulties, might normally expect to lead' – a concept known as the 'relative comparator'.

The Supreme Court disagreed with this view, as Baroness Hale explained:

> In my view, it is axiomatic that people with disabilities, both mental and physical, have the same human rights as the rest of the human race. It may be that those rights have sometimes to be limited or restricted because of their disabilities, but the starting point should be the same as that for everyone else. This flows inexorably from the universal character of human rights, founded on the inherent dignity of all human beings.

The Supreme Court rejected the 'relative normality approach' previously used in all three cases and the suggestion made in the Court of Appeal that the fact that P enjoyed a high quality of care with an active social life meant that he could not be deprived of his liberty. Baroness Hale explained:

> If it would be a deprivation of my liberty to be obliged to live in a particular place, subject to constant monitoring and control, only allowed out with close supervision, and unable to move away without permission even if

such an opportunity became available, then it must also be a deprivation of the liberty of a disabled person. The fact that my living arrangements are comfortable, and indeed make my life as enjoyable as it could possibly be, should make no difference. A gilded cage is still a cage.

The judgment suggested that if there were to be a single definition of a deprivation of liberty – an 'acid test' – it could draw on the *HL v The United Kingdom* [2004] case, which referred to HL being 'under continuous supervision and control and was not free to leave'. The judgment also agreed with the National Autistic Society and mental health charity Mind that the following had no relevance to whether the person was deprived of their liberty or not:

- the person's compliance or lack of objection;
- the relative normality of the placement (whatever the comparison made);
- the reason or purpose behind a particular placement.

The decision that all three were deprived of their liberty was unanimous in P's case and by a majority of four to three in MIG and MEG's cases.

Summarised from *Cheshire West* judgment in the Supreme Court [2014]

This judgment significantly changed our understanding of where the threshold lies when people without capacity to consent to their care and treatment in hospitals and care homes could be considered to be deprived of their liberty, including many more in its scope. This resulted in unprecedented numbers of applications for DoLS assessments received by supervisory bodies across England and Wales (see Chapter 2 for more information on the impact of the *Cheshire West* judgment on BIA practice).

Whitaker (2014) wrote cogently after the judgment about the path to the Supreme Court's judgment, informed by their experience as the independent social worker involved in the *Cheshire West* case. They identified that the previous Court of Appeal's judgment in that case had 'established a two-tier threshold for deprivation of liberty and access to human rights' and the Supreme Court's judgment that followed signified a 'long-awaited return to justice' (p 1493). Emphasising the universality of the safeguards to all those potentially subject to infringements of their right to liberty was a significant victory for people who may lack capacity to consent to where and how they are cared for but it brought huge organisational pressures as a result, which we will explore further in Chapter 2. For more detailed exploration of the cases considered in the *Cheshire West* judgment, we recommend 'Chapter 8 The Acid Test' in Series (2022, pp 156–84).

As a result of the House of Lords' (2014) report and the Supreme Court's judgment, the following actions were taken:

- The revised DoLS forms and guidance (DHSC, 2018) for England and the revised DoLS forms and guidance for Wales (Welsh Government, 2015) were published and are now widely used.
- The Law Society's guidance on identifying deprivation of liberty in health and care settings was published (Law Society, 2015).
- The National Mental Capacity Forum, chaired by Baroness Finlay of Llandaff, was created, and annual National Mental Capacity Action Days have been held since 2016.
- The Social Care Institute for Excellence (SCIE, 2020) created an MCA Directory, which includes MCA and DoLS training materials, guidance and resources, including information on the work of the National Mental Capacity Forum and DoLS resources.
- The replacement to DoLS received Royal Assent via the Mental Capacity (Amendment) Act 2019 and awaits implementation. (See Chapter 10 for more information on the LPS and its implications for the future of BIA practice.)
- The Local Government Association (LGA) and Association of Directors of Adult Social Services (ADASS) MCA and DoLS service improvement tool (LGA/ADASS, 2015) was created to help organisations implement these more effectively.

As well as the ECHR, BIAs also need to consider other international human rights conventions, such as the United Nations (UN) Convention on the Rights of Persons with Disabilities (CRPD).

UN Convention on the Rights of Persons with Disabilities (CRPD)

The CRPD (2006) was the 'first comprehensive human rights treaty of the 21st century' with the aim to 'change attitudes and approaches to persons with disabilities'. The Committee on the Rights of Persons with Disabilities was established to monitor the implementation of CRPD state parties by a body constituted by experts promoting inclusion, and advocating for the human rights of all persons with disabilities. The main consideration here for the BIA is the shift from 'substitute' decision-making to 'supported' decision-making as set out in Article 12(3) and 'that the existence of a disability shall in no case justify a deprivation of liberty', as stated in Article 14(1)(b), and how this consideration manifests itself in BIA decision-making.

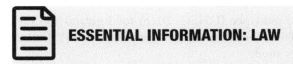

ESSENTIAL INFORMATION: LAW

UN Convention on the Rights of Persons with Disabilities (CRPD)

Article 12 Equal recognition before the law

3. States Parties shall take appropriate measures to provide access by persons with disabilities to the support they may require in exercising their legal capacity.

Article 14 Liberty and security of person

1(b) Are not deprived of their liberty unlawfully or arbitrarily, and that any deprivation of liberty is in conformity with the law, and that the existence of a disability shall in no case justify a deprivation of liberty.

CRPD (2006)

Review of the Human Rights Act 1998

The Articles of the European Convention of Human Rights (ECHR) (2010) and the UK's Human Rights Act (HRA) 1998, which gives them direct applicability to our domestic legislation, exist to protect us as individuals from actions of the state that may harm individual freedoms.

In December 2021, the UK government launched a consultation on its proposals to reform the Human Rights Act 1998, which closed in April 2022. The government's commitment to updating the HRA is driven by a desire to introduce a British Bill of Rights to 'restore a proper balance between the rights of individuals, personal responsibility and the wider public interest' (Ministry of Justice, 2021). Its assertion is that the HRA does not have this balance, as a number of European Court of Human Rights (ECtHR) decisions against the UK government, for example on the deportation of those expressing terrorist sympathies and voting rights for prisoners, have shown. It is important to remember that the purpose and strengths of the HRA are its universal applicability to all public authorities and citizens whether the government approves of that or not. One of the ways that governments find frameworks of human rights unpalatable is because they offer rights to those they find socially acceptable as well as those they do not.

One of the proposals in the consultation is to make claimants show that their case merits the court's attention and resources and that they have suffered 'significant disadvantage' as a result of the breach of their rights. It is also evident in the consultation that the government wishes to emphasise the responsibility of the individual citizen, suggesting that the person's behaviour should be considered when considering whether it should be lawful to infringe on a person's rights. This limiting of the universality of access to the UK's framework of human rights, as well as compensation if a right is judged to have been breached, suggests a willingness by the UK government to restrict the universality of rights that has been established up to now (BIHR, 2021).

The direct contradiction with the principle of universality noted by Baroness Hale in the *Cheshire West* [2014] judgment is significant. This has the potential to impact on those people with mental health issues who currently receive the protection of Article 5 (ECHR) via the DoLS and other legal frameworks in the UK if the individual's behaviour is considered not to meet the standards of personal responsibility that have not yet been specified.

It is not yet clear what the outcome of this consultation on HRA reform will be, but BIAs would be wise to pay attention to the changes that are likely to occur with the UK's human rights legislative framework and their subsequent impact on the human rights of those we work with.

In the following chapters, we explore how the current DoLS framework of legislation, ever-changing case law and guidance is applied to practice as a BIA.

FURTHER READING

To explore the historical, legal and social context of institutional care and the law that surrounds it, read:

- Series, L. (2022) *Deprivation of Liberty in the Shadows of the Institution*, Bristol, Bristol University Press

Part 1
Context for practice

2

The BIA role in practice

This chapter explores the role of the Best Interests Assessor (BIA) as an independent and accountable professional within the Deprivation of Liberty Safeguards (DoLS). This chapter will enable you to understand what is expected of you as a BIA, recognise common challenges and identify solutions and sources of support and advice. The chapter covers the following:

- What are a BIA's duties, responsibilities and powers?
- Critiques of the DoLS and perceptions of the BIA role: 'AMHP-lite' or 'highly regarded'?
- What has been the impact of the *Cheshire West* judgment?
- How do you maintain your independence and accountability?
- What are the different contexts for BIA practice?
- Local authority or independent BIA: What are the differences and challenges?
- How do you maintain the boundaries of the BIA role?
- What do supervisory bodies expect from BIAs?
- BIA practice during COVID-19.
- Key messages, knowledge review and further reading.

Introduction

BIAs are qualified, experienced and independent health and social care professionals who carry out a specific, boundaried role within the DoLS. Their role is set out in the Codes of Practice for both the Mental Capacity Act (MCA) 2005 and the DoLS amendment to that Act (2007) and has been developed through case law judgments. BIAs are employed by local authorities in England and Wales (and health boards in Wales), in their role as supervisory bodies under the DoLS, to assess people who may lack capacity to consent to their care and treatment in care homes and hospitals.

The BIA holds the power to decide whether a person with a mental disorder, whose decision-making, risk identification and management skills may be compromised, should have their right to liberty under Article 5 of the European Convention on Human Rights (ECHR) restricted for a period of time for their own safety. It is an influential and powerful role that should be wielded only with caution and reflection.

What are a BIA's duties, responsibilities and powers?

The statutory regulations for the BIA role set out who can act as a BIA.

ESSENTIAL INFORMATION: PRACTICE GUIDANCE

Who can be a Best Interests Assessor?

Eligible professions

A person is eligible to carry out a best interests assessment within DoLS if they are either (reg 5(2)) –

a) an approved mental health professional;

b) a social worker registered with the relevant registration body (Social Work England or Social Care Wales, depending on where the BIA is practising);

c) a first level nurse, registered in Sub-Part 1 of the Nurses' Part of the Register maintained under Article 5 of the Nursing and Midwifery Order 2001;

d) an occupational therapist registered in Part 6 of the register maintained under Article 5 of the Health Professions Order 2001:

e) a chartered psychologist who is listed in the British Psychological Society's Register of Chartered Psychologists and who holds a relevant practising certificate issued by that Society.

Additionally, the person must –

- not be suspended from the register or list relevant to the person's profession and
- have at least two years post registration experience in that profession (reg 5(3)).

Regulations cited from Mental Capacity (Deprivation of Liberty: Standard Authorisations, Assessments and Ordinary Residence) Regulations 2008

The list of BIA training programmes approved by the Secretary of State for Health was updated in December 2016 (DH, 2016).

The assessments that a BIA must complete and the decisions and recommendations they must make are set out in the DoLS Code of Practice (Ministry of Justice, 2008). There is a detailed legal framework, which has been adapted and refined by case law, that all BIAs must follow, and standard forms for England and Wales to complete to show what decisions the BIA has reached and why (DHSC, 2018; Welsh Government, 2015).

ESSENTIAL INFORMATION: PRACTICE GUIDANCE

What does the DoLS Code of Practice say a BIA must do?

The BIA is appointed by the supervisory body to carry out the following assessments:

- *Age:* is the person of an eligible age (18+)?
- *No refusals:* is there a valid and applicable advance decision or does anyone hold a Lasting Power of Attorney (LPA) or deputyship for health and welfare that conflicts with the planned deprivation of liberty?
- *Best interests:* is the person deprived of their liberty (according to the current definition), are the restrictions in place necessary to prevent harm coming to the person, are they proportionate to the risk of that harm occurring and, if so, are they in the person's best interests (considering the Mental Capacity Act [MCA] 2005 best interests checklist)?

The supervisory body may also ask the BIA to complete the following assessment:

- *Mental capacity:* does the person lack the mental capacity to be able to consent to the care and treatment in the place they are currently residing?

If the BIA is also an Approved Mental Health Professional (AMHP), the supervisory body may also ask them to carry out the following assessment:

- *Eligibility:* would the decision to approve the DoLS conflict with an existing power under the Mental Health Act (MHA) 1983 (amended 2007) or should the deprivation of liberty be made lawful using the MHA instead?

If the BIA recommends the DoLS be authorised, they must also recommend:

- *How long* the DoLS should be authorised for (up to one year).
- Whether any *conditions* should be attached to the authorisation that the managing authority must address or whether any *recommendations* should be made to other involved professionals, such as social workers or health professionals.

- Who the *Relevant Person's Representative* (RPR) should be, taking into account:
  - whether the person has the *capacity* to decide this for themselves;
  - whether the *LPA/deputy* for Health and Welfare could decide;
  - whether the *BIA* should decide;
  - whether the nominated person is *eligible*; if the nominated person will need an Independent Mental Capacity Advocate (IMCA) under *Section 39D MCA*; and
  - if no one is suitable to recommend, to notify the supervisory body that a *paid representative* will be required.

If the BIA decides that the person they have assessed is not eligible for DoLS, they should provide evidence for the specific assessment the person has not met as to why they consider they have not met it. They can also make recommendations on how any restriction the person is subject to can be reduced.

The BIA has duties under the DoLS Code of Practice to:

- identify if a *DoLS IMCA* is needed during the assessment or after, if the DoLS is authorised (see Chapter 4 regarding types of IMCA and RPR roles);
- abide by the MCA *best interests checklist* as set out in Chapter 1;
- *consult* with all those interested in the person's welfare including those with powers under the MCA, such as LPAs or deputyships or Section 39A IMCAs and existing RPRs if appointed;
- consider the views of the *Mental Health Assessor*, the doctor qualified under Section 12 MHA who carries out the mental health assessment (and may also have carried out the eligibility and mental capacity assessments).

BIAs may also be asked to:

- *review* assessments that are part of an existing DoLS authorisation, for example whether the person has regained capacity to consent to the deprivation of liberty or whether the restrictions the person is subject to have increased or decreased and therefore whether the DoLS is still needed or whether new conditions are required;
- assess whether a person is being deprived of their liberty as part of a *third party* application for DoLS (which can be made by other than the managing authority if they have not made an application).

Summarised from the DoLS Code of Practice (Ministry of Justice, 2008)

In reality, if all the BIA does is to follow the instructions of the legal framework, an appropriate assessment can be completed. However, if a BIA were to choose to complete the process by merely filling in the forms, there is a risk that the scrutiny and questioning of decisions made about the person's care in the past would be lost. A considerable amount of the human rights, person-centred spirit that the MCA and DoLS law has embedded in it would be ignored and would merely 'rubber stamp' the care plan, as highlighted in the *Hillingdon v Neary* judgment [2011]. See Chapter 8 for more information on this case and its implications for BIA practice.

Critiques of the DoLS and perceptions of the BIA role: 'AMHP-lite' or 'highly regarded'?

Since the DoLS were implemented on 1 April 2009, they have come in for a significant amount of criticism. The House of Lords (2014) post-legislative scrutiny report (summarised in Chapter 1), published one week before the *Cheshire West* judgment in March 2014 (see also Chapter 1), noted that the DoLS are 'poorly understood by practitioners', are 'frequently not used when they should be', and have received a 'level and breadth of criticism ... that the legislation is not fit for purpose' (p 92), and it recommended that the government 'undertake a comprehensive review ... with a view to replacing it' (House of Lords, 2014, pp 92–3). At the time of that report, low numbers of applications were of significant concern, an issue that the subsequent *Cheshire West* judgment has decisively laid to rest. The report quotes Professor Richard Jones, who describes the DoLS as 'hugely complex, voluminous, overly bureaucratic, difficult to understand and yet [providing] mentally incapacitated people with minimum safeguards' (p 96). The report did note 'nevertheless, support for the purpose underlying the safeguards' (p 96).

Despite input from BIAs *to* the House of Lords report, there was no reference *in* the report to the role. Considering the key role BIAs play in the effective implementation of the DoLS, this lack of attention was curious. It has been noted that the AMHP role under the MHA and the BIA role have widely differing status, as well as length and standard of training. The AMHP role has been well established for some years and a tendency for BIAs to be 'underappreciated' or 'treated as poor relations' has been highlighted (Hubbard, 2012, p 24). They suggested that some BIAs were initially dismissive of the BIA role and saw no value in the safeguards it offered. Some AMHPs, it appeared, considered that the MHA offered more robust protection to people with mental health issues than the DoLS, and the BIA role was not valued as a result. Hubbard (2018) noted that the role 'has shone a spotlight on the rights and lives of people in care homes and hospitals' (p 84).

Evidence from BIAs themselves suggests that whichever route into qualifying and practice is taken, many value the role highly. Hemmington et al's (2021) focus group of BIAs reported a range of reasons for undertaking qualifying education:

> For some social workers it was an expectation of their local authority employer ... Some participants undertook the training reluctantly

or stated that they were not fully aware at the time of what the role entailed, but that generally they came to value the role once they had undertaken the training and were more confident. These views align with the data obtained from the BIA surveys where the benefit of the role and understanding of its professional context developed as time progressed.

Others had completed the training because they were interested in finding out more. Some became interested in the role through discussions with other BIAs or observations about the impact of DoLS in practice; they regularly cited the human rights aspect of BIA work and the focus on autonomy and independence. Seeing other BIAs practising and how much they enjoyed or valued the role was also a factor. There was also an element of anti-oppressive practice identified and there were some concerns about the way people had been treated. They saw BIA work as a way of bringing positive change ... These views connect with the literature which suggest that BIAs have a clear view that their role is to safeguard the legal rights of people whose care amounts to a deprivation of liberty. (p 101)

Others saw the BIA role as a route to promotion, a way to gaining a more independent working life or a way of reconnecting with a social work role they had lost in otherwise bureaucratic and managerialist practice. Many valued the independence of BIA practice:

The independence of the role was [seen as] essential in upholding the human rights element of the DoLS, a theme that was frequently repeated. This independence was expressed in several ways. There was a strongly held belief that because DoLS was underpinned by human rights legislation and case law this offered a degree of protection when making decisions. The adherence to a procedure prescribed by law enabled them to resist pressure from managing authorities and their own employers or managers. This was described as very different to the day-to-day care management that was procedural, constrained by budgets and dependent on higher management approval. (Hemmington et al, 2021, p 102)

Series (2022, p 28) describes BIAs as 'champions of social care detention, viewing its conceptual and regulatory machinery as tools to challenge, rather than promote, restrictive practices'. Although this could be considered damning with faint praise, the core function of 'reducing restrictions to the greatest extent possible within the constraints of the contemporary landscapes of care' (p 28) often offers greater potential for change – what Series calls 'small (but often significant) changes' (p 28) – loosening restrictive care on an individual level more effectively than many government policy initiatives have achieved.

The BIA role was supported by the Law Commission in its consultation on a replacement for the DoLS in 2015. It identified the 'role of the Best Interests Assessor as a particularly important one' (Law Commission, 2015, p 72), making many of the key decisions required for a DoLS assessment and consulting more widely than an AMHP, who is required to consult the person's nearest relative at the bare minimum with wider responsibilities to consult under human rights law. The Law Commission stated that 'the role and expertise of the best interest assessor is a highly regarded aspect of the DoLS' (p 75) and quoted a '2014 report by the Care and Social Services Inspectorate Wales and Healthcare Inspectorate Wales [that] found that they were often the "linchpin" of the system, and a "skilled and valuable resource"' (p 75). During its initial consultations, the Law Commission (2015, p 75) was 'highly impressed by the skills and commitment of individual best interest assessors, including their in-depth knowledge of the law' and believed that BIAs have 'developed into a knowledgeable and well-respected quasi profession, which is comparable to the role of Approved Mental Health Professional'.

The Law Commission (2015, p 75) also noted the impact of the *Cheshire West* judgment on the role of BIAs as follows:

> The expansion in the numbers of DoLS referrals in the wake of *Cheshire West* has placed immense pressure on this resource. Many have argued that the existing role of the Best Interests Assessor is no longer sustainable, and that an independent best interests assessment for every referral cannot be guaranteed (and that, in some cases, it may not be necessary).

The Law Commission (2015, p 77) planned an expanded role for BIAs with a new title 'Approved Mental Capacity Professional (AMCP)', which would 'reflect the equivalence of the level of skills and knowledge' with the AMHP. However, the Department of Health made it clear that it expected a more streamlined and cost-effective replacement for DoLS to meet the significantly increased demand for assessments following the *Cheshire West* judgment. The Law Commission (2016, p 9) noted that 'owing to the vast number of people now considered to be deprived of their liberty following *Cheshire West*, it would not be proportionate or affordable to provide [the oversight of an AMCP] to all those caught by article 5 of the ECHR'. The Mental Capacity (Amendment) Act 2019 that finally made its way onto the statute books includes a drastically reduced role for the AMCP. The specialist scrutiny of the AMCP within the Liberty Protection Safeguards (LPS) will now only be available where the person is objecting to their care plan, where they are placed in a private mental health hospital and in discretionary circumstances. (For more information on the plan for replacing DoLS, see Chapter 10.)

What has been the impact of the *Cheshire West* judgment?

The event that has had the greatest impact on BIA practice since the DoLS was implemented was the Supreme Court's judgment in the *P v Cheshire West and Chester Council and another* and *P and Q v Surrey County Council* cases in 2014 (see Chapter 1). The precedents set in the judgment were authoritative and their impact has been felt across England and Wales.

The judgment clarified the following:

- *Universality:*

  What it means to be deprived of liberty must be the same for everyone, whether or not they have physical or mental disabilities. If it would be a deprivation of my liberty to be obliged to live in a particular place, subject to constant monitoring and control, only allowed out with close supervision, and unable to move away without permission even if such an opportunity became available, then it must also be a deprivation of the liberty of a disabled person. The fact that my living arrangements are comfortable, and indeed make my life as enjoyable as it could possibly be, should make no difference. A gilded cage is still a cage. (para 46)

- *Definition of deprivation of liberty:* Quoting from the *HL v The United Kingdom* (2004) judgment, the 'acid test' of deprivation of liberty hinges on whether the person 'was under continuous supervision and control and was not free to leave' (para 49).

- *Irrelevant factors:* 'The person's compliance or lack of objection is not relevant; the relative normality of the placement (whatever the comparison made) is not relevant; and the reason or purpose behind a particular placement is also not relevant' (para 50).

The impact of this judgment effectively lowered the threshold for those who would be considered to be deprived of their liberty – from very few living in care homes and hospitals to most of those who lived in care homes and hospitals without the capacity to consent to remain there.

The *Cheshire West* judgment had a huge impact on the number of DoLS applications received by local authorities in England and Wales. In the first full year following the judgment (2014–15) a 10-fold increase in DoLS applications was noted in England (HSCIC, 2015, p 5) and a 16-fold increase in Wales (CSSIW/HIW, 2016, p 2). DoLS applications continued to increase year on year after that and a wide gap between applications received and assessments completed has remained an ongoing issue since then for many supervisory bodies across England and Wales (CQC, 2022a; HIW/CIW, 2022). Later in this chapter we will consider the impact the COVID-19 pandemic had on DoLS applications and assessments.

Part of the way that the increasing numbers of assessments post-*Cheshire West* had been managed was via training more BIAs. Demand for qualified BIAs significantly increased in the immediate aftermath of the *Cheshire West* judgment in order to be able to meet this ongoing increase in DoLS applications, although this demand had tailed off in anticipation of the implementation of LPS. Demand for BIA training places increased again when LPS implementation was postponed from April 2022 as local authorities and particularly NHS trusts sought to be as prepared as possible for the likely increase in those needing the knowledge required for LPS practice, even if conversion training will be required for those who will go on to become Approved Mental Capacity Professionals (AMCPs).

A wider model of BIA employment also developed to meet the increased demand following Cheshire West. More independent and agency BIAs were commissioned by supervisory bodies alongside those working for local authorities.

Concerns were initially expressed, alongside those noted by the House of Lords about the DoLS framework itself, that the Supreme Court's judgment has rendered DoLS an ineffectual safeguard as it 'has left a "worryingly high" number of vulnerable people without legal checks on their care arrangements' (McNicoll, 2015), as reported by the Care Quality Commission (CQC). Without sufficient BIAs (or other assessors, such as Section 12 doctors, or advocates, such as IMCAs), the protections offered by the DoLS are limited as the full framework is not being implemented. The Association of Directors of Adult Social Services (ADASS) and Local Government Association (LGA) responded to the increasing number of applications with a number of resources including a prioritisation tool to help supervisory bodies decide which applications should be assessed most urgently (ADASS, 2014) as well as developing streamlined DoLS forms (ADASS, 2022).

Other measures, including £25 million of funding from the Department of Health, were also used to try to manage the gulf between the number of people needing DoLS assessments and the number of BIAs able to assess. The Department of Health (DH, 2015b) noted that much of this funding was used to increase the number of assessors, including BIAs, who were available to carry out DoLS work, amid concern that this increase did not address the full cost of meeting the increased demands for DoLS.

Alistair Burt, Minister of State for Community and Social Care, gave a timely reminder in the House of Commons on 17 June 2015:

> Although some may baulk at the idea of 100,000 DoLS applications a year, we should remember that every one of those applications represents a person having their care independently scrutinised. DoLS can help shine a light on care that is unnecessarily restrictive and does not put the person's views first and foremost. (cited in Mughal and Richards, 2015, p iii)

Four local authorities in England (Liverpool, Nottingham, Richmond and Shropshire) started judicial review proceedings to challenge the Department of Health's decision not to increase more significantly the funding to local authorities since the Supreme Court's judgment (McNicoll, 2016). Their case was that this has left councils to face the risk of illegally depriving people of their liberty without the financial ability to fund assessments and other work needed to apply the DoLS framework in all cases. However, the High Court decided in *Liverpool City Council and others v the Secretary of State for Health* [2017] that the Department of Health had acted lawfully as local authorities could decide to meet the cost of the DoLS from within their overall funding from central government (McNicoll, 2017).

Cases heard by the Local Government Ombudsman suggested that this did not solve the DoLS application backlog. In 2019, Staffordshire County Council was found to be at fault as it had chosen to adapt the ADASS prioritisation tool and state that 'low and medium priority' DoLS applications would go without assessments altogether as a result of lack of funding for DoLS. This was ruled unlawful and the local authority had to meet its legal obligations to complete all DoLS assessments (Local Government and Social Care Ombudsman, 2019).

How do you maintain your independence and accountability?

In such pressured circumstances, BIAs need to remain calmly focused on the person they are assessing, not the hundreds the supervisory body may still need them to assess. The DoLS Code of Practice (Ministry of Justice, 2008) sets out the following regulations designed to ensure that BIAs are independent from influence in their role.

ESSENTIAL INFORMATION: PRACTICE GUIDANCE

Appointing BIAs and avoiding conflicts of interest

The supervisory body must consider the following when appointing BIAs and other assessors:

- the best interests assessor can be an employee of the supervisory body or managing authority, but *must not* be involved in the care or treatment of the person they are assessing nor in decisions about their care;
- a potential best interests assessor should not be used if they are in a line management relationship with the professional proposing the deprivation of liberty or the Mental Health Assessor;

- none of the assessors may have a financial interest in the case of the person they are assessing (a person is considered to have a financial interest in a case where that person is a partner, director, other office-holder or major shareholder of the managing authority that has made the application for a standard authorisation);
- an assessor *must not* be a relative of the person being assessed, nor of a person with a financial interest in the person's care [the DoLS Code sets out a list of those it considers relatives in this context];
- where the managing authority and supervisory body are both the same body ... the supervisory body may not select to carry out a best interests assessment a person who is employed by the body, or providing services to it; and
- the supervisory body should seek to avoid appointing assessors in any other possible conflict of interests situations that might bring into question the objectivity of an assessment.

DoLS Code of Practice (Ministry of Justice, 2008, p 42, para 4.13)

If you think any of these conditions apply to an assessment you are asked to complete by a supervisory body, it is your professional duty to let your supervisory body know so they can consider whether it is appropriate for you to assess. It is also advisable to notify the supervisory body if there are any other circumstances that might affect you carrying out an independent assessment as a BIA.

REFLECTIVE ACTIVITY

- What impact might the situations outlined in the preceding panel have on the independence of your assessment as a BIA? Consider your independence from care and support decision-making, the management of managing authorities and the demands of your everyday health and social care employer, where relevant.
- What other circumstances might have an influence on the decisions you make as a BIA?
- In the complex realities of practice, what does independence and accountability mean for BIAs?

It can be a challenge for BIAs to step outside their day-to-day experience of care management or medical decision-making to see the person from a BIA perspective. To see the person's current experience of care and treatment and the impact of those restrictions without the ever-present knowledge of budgetary limitations and local policies takes effort and reflection on the part of the BIA. In our experience, BIAs working for local authorities or the NHS are very aware of the pressures on those agencies, so it takes a practitioner of courage to step back from their organisation and question the practice and decisions of others. The BIA role requires them to note poorly thought-through decisions, prioritise the person's views and hold commissioners and providers to account. This requires distance, independence, professionalism and, at times, bravery, as the BIA has to think with a different emphasis to their everyday practice and be prepared to make unpopular decisions or challenge well-established views.

The risk is that, without BIAs who are prepared and able to challenge practice orthodoxy, cases like that of the *London Borough of Hillingdon v Steven Neary and others* [2011] (see Chapter 8) and *Essex County Council v RF and others* [2015], outlined in the following panel, will continue to appear in the Court of Protection.

 ## ESSENTIAL INFORMATION: LAW

Essex County Council v RF and others [2015]

RF was a 91-year-old man, a retired civil servant, who had served as a gunner with the RAF during the war. He had lived alone in his own house with his cat Fluffy since the death of his sister in 1998 and was described as being a very generous man and was a regular attendee at a local church where he had many loyal friends. He had dementia and other health problems that affected his mobility.

In May 2013, RF was removed from his home by a social worker in undignified circumstances because of reported concerns about his welfare and placed in a locked dementia unit. It was not clear that RF lacked capacity at the time and he was removed without any authorisation. The local authority eventually accepted that RF had been unlawfully deprived of his liberty for approximately 13 months (as there was disagreement as to whether he lacked capacity to consent to be in the care home and gaps in the DoLS authorisations in place), during which time he paid for his own care at the home. A settlement in court included £60,000 damages for RF's unlawful detention.

REFLECTIVE ACTIVITY

Imagine that you are the BIA assessing P at the care home:

– How might you have noted during your assessment the decisions made to admit him to the home?
– What role could you play as a BIA in addressing this situation?

We would have started our assessment by identifying the path that brought RF to the care home, which hopefully would have identified the decisions made on admission. We would hope to have identified his friends to find out more about his views and wishes regarding his care and residence. We would also consider how to address the actions of the social worker that led to his placement in such undignified circumstances, potentially via adult safeguarding.

What are the different contexts for BIA practice?

Although the BIA role and processes are set out clearly in statute and guidance, the context that BIAs practice in can vary considerably. Consider the various settings in the following activity. What issues and challenges might arise in these different contexts and how would you deal with them?

REFLECTIVE ACTIVITY

What difference does it make to your practice if you are a BIA:

– In England or Wales?
– Assessing in a hospital or assessing in a care home?
– Assessing as a nurse, social worker, occupational therapist or psychologist?
– Newly qualified or experienced?
– Assessing in a service that is well known to you?
– Assessing outside your usual work location?
– Assessing outside your area of expertise; for example, if you are not familiar with dementia, learning disabilities, autism, adult mental health and so on?

Will you need additional support, supervision, assistance or information for:

- – Contacting the right people?
- – Accessing training?
- – Finding an experienced BIA for advice?
- – Accessing different forms and guidance?
- – Complex decision-making?
- – Having the confidence to say no to completing an assessment that you do not have the skills or knowledge to complete effectively?

Other chapters in this book will give you information on these challenges and provide suggestions for ways to work effectively in these circumstances.

BIA practice draws on a wide range of practice skills and knowledge (as discussed in Chapter 6), and it is unlikely that BIAs have all those needed to assess and make decisions effectively with every person. It may be that you have skills, knowledge and expertise that your supervisory body can use to ensure that the person is assessed as expertly as possible. In the Mental Health Alliance's first report on the implementation of the DoLS (Hargreaves, 2010, p 8), it was noted that:

> Supervisory bodies were failing to ensure that assessors had skills and experience 'suitable to the particular case'. This is rather surprising given that they [were faced at the time] with a much lower number of assessments than most of them planned for, and they should therefore have had less difficulty in allocating assessors with the necessary specialist background, for instance in the care of people with dementia. However, the Code guidance tends to give the impression that the appointment of suitable assessors is just 'good practice' when it is in fact a requirement of the statute.

In the world of BIA scarcity post-*Cheshire West*, the likelihood of supervisory bodies being able to match assessor expertise to the needs of those they are assessing appears even more difficult. The professional responsibility of BIAs to recognise and develop their knowledge and skills remains to ensure that the person they are assessing benefits from a tailored assessment and evidence-informed decisions.

ESSENTIAL INFORMATION: PRACTICE GUIDANCE

Selection of BIA

4.14 Other relevant factors for supervisory bodies to consider when appointing assessors include:

- the reason for the proposed deprivation of liberty;
- whether the potential assessor has experience of working with the service user group from which the person being assessed comes (for example, older people, people with learning disabilities, people with autism, or people with brain injury);
- whether the potential assessor has experience of working with people from the cultural background of the person being assessed; and
- any other specific needs of the person being assessed, for example, communication needs.

4.15 Supervisory bodies should ensure that sufficient assessors are available to meet their needs, and must be satisfied in each case that the assessors have the skills, experience, qualifications and training required by regulations to perform the function effectively. The regulations also require supervisory bodies to be satisfied that there is an appropriate criminal record certificate issued in respect of an assessor. It will be useful to keep a record of qualified assessors and their experience and availability. Supervisory bodies should consider making arrangements to ensure that assessors have the necessary opportunities to maintain their skills and knowledge (of legal developments, for example) and share, audit and review their practice.

DoLS Code of Practice (Ministry of Justice, 2008, p 43)

See Chapter 9 for an activity to explore your knowledge and skills for the BIA and ways to plan your continuing professional development (CPD).

Local authority or independent BIA: What are the differences and challenges?

Since the DoLS were implemented, the ways that BIAs are employed have changed most significantly in response to the increase in demand for assessments since the *Cheshire West* judgment in 2014.

The main models for employing BIAs are:

- BIAs *employed by local authorities*
  - directly in specialist teams either on a fixed term temporary or permanent basis or on contract from an employment agency; or
  - expected to complete a certain number of BIA assessments alongside usual working roles, for example as social workers, nurses or occupational therapists, often on a rota basis.
- *Self-employed* BIAs working independently for a number of supervisory bodies, with responsibility for their own liability insurance, data protection, Disclosure and Barring Service (DBS) checks and so on.

So what difference does how you are employed make to qualifying and practising as a BIA?

Local authority BIAs

A time study for Cornwall Council (Goodall and Wilkins, 2015, p 41) found 'that a majority of BIAs work for and will be trained by local authorities (78%)'.

Training as a BIA can be an attractive means of career development in a specialist area for adult social workers, with training often funded by local authorities for their employees. Local authority BIAs also have the advantage of easy access to the supervisory body and the support and guidance they can offer, including free ongoing training and peer supervision as well as access to internal record systems and ease of contact with colleagues in other teams involved with cases.

In our experience, BIAs who are employed by local authorities and practise alongside their usual working roles are not always supported by their managers to carry out what is often perceived as an additional task. This can mean managers ask BIAs to complete tasks from their usual role during time set aside for BIA work and there may be little recognition of the need to adjust the worker's caseload because of the high demand on their usual team. It may also mean that if the supervisory body asks the BIA to revise their assessment to improve the quality of recording, there is no time in the working day to do this. Goodall and Wilkins (2015, p 47) reported that:

> Many suggest that they are not given enough time by their employers to complete assessments, particularly when their work as a BIA is not their primary or 'core' role. For some, this results in having to work in their own time to meet assessment timescales.

In some areas, BIAs working on rotas may be given 'less complex' DoLS assessments that are more likely to be completed in the time available, although it can mean that people who are living in less settled arrangements may have to wait longer for a BIA assessment. This can mean that the BIA's skills are not challenged by the experience of complex casework.

In our experience, there is often a high turnover of BIAs on local authority rotas and if BIAs only complete one assessment a month for their supervisory body, even with 30 BIAs on a rota, the number of assessments completed per month are unlikely to significantly reduce the waiting lists of hundreds of DoLS applications that some supervisory bodies are currently managing. It can also be a challenge for rota BIAs to meet their annual CPD requirements, for example for refresher training or peer supervision, when their manager may already perceive their BIA work as an unnecessary absence from their usual role. Supervisory bodies are under pressure to meet their statutory obligations to assess and the teams that BIAs are already employed in have their own caseload pressures to manage. It is little wonder that BIAs report finding it difficult to say no to pressure to take on assessments.

There can also be a higher risk of conflicts of interest over involvement in care decision-making, especially in smaller local authorities and specialist services, so BIAs and supervisory bodies need to be vigilant about distance from those who have made decisions about the person's current and future care. For instance, where a person is well known to a specialist service, for example in the case of people with autistic spectrum conditions, a BIA whose day-to-day job is in that team may have the specialist skills required for the assessment but may be too close to the decision-making that has already occurred to be truly independent. It may then be a challenge to find a BIA with that same specialist knowledge, so a supervisory body may appoint a less skilled BIA or would have to look for a similarly skilled independent BIA instead.

These issues should be less of a challenge for those who are employed as BIAs in specialist DoLS teams, separate from local authority care management. Specialist BIAs have the time to manage caseloads of more complex assessments and adapt to specific needs, such as different communication methods and pressing timescales for assessment, for example when courts are involved in decision-making. These BIAs can also develop greater confidence in complex decision-making and receive BIA-focused supervision.

Independent BIAs employed by the supervisory body on a 'per assessment' basis face different challenges. These include access to information about the person, especially contacting care management who will be aware of less restrictive options that have been explored previously, and what potential best interests options could be considered or may be available. We have experienced difficulties when working outside a local authority with contacting social workers or gathering information from local authority databases. Independent BIAs should link up with supervisory bodies to access support, supervision and annual refresher training or link up with other independent BIAs for peer support.

Independent BIAs

Independent BIAs are self-employed, so they must take on responsibility for their own tax, national insurance, insurance liability, data protection, costs, invoicing and DBS checks and for managing their own time into their work schedule. They rely on informal contacts in supervisory bodies to ensure they have enough work and some use social media, such as the Mental Capacity Act and Liberty Protection Safeguards – Discuss! Facebook group, to maintain support, peer supervision and CPD.

It is not yet clear to date what role there may be for independent assessors within the Liberty Protection Safeguards (LPS). (See Chapter 10 for a more detailed explanation of the roles that those with BIA expertise might be able to fulfil in the future.)

How do you maintain the boundaries of the BIA role?

It is essential to remember that the BIA role is a boundaried and specific one that sits solely within DoLS. BIAs assess the person, gather information, consult relevant people, make assessment decisions (see Chapter 5 regarding the decisions that BIAs make), make recommendations and complete a report. The role should have a clear beginning, middle and end. Unlike casework, you are not asked to take an ongoing role in the monitoring or decision-making about the person's care and treatment, although you may be asked to complete a review or a reassessment of the same person in the future.

Those responsible for the person's care, that is, the managing authority, social worker or health professionals, if they are involved, should consider your decisions, conditions and recommendations in their ongoing planning.

If you find yourself doing the following you may have stepped outside the BIA role:

- planning the person's ongoing care, for example discharge from hospital or deciding on which care home a person should move to, beyond identifying and considering best interests options;
- being asked to chair a best interests meeting considering decisions outside the DoLS;
- unless you are assessing for a standard authorisation in advance of a placement, finding yourself exploring discharge options rather than the restrictions the person is currently subject to in hospital;
- advising on medication options or identifying assistive technology.

If you find yourself involved in these decisions, remind yourself of the decisions that BIAs need to make and the information you need to make them. As Johns (2014, p 118) stated when summarising the *Hillingdon v Neary* [2011] judgment, 'in all cases, the BIA should be independent of the care team' and the decisions they make about the person's care. Your supervisory body should advise you on whether what you are being asked to do is appropriate for your role.

What do supervisory bodies expect from BIAs?

Supervisory bodies have significant organisational challenges to meet and are very aware of the considerable number of people who are considered to be deprived of their liberty without a legal framework in place, both in terms of the potential legal consequences for local authorities who are responsible for the decisions made to deprive and the personal impact of being illegally deprived without recourse to appeal. When the managing authority has made an application to the supervisory body for DoLS, it is effectively saying that the person is currently being deprived of their liberty, and the legal framework, under the urgent authorisation, only offers protection for 7 days (now, in many areas, routinely extended to 14 days). This accounts not only for the pressure to get assessments completed but also for the risk of poor quality assessments being completed as quickly as possible and losing sight of the views of the person.

The challenge for those completing BIA assessments post-*Cheshire West* is maintaining the balance of quality versus quantity of assessments. Goodall and Wilkins (2015, p 47) identify from their BIA time study that 'in the narrative data 53% of the [BIAs] told us about "time", with many citing an increased emphasis [from supervisory bodies] on assessment productivity and "time standard" measures with their employer'. This suggests that supervisory bodies are potentially valuing the completion of assessments in limited timescales over the thorough and considered completion of assessments. With the potential for complexity identified in the Goodall and Wilkins study, this suggests that supervisory bodies are risking losing the quality of assessments in the rush to get as many assessments completed as possible. BIAs have a responsibility to ensure that they do not lose sight of the importance of the quality of their decision-making in the rush to complete assessments. Ripfa (2014, p 3) noted that 'adults and carers want assessments that are both technically competent (in terms of following a process) and professional (in terms of containing critical thinking'. It is the BIA's responsibility to ensure that they can maintain both in the face of significant workload pressure.

To help focus practice on those in most need of DoLS assessments, many supervisory bodies use the ADASS prioritisation tool (ADASS, 2014), developed after the Supreme Court's *Cheshire West* decision, to triage the DoLS applications they receive. This asks them to take the following conditions into account to decide which applications should be assessed most urgently:

- whether the person or their family objects to the restrictions or if the person tries to leave;
- what level of restrictions the person is subject to, including one-to-one supervision, sedating medication, physical restraint and restrictions on contact with family or friends;

- whether the placement is new or unstable;
- whether there is a Court of Protection appeal, safeguarding concerns or complaints about the person's care;
- whether the person is in an acute or psychiatric hospital;
- if an existing DoLS authorisation is going to expire.

Applications are rated as high, medium or low priority and the supervisory body may choose which assessments to prioritise. There is always a risk that circumstances may change or the information provided to supervisory bodies is incomplete. In light of this, supervisory bodies and managing authorities should maintain communication to ensure that any changes in the person's care needs, especially increases in restrictions or objections, are notified.

Misuse of the ADASS prioritisation tool was criticised by the Local Government Ombudsman (LGO) (2019) in the case of Staffordshire County Council who chose to reinterpret which cases were high priority and only assess those screened as high priority for financial reasons. They noted that 'Resource constraints can never be a legitimate reason for not carrying out the assessments required by law or statutory guidance. While councils may decide how to prioritise cases, it is not acceptable that the only way low and medium priority applications are resolved is because the people involved move away or die.'

It is also worth being aware that the new powers that the CQC will acquire under the Health and Care Act (2022) (given Royal Assent in May 2022) to review, assess and report on local authority provision under the Care Act 2014 will also include how well local authorities are applying the MCA 2005 and DoLS. This is likely to mean that where long waiting lists for DoLS assessments remain they are going to come under increasing scrutiny.

There is also the risk that measures that BIAs take to encourage the review of care planning and decision-making following their assessments, such as conditions attached to an authorisation or recommendations to health and social care staff, may be neglected or ignored. Managing authorities may not be clear on what they are being asked to do when conditions have not been written clearly, or they may be unaware of their duty to address them. Social workers in overburdened local authority teams may not have the time to address these issues with service users, who may be left in review limbo or have no resources available to address issues relating to the availability and costs of care. However, the safeguard offered by conditions and recommendations regarding reducing restrictions on liberty and exploring less restrictive alternatives to current care provision for the person is an essential element of the protection of rights offered by DoLS as a whole and should be prioritised by both managing authorities and those with responsibility for planning the person's ongoing care.

BIA practice during COVID-19

The COVID-19 pandemic brought significant new challenges across health and social care from when its impact was first felt in England and Wales in March 2020. The challenges of conducting person-centred assessments and balancing individual risks and rights in institutional care have been significant and have directly impacted on the practice of BIAs.

UK government guidance emphasised from the start that the legal safeguards within the MCA and DoLS still applied across hospitals and care homes:

> The care and treatment of people who may lack the relevant mental capacity must always be guided by important principles of the Mental Capacity Act 2005 (MCA) and may in some cases include the safeguards provided by the Deprivation of Liberty Safeguards (DoLS). This was and is the case, before, during and after the pandemic. (DHSC, 2021)

However, for possibly understandable reasons, it became evident that these measures were not given quite as high a priority as infection control measures. The discharge of patients from hospital to care homes with insufficient infection control resources and testing in place in March and April 2020 was identified as a decision that had a huge impact on care home residents' health and wellbeing (Amnesty International, 2020, p 18). The first year that DoLS applications did not increase overall in both England and Wales was 2020–21, which the CQC (2022a) and the HIW/CIW (2022) both ascribed to care home providers and hospitals shifting to managing COVID-19 infections and responding to the measures taken in the initial response to COVID-19. At the same time, increasing completion of DoLS assessments also tailed off, which may also reflect shifting priorities for supervisory bodies during the early months of the pandemic. This reduction in DoLS applications during 2020–21 by managing authorities and measures that closed care home and hospital doors to all but essential staff meant that BIAs' access in person to those they have a legal duty to assess ceased.

The House of Commons and House of Lords Joint Committee on Human Rights report (2021, para 132) emphasised that the

> Deprivation of Liberty Safeguards provide 'indispensable safeguards' for those who are subject to them. Indeed DoLS are more important than ever when those who lack capacity to consent to new restrictions on their freedoms may be subjected to such new restrictions intended to protect their right to life. DoLS provide a framework for verifying that such restrictions are necessary and proportionate. It is vital that DoLS authorisations are in place to ensure persons deprived of their liberty on the ground of mental incapacity have safeguards in place and the means to challenge their deprivation of liberty.

In this context, it has been the BIA's responsibility to ensure that the vital protections of Article 5 (ECHR) relating to restrictions for both mental health and containment of infectious diseases are balanced alongside the Article 8 right to privacy and family life, while the Article 2 right to life is of high priority. Balancing these rights in the interests of the person's physical and mental health and wellbeing has often been challenging, as is aiming to conduct assessments in a manner that accords with the principles of the MCA 2005. Principle 2 regarding taking all practicable steps to support the person to make decisions themselves has challenged BIAs to conduct assessments in a range of formats to safeguard the person's human rights while risk to life from COVID-19 has been at its height.

At the time of writing (May 2022), COVID-19 public health measures are now a matter of personal preference in wider public life. However, continuing restrictions on access to care homes and hospitals for health and social care assessments, including for DoLS, are no longer supported by government guidance (DHSC, 2022a). Care and health settings, like care homes and hospitals, continue to have a responsibility to protect their residents and patients from ongoing waves of infection. However, unless there is an outbreak of infection, restrictions on contact between residents and their families as well as professionals visiting to perform essential functions in relation to the person's rights should not be interfered with as this may constitute a breach of the person's Article 8 right. Measures such as the use of personal protective equipment (PPE) and social distancing may still be necessary to reduce the risk of infection to vulnerable people but infection risk no longer justifies the use of remote assessments by professionals where face-to-face assessment is possible.

Balancing Articles 2, 5 and 8 (ECHR)

The House of Commons and House of Lords Joint Committee on Human Rights (2021) report noted the 'obligation on the State to secure the right to life [as] imposed by Article 2 ECHR ... [which in this situation focuses on] the substantive obligation to take appropriate steps to safeguard the lives of those within the state's jurisdiction' (para 64). It noted that: 'Overall, there were 57,588 deaths in care homes during the period from 2 March to 12 June 2020 which represents approximately 26,230 "excess" deaths compared with previous years. The Covid-19 mortality rate for care home residents was significantly higher than for other people of the same age' (para 95). The report identified that 'the very high number of deaths from COVID-19 in care homes is a matter of deepest concern to us and engages the operational duty to secure life (Article 2 ECHR)' (para 97).

In this context of high risk to care home residents and hospital patients, restrictive measures within care settings, such as restricting freedom of movement, contact between residents and closing their doors to visitors, whether families, friends or professionals, were considered justified, at least at first, to maintain the physical safety of residents.

The risks of the care home setting during the early period of the pandemic weighed against the risks of going home to inadequate care but with much desired contact with family was considered in two hearings in *BP v Surrey County Council and RP* [2020]. The first hearing in March 2020 judged that the risk to BP's health was far greater at home without a care package beyond his daughter's willing support than remaining in a care home with no COVID-19 cases at that time. Measures to improve BP's contact with his family while he remained in the home via video call and window visits using his preferred communication method were planned. One month later, at the second hearing in April 2020, the circumstances had significantly changed. The daughter had found carers to assist her to care for her father in her home and the COVID-19 risk in care homes had increased nationally, so the judge agreed to BP's swift discharge to his daughter's care. The intersecting demands of BP's right to have his physical health protected from serious illness, to exercise his right to a family life through the regular contact he so valued and his right to liberty came together acutely at this time. This case shows the judge weighing evidence of each of the risks afresh at each hearing and shifting his decision-making according to the new circumstances he was presented with on each occasion – a useful model for BIA decision-making regarding changing risk in the wider context as much as in the context of the COVID-19 pandemic.

Kuylen et al (2022) noted from their survey of capacity professionals, including BIAs, during the COVID-19 pandemic that restrictions on liberty and contact on care home residents had caused widespread negative impacts, including increased anxiety, depression and cognitive impacts observed by the majority of respondents (p 4). A 'massive discrepancy' in the ways that different care settings balanced the risk of infection against the risk of increased restrictions was also noted (p 5), which was attributed to poor guidance to care homes and the different ways these were interpreted. The difficulties of checking information given by care homes about people deprived of their liberty for accuracy in person was a concern of many respondents (p 7).

BIA assessments and Principle 2 MCA 2005

Principle 2 MCA 2005 1(3) states that: 'A person is not to be treated as unable to make a decision unless all practicable steps to help [them] to do so have been taken without success.' It is a vital underpinning to all BIA assessments, especially DoLS mental capacity and best interests assessments, and we consider this more broadly in Chapter 4. Although COVID-19 restrictions on conducting assessments have now been lifted (DHSC, 2022a) the learning from this experience remains valuable for priorities in BIA assessment practice. BIA assessments must prioritise Principle 2 MCA 2005 to enable positive rights-driven practice. When the doors of care homes and hospitals were closed to BIAs and other health and social care professionals in March 2020, the need to use safer methods to assess became a priority. It has always been lawful to conduct video assessments within the MCA 2005, unlike for the MHA 1983 (2007) where remote assessments are unlawful.

There was a sharp increase in the use of video calling software for both social contact for care home residents and hospital patients and assessment practice as this allowed face-to-face, if virtual, contact between BIAs and those they assess. However, confidence in using phones, tablets, reliable Wi-Fi or data connections and the challenges of communicating with those who may lack capacity, have communication issues and be unfamiliar with using these communication methods made video calls for remote assessment a limited tool in terms of effectiveness. BIA respondents to the Social Work England survey highlighted 'how important it is to "use our senses" in person to get a full picture of the person they are assessing' (p 87) and noted how difficult this was when assessing via video call (Hemmington et al, 2021). The ability to use sight, sound, smell, hearing and touch to understand the risks and restrictions to the person and to explore the care environment where the person resides is vital to the assessments that BIAs complete and the limitations of what is seen and experienced when conducting assessments remotely must not be underestimated.

In person but socially distant assessments had the potential to be more effective in terms of the sensory understanding of the person in their environment and their interactions with care staff, and perhaps also their family, but there were other challenges. The need to wear a mask to reduce the risk for both assessor and assessed person interfered with communication and risked causing anxiety. The use of evidence from other assessments, from those who care for the person regularly were suggested as alternatives to support decision-making. However, these are little substitute for actually meeting the person where they live.

In the end, the principle remains that you as an assessor must take all practicable steps available to you at the time. How much evidence can you gather in as many different forms as close to the person as possible to confidently establish the person's level of mental capacity or best interests in as practicable manner as possible? This has been and remains a matter for your professional judgement and ethics to decide. However you complete a BIA assessment, you need to be able to justify your approach in the context of prevailing guidance. Doing whatever is easiest or quickest is not a sufficient argument for limited effort in assessment practice.

KEY MESSAGES

- BIAs work in a legally contested and ever-changing area of health and social care practice.

- BIAs' knowledge, skills and critical reasoning are essential to maintaining the ethical and rights-based requirements of DoLS.

- **BIAs** need the support of their supervisory body to manage competing demands and professional qualities, including support from their organisation, access to crucial information and critical reflection to practise effectively.

- **THE** future of the BIA role is changing, but the skills, knowledge and expertise of BIAs will remain in great demand as they form the core of rights-driven health and social care practice.

- **POSITIVE** rights-driven assessment and decision-making practice should always be at the heart of good BIA practice, no matter how challenging the circumstances.

KNOWLEDGE REVIEW

- **WHICH** decisions will you be making as a BIA?

- **WHAT** law and statutory guidance sets out the framework for the role?

- **WHAT** changes have affected BIA practice most recently and why?

- **WHY** is it important to maintain boundaries between your usual work and BIA practice?

- **WHAT** guidance, information and support do you need for BIA practice and who should provide this?

- **WHAT** impact might your BIA employment status have on your work?

- **HOW** can you prioritise the person's rights where public health measures reduce your ability to assess the person, their relationships and environment?

FURTHER READING

Your first sources of information about your role as a BIA should be:

- Department for Constitutional Affairs (2007) *Mental Capacity Act 2005 Code of Practice*

- Ministry of Justice (2008) *Mental Capacity Act 2005: Deprivation of Liberty Safeguards: Code of Practice*

You can also find comprehensive practice guidance for the BIA role in:

- Mughal, A. and Richards, S. (2022) *Deprivation of Liberty Safeguards Handbook*, 2nd edn, Hounslow, BooksWise

- Mental Capacity Act and Liberty Protection Safeguards – Discuss! Facebook group. Ask the group admin if you can join

Independent BIAs may find the following useful:

- British Association of Social Workers (2014) *Code of Ethics Addendum: Additional Guidance for Independent Social Workers* gives useful guidance for those practising as independent BIAs, whether social workers or not

Where these are online resources, web links are available in the References section.

3

The multi-professional BIA role

This chapter focuses on the multi-professional nature of the Best Interests Assessor (BIA) role and the benefits and challenges of the range of professional backgrounds and contexts that BIA practice is drawn from and operates in. The chapter explores the following:

- The value and challenges of the BIA role as a multi-professional identity.
- What social work brings to the BIA role.
- The links and overlaps between the Approved Mental Health Professional (AMHP) and BIA roles.
- The contribution nurses and occupational therapists make to the knowledge and skills available for BIA practice.
- Why there are so few psychologist BIAs.
- Other perspectives relevant to BIA practice.
- Key messages, knowledge review and further reading.

Introduction

BIAs must be qualified and registered as one of the four eligible professional groups (social work, occupational therapy, nursing and psychology). The following sections explore the reasons behind the decision to focus on these professions, the impact of different professional backgrounds on BIA practice, and the experiences of some of these professionals when training and developing their identity in the BIA role.

The value and challenges of the BIA as a multi-professional identity

The reasoning behind the government decision to enable a broad range of professionals to be eligible to undertake the BIA role (see Chapter 2) can be viewed from several different positions. From a social policy perspective, not aligning the BIA to one professional background ensures that, at least in principle, there should not be a shortage of workers for local authorities to draw on. Moreover, professionals in the same four fields are also eligible to qualify as AMHPs, as noted in Schedule 1 of the Mental Health (Approved Mental Health Professionals) (Approval) (England) Regulations 2008 and Schedule 1 of the Mental Health (Approval of Persons to be Approved Mental Health Professionals) (Wales) Regulations 2008, which can be seen as a pragmatic approach that maintains an equivalence between these roles. It was reported, at the time of the change that introduced both the AMHP and BIA roles, that 'the intention was to move away from a "closed shop" to the opening up of roles to "approved professionals" including nurses' (David Pennington, a civil servant in the Department of Health involved in defining these roles, cited in Pulzer, 2008). This was in reference to the fact that prior to the amendment of the Mental Health Act in 2009, there was only the Approved Social Worker role, and the intention was to broaden out the professional backgrounds of those taking on this key element of statutory mental health practice.

REFLECTIVE ACTIVITY

Research that recruited as many BIAs as possible has found a distinct professional profile to BIA demographics:

–   Cornwall Council's BIA time study (Goodall and Wilkins, 2015, p 17) recruited the following participants: '507 BIA respondents, 87% (443 respondents) are Social Workers; 9% (49 respondents) are Nurses; 4% (22 respondents) are Occupational Therapists and 1% (5 respondents) are Psychologists'.
–   Social Work England's study (Hemmington et al, 2021, p 9) recruited the following participants: 'All 248 respondents were practising BIAs. There were 221 social workers [89%], 22 nurses [9%] and 5 occupational therapists [2%].' No psychologists were recruited to this study.

Think about your own professional background:

–   Is your profession in the majority or minority among BIA practitioners? What impact might that have on the continuing professional development (CPD) you will need for the role?
–   What knowledge, skills and experience do you have that you think are relevant for BIA practice?
–   What impact does your profession's value base have on your confidence and understanding of the BIA role?
–   What might you find challenging and how will you seek to address this?

It is vital to recognise that each BIA profession brings with it a standard set of skills, knowledge and worldview associated with the professional training and experience linked to that role. Each of these professions expects a rigorous academic qualification to have been completed before individuals begin to practise, so must have roots in academic study and evidence-informed practice.

Each profession requires its members to register with a professional body and adhere to the regulator's codes and standards of conduct and professional ethics, which suggests that those coming to the BIA role have a diverse but clearly defined professional identity. Each profession brings a distinct set of values that have at their heart a person–centred approach to care and support of others. The work that BIAs carry out is the same, but it would be foolish to suggest that there is a generic BIA workforce. The unique experience that each professional has as part of their practice experience, working contexts and range of human experience means that each individual professional contribution enriches the identity of BIAs; if these can be shared within the profession, the role is enriched. As we explore further in Chapter 6, one of the key decisions that BIAs make is to identify instances of deprivation of liberty. This is a good example of how the different BIA professions can contribute skills and knowledge from their knowledge bases. For example:

- How can nurses contribute to the exploration of the impact of medical treatments? For example, medications that may sedate, alter behaviour or manage the person's mood, or the nature of inpatient hospital care?
- How can occupational therapists use their skills to identify less restrictive alternatives to physical restriction and restraint and make use of assistive technology?
- Are social workers more aware of the social circumstances of people and the potential for community-based solutions to those restricted in care environments?
- What untapped potential contribution might psychologists make that, as yet, has not had a significant impact on the BIA role?

Each of these areas is valuable in itself, but how do those acting as BIAs respond when they do not share the experience and knowledge of their BIA colleagues? What impact does not sharing a professional background have on feelings of, and actual, competence?

The structures that BIAs work within also have a significant impact on how professional practice is formed and develops. Those who are used to working for a local authority are likely to find that the supervisory body is a familiar environment, with working practices and expectations similar to those in their usual workplace. However, a nurse based in a National Health Service (NHS) hospital or a psychologist used to an integrated community mental health or learning disability team might find the broad range of Deprivation of Liberty Safeguards (DoLS) work and local authority context strange and alienating. The fact that the Department of Health originally located English BIA training programmes within universities providing post-qualifying social work programmes means that a sense of alienation from your profession, if you are not a social worker, may be compounded from the initial point of training for the role. What is essential is to find the essence of the BIA identity that is most closely aligned to your professional experience and knowledge base and learn from your colleagues and your supervisory body about how to understand and implement the valuable contribution you can make.

What social work brings to the BIA role

Social work as a profession is a contested idea. Parker and Doel (2013, p 2) suggest that: 'When we pose the question "What is social work?" we expose ourselves to multiple interpretations and associated queries.' This is because 'social work is not a homogenous entity' (p 2) – it mirrors the diversity and complexities of the communities, experiences and locations it serves. International efforts to define social work as a profession have taken a very broad view, as shown in the International Federation of Social Work's (IFSW, 2014) global definition, which we recognise is far wider than the specific context for practice in England and Wales where DoLS applies. However, even in the context for practice in England and Wales where BIAs work there will be variation in expectation and experiences for social workers as individual practitioners.

Much of how social work as a profession identifies itself is bound up in the roles that social workers do and the actions they take. Parker and Doel (2013, p 3) identify that, in the UK, 'social workers apply balm to social and individual troubles, challenge disadvantageous social structures and practices while, somewhat paradoxically, also being an integral part of those social structures by virtue of being (predominantly) employed by local government'. Interestingly, this also describes the role, and paradox, of the BIA, which does suggest that there is a powerful symbiosis with the social work profession at work.

Could this be why there is a tension at the heart of BIA practice? Is acting on behalf of a local authority (in its role as a supervisory body) a contradiction when also asked to scrutinise and challenge decisions made by that local authority on behalf of the person who may be deprived of their rights because of those decisions? If that is the case, then how do social workers (and BIAs) work effectively across both contradictory activities?

PERSPECTIVES: PROFESSIONAL

Interview with a social worker and BIA, practising in England

I think that the Best Interests Assessor role is a natural development from social work with adults. I have experience of working with people with mental health issues, people with dementia, people with learning disabilities and brain injuries and when I started thinking about the BIA role it just felt like a natural development from that. I could use my observation skills, my reflection and analysis skills, my assessment and recording skills and my knowledge of the law to help the people I assess fight for a less restricted life. It feels like the social work I couldn't do when working in care management. It has also really suited me as I like working in an intensive short-term way – just getting a snapshot of the person's life and working out what could be less restrictive. It feels like the social activism I had hoped to be doing when I first got into social work.

I get to apply the social model of disability in a real way and find I really value when the case law we have to work to as BIAs lines up with my values. For example, when the Court of Appeal judgment in the *Cheshire West* case came out [see Chapter 1], I was unhappy that I might have to apply what I felt was a discriminatory decision. There is no way that I was going to agree that a deprivation of liberty for a disabled person was in any way different from any other person – it felt like I had to say that a disabled person has no right to expect equality. So, I was delighted when I read Baroness Hale's words in the Supreme Court's judgment on the same case – you know, 'a gilded cage is still a cage'. It was such a positive message and restored my sense that the BIA role is a valuable one that I do because (when it works) it promotes positive change in people's lives, protects them from unnecessary restriction and gives them hope that things can improve.

From our experiences of working with BIA students and practitioners, social workers often mention the following as being a valuable intersection between their two professional roles:

- working knowledge of the social model perspective to promote rights, develop strengths-based approaches and person–centred practice;
- experience of working with the law, whether statute or case law, to promote rights;
- knowledge of social care resources available to support alternatives;
- experience of working to safeguard rights;
- more confidence in assessing mental capacity and making best interests decisions in risky situations where risk aversion may be an issue.

Those surveyed by Social Work England (Hemmington et al, 2021, p 81) agreed: 'Respondents believe that social work connects well with the BIA role, with an emphasis on safeguarding, person–centred practice and self-determination. The social model and a holistic view of the service user were clearly articulated.'

The kinds of challenges social workers often face when acting as BIAs include the following:

- getting drawn into 'care managing' assessments, such as finding long-term solutions to issues, rather than focusing on the detailed and time-limited nature of BIA assessments and decision-making;
- less confidence in working with the restrictions that medication and medical treatment may contribute to deprivation of liberty.

Social work has the advantage of being most closely identified with the BIA role, but it is vital to recognise that other professionals also make essential and distinctive contributions to the wider BIA role and that social workers have much to learn from other professions acting as BIAs.

The links and overlaps between the AMHP and BIA roles

Many BIAs are also qualified AMHPs under the Mental Health Act (MHA) 1983 (2007) and often act in both roles. As the DoLS was designed to fill a gap in the legal protections offered by the MHA, there are certainly some advantages in already having the knowledge and skills to apply the law to detain people with mental disorders at times of risk to their safety. It is our experience, however, that AMHPs who are BIAs can find that the different roles present additional challenges, especially if their employer expects them to act in both roles. These challenges may include:

- moving between two complex legal frameworks with different requirements for decision-making and recording;
- understanding and applying the complex interface between the MHA, DoLS and other legislation;
- seeing the BIA role as distinct, valuable and separate from the AMHP role.

PERSPECTIVES: PROFESSIONAL

Interview with a social worker, AMHP and BIA, practising in England

How did your professional background prepare you for BIA practice?

Social work practice had prepared me by instilling an understanding that service users can need advocates to uphold their rights and care providers do not always have their service user's best interests at heart. This was coupled with the legal education I had studied to become a social worker and, through CPD [continuing professional development], I had a sound knowledge of the MCA, its relationship with the Human Rights Act and our legislative development in this country in its response to mental disorder.

What benefits did your professional background give you for BIA practice?

As an AMHP I was already familiar with the responsibility of being required to make decisions relating to the person's deprivation of liberty and weighing up the associated judgments and decisions associated with that. I felt that I was able to bring a social perspective to each assessment due to my social work background. As an AMHP I was also able to understand the interface between the MHA and the MCA, particularly when considering if using the DoLS is a less restrictive approach. The skills that all AMHPs use in recording and formulating arguments is invaluable in BIA work, as evidencing how you reached a decision is vital to defensible practice. As an AMHP you are acutely aware of the need to produce court-worthy recording and reports that can withstand legal scrutiny as a result of well-considered and evidence-informed practice. Both roles ask you to decide whether depriving the person of their liberty is in their best interests but as a BIA you are also asked to establish if the deprivation of liberty which is occurring is proportionate to the risk of harm the person poses to themselves.

What challenges did the BIA role present for you, bearing in mind your professional background?

The role of the BIA is different to that of an AMHP; as an AMHP I can make an independent decision from the local authority. This is different for the BIA, as although the local authority acting as supervisory body cannot refuse to authorise DoLS, it can ask for more evidence for the judgement you have reached. This is unlike the role of the AMHP; I am solely responsible for the decisions I make. The other challenge for the AMHP when undertaking BIA work is that the starting point is different. As an AMHP, you are being asked to decide if a deprivation of liberty is needed or needs to continue if the person is still in hospital, as no such restrictions may be in place. As a BIA, you are being asked to validate if a current deprivation of liberty is justified or is actually occurring.

What would you advise professionals from a similar background to you about coming into the BIA role?

As a BIA, understanding the Mental Health Act can be very beneficial, even if you are not an AMHP. Knowing about the alternative legal framework of the MHA can help you see whether DoLS offers the legal framework that is most supportive of the person's rights. The application of the social perspective in mental health is just as important in BIA work. You will be familiar with

> completing legal paperwork, and needing to produce court-worthy documentation which is a transferable skill to the BIA role; you may find it a different experience though and disempowering to be commissioned by a supervisory body, and be responsible to them, but this can also add some reassurance as well.

This AMHP identifies that there are distinct similarities between the AMHP and BIA roles they fulfil. They identify the following key elements:

- Legal knowledge is required in both roles to ensure that the law is applied in the least restrictive manner and in the person's best interests.
- Identifying where the burden of responsibility lies for decision-making is similar in both roles, but not the same: the AMHP is solely responsible for their decisions, albeit they are reached with other professionals and families; the BIA also has to consult others to reach a decision, but the supervisory body retains ultimate accountability for the decision the BIA makes.
- In both cases there is a requirement for well-evidenced and thought-through decisions recorded clearly with the expectation that they may be considered in a court environment.

The contributions nurses and occupational therapists make to the knowledge and skills available for BIA practice

In our experience, nurses and occupational therapists on BIA qualifying training often find the experience challenging, at times because it appears to ask them to abandon their existing professional knowledge and skills in favour of adopting a 'social work' way of thinking.

It is essential that nurses from all specialisms and occupational therapists recognise the core skills, knowledge and values they bring from their profession that are directly relevant to the BIA role as well as bringing an open-minded attitude to developing the new ways of working and thinking needed to be a BIA.

Nursing

The Royal College of Nursing (RCN, 2022) set out eight principles that define what nurses do, 'describe what constitutes safe and effective nursing care, and cover the aspects of behaviour, attitude and approach that underpin good care'. These include 'nursing staff treat[ing] everyone in their care with dignity and humanity – they understand their individual needs, show compassion and sensitivity, and provide care in a way that respects all people equally'.

PERSPECTIVES: PROFESSIONAL

Interview with a mental health nurse and independent BIA, practising in England

What benefits did your professional background give you for BIA practice?

Wide experience of mental health issues particularly those of older adults. Nursing experience particularly helpful with psychotropic medication issues. Community nursing experience of a wide range of hospital and nursing homes (admissions and discharges). Mental health community nursing experience of working closely with social workers, psychologists, general nurses and allied health professionals.

What challenges did the BIA role present for you, bearing in mind your professional background?

As nurses form a minority of BIAs and most authorities were already used to working with social workers and Approved Mental Health Professionals in the application of the Mental Health Act, it took a while for me to develop an acceptable (to different local authorities) language and format for completion of DoLS assessment forms.

What would you advise professionals from a similar background to you about coming into the BIA role?

Try to be familiar with the way social workers work with and complete appropriate paperwork and develop a strong idea of the 'least restrictive intervention or option'. Be careful to hang on to your values around keeping the individual at the heart of things and don't get swamped by the DoLS bureaucracy or by nursing home's nursing processes and duty of care.

This mental health nurse recognises core elements of their expertise (such as psychotropic medication and the context for care) and values (for example focus on the person) that they bring to the role, while offering a willingness to be flexible and adapt to differences from their experience in a way that is open to these new ways of thinking.

PERSPECTIVES: PROFESSIONAL

Interview with a learning disability nurse and BIA, practising in England

How did your professional background prepare you for BIA practice?

Learning disability nursing work has empowerment of individuals as one of its core values. My work in a community team was primarily about supporting individuals to remain in their own properties within the community. As such there are strong similarities with the work of a Best Interests Assessor in deciding what the least restrictive care and residence for a person is. The question I often start with when completing my BIA work is 'Can the person live in their own home? If not, why not?'

What benefits did your professional background give you for BIA practice?

Working within an inpatient environment I experienced decisions being made on behalf of others by family members with the loudest voice or professionals with the highest 'status'. Although this could be perceived as a negative, it served to develop my interest and engagement initially with the MCA, then later with DoLS as a Best Interests Assessor. Specific knowledge that comes in useful daily with assessments includes knowledge of relevant medication and behaviour management. Part of my previous clinical role was the implementation of a positive behaviour management package. The focus of this was primarily around the avoidance of restrictive practice and therefore fits with the principles of the MCA/DoLS.

What challenges did the BIA role present for you, bearing in mind your professional background?

I spent a large proportion of my pre-BIA career in a secure hospital setting. As such, I was aware of the challenges that staff face in these environments, both in terms of the resources available and some of the cultural and hierarchical barriers to change. I think at times this experience can affect my decisions, allowing me to accept more pragmatic compromises rather than pushing for the ideal solution.

What would you advise professionals from a similar background to you about coming into the BIA role?

That the role of BIA is as much 'art' as 'science'. When I first qualified I would often get hung up on processes and then struggle when definitive answers were not available. As time went on, I began to realise that what was important was the values you worked by. Although process is important, it is arguably more important to stop and ask yourself, 'Why am I making this decision and for whose benefit?' If you are person-centred in your answers, then you can reassure yourself that you are on the right track. What is particularly important for me as a nurse was to reframe their duty of care. I still view that I have a duty of care to ensure someone's physical safety. Now, however, I am aware that this duty extends to include their emotional wellbeing and is not used to override their human rights and right to self-determination.

This learning disability nurse has identified that their professional values have a strong role to play in acting as a BIA and that explicitly considering how their values contribute to their work enables them to think more about the person as a whole, not just their physical safety. They recognise that their work has given them specific knowledge of value to BIA practice, including knowledge of medication and the use of techniques to manage behaviour that challenges staff positively.

PERSPECTIVES: PROFESSIONAL

Interview with a general nurse and independent BIA, practising in England, including for the Court of Protection

How did your professional background prepare you for BIA practice?

Coming from a general nursing background to BIA practice has meant I can assess the person's complex health needs, including the nature of their diagnosis, the likely progression of their condition, any advance care planning or end-of-life care decisions, and can identify any areas of concern about how they are being cared for. My experience has been with older adults and dementia, which has been invaluable for BIA work as so much of my work has been in this context. I can also talk 'nurse speak' to nurses in care homes and hospitals, and have them be less defensive about how they are caring for the person as they know I understand where they are coming from. I know there are times when nurses are more defensive towards other professions as they feel that their actions are being criticised and this hinders the honest sharing of information that is needed.

What benefits did your professional background give you for BIA practice?

I have knowledge and understanding of a range of medical conditions, a range of medication and when it should or shouldn't be used, the pressures that operate on clinical staff that can drive their decision-making, how to use the MCA as a nurse, skills to read medical notes including doctors' handwriting, and can interpret and explain DoLS in a way that medical staff can understand. It has helped me to develop as a nurse as, in line with the NMC [Nursing and Midwifery Council] code, I feel more confident to challenge poor practice as a BIA and I know that I can advocate for people more as a BIA than I have in the past. I am able to look at the whole person, including any social issues having an impact on the person, and they all interact.

What challenges did the BIA role present for you, bearing in mind your professional background?

I have needed to learn about conditions that I had no experience of (for example learning difficulties) and have needed to ask for advice from others. I am aware that at times I have fallen into the trap of being risk-averse and being more understanding of the pressures on hospital and care home staff, which has led me to be more inclined to agree with their plans rather than challenging decisions. I think social workers are often braver at challenging these decisions.

What would you advise professionals from a similar background to you about coming into the BIA role?

You need to learn a lot of stuff, especially about the law and how it will impact on your everyday practice. BIA work is time-consuming, there is a lot of procedure and process involved with tight timescales and you will have to work to improve your documentation skills. It is massively rewarding and challenging. It will take you out of your usual work bubble and give you a much better understanding of the MCA and how to make best interests decisions to enable people to make their own decisions. I heartily recommend the role but advise that you need at least five years' experience in practice, ideally with older people in a community setting.

Social Work England's research into BIAs (Hemmington et al, 2021, p 110) found that:

> there was some speculation from social workers that nurses would default to a 'medical model' approach and be less likely than social workers to use a social perspective. Equally, there was a concern that nurses might be less likely to act with the requisite independence and capacity to challenge where people's rights are not being upheld. These ideas were challenged within this research. Despite concerns about nurses' proximity to, and deference within, hierarchical 'health systems' and the ways in which these might hamper their capacity for challenge, there was interesting emerging evidence that an aspiration to challenge hierarchies, or oppressive and poor practice, was of itself a motivating factor for nurses to seek the specialist training in the first instance. Contrary to perceived wisdom, then, some nurses may be attracted to the roles precisely because they are interested in furthering a rights-based agenda through their ability to take an independent stance with an enhanced capacity for challenge.

These findings align with how the nurses interviewed above integrated their professional backgrounds, their values and their understanding of health and social care contexts with the rights-driven approach required for BIA practice. Hemmington et al (2021, p 81) noted that (in common with those nurses interviewed above) 'a small number of nurses thought that their own practice was becoming more attuned with social work ideas because of their time as a BIA'. This was presented in a positive light: 'The values and ethos of social work are reflected in this role ... Empowerment, principles of social justice, human rights providing vulnerable people with a voice, addressing inequalities, determination, supporting people's right to choice and involvement in their life, challenging discrimination (nurse BIA)' (p 81).

Occupational therapy

The World Federation of Occupational Therapists (WFOT, 2012) defines occpational therapy as follows:

> a client-centred health profession concerned with promoting health and well being through occupation. The primary goal of occupational therapy is to enable people to participate in the activities of everyday life. Occupational therapists achieve this outcome by working with people and communities to enhance their ability to engage in the occupations they want to, need to, or are expected to do, or by modifying the occupation or the environment to better support their occupational engagement.

This aligns occupational therapy as a profession focused on practical solutions to help people get what they want out of their lives, whether physically or psychologically.

PERSPECTIVES: PROFESSIONAL

Interview with an occupational therapist and local authority rota BIA, practising in adult social care in England

How did your professional background prepare you for BIA practice?

As an occupational therapist [OT] I need to have a good idea of applying the Mental Capacity Act, assessing capacity and consent in my practice, though not every day as the focus in my usual role is on providing equipment to enable the person to move as freely as possible in their environment, which can include reducing any restriction of movement. My values as an OT are very like the values I have as a BIA. As a BIA, I am focused on finding out if care is unnecessarily or overly restrictive and reducing that restriction to improve the person's quality of life. As an OT working in adult social care, I look at the person's home environment and find ways to improve their access to the world outside and work in a holistic and client-centred way to make sure that the person is able to get to where they want.

What benefits did your professional background give you for BIA practice?

I have experience as an OT of working to get family carers on board with best interests decision-making, which has been helpful when thinking about how to explain what I am doing as a BIA with family members. My approach has been to focus on explaining in simple terms what I do, as you can never be sure of their reaction or how much they understand about DoLS. I have found that I need to prepare a way to explain DoLS that starts with my involvement being nothing to worry about and being focused on the person being cared for without too much restriction.

What challenges did the BIA role present for you, bearing in mind your professional background?

I have found that I need to be far more aware of issues of capacity and consent – usually as an OT I am doing 'nice things' for people, helping them to get things that will help them to get out more or to be more independent at home, but the BIA role has asked me to think more about balancing the risk of harm with the person's physical safety. I have also needed to encourage care homes to apply for DoLS for people, educate them about what DoLS is for and learn more about how to use the MCA to give covert medication correctly.

What would you advise professionals from a similar background to you about coming into the BIA role?

I would think about what kind of training suits you, as I did a short intensive course which suited me, but I am aware it is not for everyone. I also work on a monthly rota where I rarely have enough time to complete my assessment in the time allowed and the four weeks [between BIA assessments] always goes very quickly.

Hemmington et al (2021, p 84) noted that occupational therapy BIAs were:

> thought of as using a biopsychosocial and holistic approach to their work. Their particular knowledge of equipment, mobility issues and how to help people function in their lives were seen as well-matched to the BIA role. Promoting independence and looking for less restrictive options were areas of their usual practice that occupational therapists could bring to the role. ... positive comments includ[ed] ... specialist knowledge of equipment and aids that can help reduce restrictions allowed people more freedom. A number of people reported that occupational therapists were good at writing well-structured reports and used a solid analytical approach.

Interestingly, many of those interviewed considered their profession to take a uniquely holistic view of the person, although each acknowledged a specific focus to their thinking based on their profession's main purpose. Other issues that nurses or occupational therapists have mentioned to us as challenges in acting as a BIA include the following:

- maintaining an up-to-date knowledge of applied case law;
- balancing the risk of harm coming to the person with their rights to autonomy and freedom from restrictions;
- challenging hierarchies and power or status held by those who control decision-making and what influence their professional background might have in their confidence in disagreeing with these established viewpoints.

Social work as a profession is very aware of the operation of power in these forms as part of its values and ethical framework (see Chapter 7) and this might be something that BIAs from other professions might want to explore.

Why there are so few psychologist BIAs

It was our intention when initially writing and revising this book for the second edition to ensure that all professional groups able to practise as BIAs would have their voices represented. We struggled to contact psychologists who have trained and are practising as BIAs and suspect that this is because there are so few trained and in practice. We have had experiences that suggest that, anecdotally, there is an underrepresentation of psychologists acting as BIAs. For example, in the 14 years to date that we have run BIA qualifying education, only two psychologists have completed the course (both in the first year). In our practice experience, we have never met a practising psychologist BIA and had no response when we previously asked the DoLS Facebook group for psychologists who are qualified as BIAs to talk about their experiences. Responses to our question suggested that others involved in BIA education had had similar experiences and suggested various explanations, including a lack of interest in the role based on a perceived lack of status, lack of time to assess and lack of professional and employer support for involvement in both the AMHP and BIA roles.

We heard from those within The College of Social Work who originally developed the BIA capabilities in 2013 and training endorsement scheme, in conjunction with the College of Occupational Therapists and Royal College of Nursing, that the psychology professional body did not engage in the consultation process. We spoke to a psychologist at a conference who said she had been interested in training as a BIA when DoLS first started, but that her employer refused to release her for the training as they did not want to release such a highly paid professional to act as a BIA. This suggests that even where there has been some interest in the role from the profession, psychologists may not have been supported by their employers to train or practise.

It is difficult to establish exactly how many psychologists are qualified and practising as BIAs as there is no national data on the role available at present. Efforts were made to contact BIAs for three studies into BIA practice. The Cornwall Council BIA time study had 1 per cent (five respondents) who identified themselves as psychologists (Goodall and Wilkins, 2015, p 17). Social Work England's research (Hemmington et al, 2021, p 76) had no psychologists responding to its survey of practising BIAs. An unpublished BASW Wales survey of Welsh BIAs conducted in 2020 also had no psychologist BIA respondents.

As a result of this limited information and lack of contact with practising psychology BIAs, it has been difficult for us to identify what resources and knowledge are lacking from BIA practice as a result of the lack of a professional psychology perspective.

Other perspectives

BIA practice in Wales

Devolved government in Wales allowed the Welsh Assembly Government to adapt the application of the DoLS in Wales from that of England. Health is a devolved government responsibility, although criminal justice and other areas of Home Office responsibility, including the MCA and DoLS, are not. The legislative framework, Codes of Practice and application of case law is the same but some elements of guidance and implementation of DoLS in practice differ, including how BIAs are trained.

Guidance

The Welsh Assembly Government (2009a, 2009b) published its own guidance for managing authorities and supervisory bodies in Wales at the same time that the DoLS Code of Practice was published, but we understand that these are rarely referred to in practice even though they set out some of the differences in context. These include timescales for completion of assessments where the clock starts ticking when the assessor is instructed by the supervisory body to complete the assessments (Welsh Assembly Government, 2009b, p 17), rather than when the application is received by the supervisory body as in England.

DoLS forms

The Welsh Government (2015) made use of its devolved powers to develop its own streamlined DoLS forms post-*Cheshire West*. It is not evident that the minor differences between the English DoLS forms developed by ADASS (DHSC, 2018) and the Welsh forms (Welsh Government, 2015) make a significant difference to practice beyond causing confusion where numbering of forms differs. Having a separate form for the mental capacity assessment (Form 3a) that either the BIA or Mental Health Assessor can complete (or facilitate the use of equivalent mental capacity assessments) can be valuable. However, other differences appear to be more designed to highlight the ability of the Welsh Government to exercise its devolved powers.

Supervisory bodies

Where English supervisory bodies are now solely local authorities as a result of the abolition of primary care trusts, Welsh supervisory bodies remain the responsibility of local authorities with respect to DoLS in care homes and local health boards (LHBs) with regard to DoLS in hospitals, whether NHS or privately run. As in England, when there was health involvement in supervisory bodies, sometimes these are jointly run in order to share resources and knowledge and are sometimes hosted by LHBs.

Training and registration of BIAs

The main difference for BIAs in Wales is that there has never been a requirement to complete an academically assessed BIA course in order to qualify to practise. The reasoning for this was reported to be the likely inaccessibility of university BIA qualifying courses in rural Wales. In the current context of hugely increased provision of online learning and a notable number of Welsh BIA students accessing English university BIA qualifying education, this reasoning seems rather antiquated.

BIA training in Wales, as a result, has been a patchwork of internally taught non-accredited training courses, often taught by lawyers or university teaching staff, and prospective Welsh BIAs seeking places on English BIA courses. Supervisory bodies in Wales were given control over their standards for training BIAs and some chose to support their training BIAs to access assessed university courses run by English universities in the interests of supporting more evidence-based decision-making that could be more justifiable in court. An unpublished survey of Welsh BIAs conducted in 2020 by BASW Wales, which we have had sight of, suggested that the majority (more than 70 per cent out of 159 respondents) had completed English BIA qualifying courses.

There is also no requirement for annual BIA refresher training as there is in the English BIA statutory regulations. However, in the unpublished survey of Welsh BIAs (BASW Wales, 2020), at least 75 per cent of respondents stated they completed annual training relevant to their role.

The only regulatory requirement is that the BIA is registered with the relevant professional body. For OTs, psychologists and nurses, these professional regulators cover both England and Wales (HCPC and NMC). However, social workers must be registered with the professional body for the country they are practising in, meaning that social workers practising in Wales must be registered with Social Care Wales and social workers practising in England must be registered with Social Work England. Social workers who practise in both nations can register for both professional bodies, but it is not clear that all supervisory bodies pay attention to the requirement that they should be registered with the professional body for the nation in which they are practising. It is also worth noting that the annotation of BIA qualified status that Social Work England has recently adopted within its regulation of social workers in England has not been matched by a similar process with Social Care Wales.

PERSPECTIVES: PROFESSIONAL

Interview with registered social worker and DoLS lead practising in Wales

What do you see as the particular challenges and benefits for practice as a BIA in Wales?

If DoLS in England is a mess, DoLS in Wales is a bigger mess by any measure or metric you can consider! There seems to be an ongoing lack of interest in the DoLS in Wales. Social Care Wales (SCW, the Social Work regulator), Care Inspectorate Wales (CIW, the social care standards body), Health Inspectorate Wales (HIW, the hospital and health care inspectorate) and the Welsh Government have not provided effective leadership about DoLS practice. Staff in these bodies during implementation who had an interest in DoLS left or got promoted. There was a further spike of interest in 2014 with a thematic inspection from the Care and Social Services Inspectorate Wales and Healthcare Inspectorate Wales (CSSIW/HIW, 2014), which was prompted by the House of Lords MCA legislative impact report (House of Lords, 2014) and the *Cheshire West* judgment [2014], but this focus was not maintained.

My personal interest in DoLS practice is as a strategic wedge in making professionals more aware of the MCA and rights-based practice and to encourage more caution when concern about managing risk might lead to overreach in interventions. This is happening, slowly. In my area, this is because of increasing exposure to the Court of Protection but I suppose that is mostly due to Section 21A DoLS appeals and welfare applications seeking to authorise placements in response to hospital discharges.

The initial decisions about not mandating training for the BIA role as university-assessed courses have had ongoing effects. This has been generational. A cohort of Welsh professionals have had a lower level of training than their England-based peers. I believe this is a large part of the reason MCA-focused practice has been given less priority in professional culture and workforce development as well as in social care and health policy. I think this is what has ultimately led to lower levels of referrals for initial DoLS assessments in Wales; to lower levels of referrals to the Court of Protection for the authorisation of deprivation of liberty in non-registered settings, lower levels of referral to the court for Section 21A appeals and welfare rulings and, sad to say, lower standards of BIA practice. This is not a criticism of staff. It is an observation about how the effects of initial policy in Wales signalling that DoLS was a less

> serious consideration has had an effect over time focusing the attention of managers and leaders, which has had consequences.
>
> The main challenge is now catching up from a lower standard of training, which has had a negative impact on wider professional culture and practice for adult social care and clinical decision-making in Wales.

It is also important to reflect on the impact of majority English-speaking BIA assessments in majority Welsh-speaking areas of Wales. Where BIAs are assessing in English when the person's first language is Welsh, there is likely to be, as with other translated assessments, an impact on the understanding in communication that may risk being confused with a lack of capacity. There are limited resources available on the DoLS in Welsh beyond the DoLS Code of Practice (Y Weinyddiaeth Gyfiawnder, 2008).

Speech and language therapy

In our experience, there are other professions that play a significant part in improving the quality of BIA decisions. In particular, the skills and knowledge of speech and language therapists (SLTs) have great value when supporting the person's decision-making, considering how to assess their capacity and gather the person's views in making a best interests decision, where the person's ability to communicate is compromised.

SLTs' expertise in assessing communication issues and their knowledge of communication techniques and aids can be invaluable in ensuring that communication difficulties do not mask a person's ability to make decisions for themselves or remove the opportunity to improve their engagement in decision-making through a lack of support for their communication needs. The Royal College of Speech and Language Therapists (RCSLT, 2022) identifies that: 'SLTs can use their expertise in communication assessment and facilitation to ensure that people with speech, language and communication needs receive the specific support they need to understand, think and talk about decisions during mental capacity assessments.'

When might SLTs be useful in assessing capacity?

SLTs can be involved in supporting the managing authority to explore with the person, over time, their ability to make an informed choice in the following ways:

- establishing exactly which level of decision a person might be able to make and with what support, for example identifying which decisions the person can make on a range of complexity from choosing between two hot drinks to choosing where they live;

- identifying the options relevant to the decision and enabling the person to express their views, with regard to the context in which the questions are being asked, and interpreting the person's responses;
- exploring the person's life, opportunities to make choices and behavioural responses, as noted by carers through observation and engagement;
- identifying tools and resources that the person will use most consistently to communicate, such as objects of reference, pictures, symbols or words;
- spending time exploring the person's level of ability to make choices through regularly repeating the same choices and using the same communication aids, if necessary, to establish consistency;
- taking time to enable the person to learn to make new or unfamiliar choices.

For these and other reasons, SLTs are planned to be eligible to become Approved Mental Capacity Professionals (AMCPs) within the Liberty Protection Safeguards (LPS) once the regulations have been ratified by parliament. (See Chapter 10 for further exploration of the AMCP role.)

What conditions can SLTs assist with?

SLTs work with people across the life course, but in terms of relevance to BIA practice, the groups they are often involved with include the following:

- people with aphasia that affects speech following stroke;
- people with communication difficulties as a result of acquired brain injury and conditions such as dementia, motor neurone disease, Parkinson's disease and Huntington's disease;
- people with developmental disorders such as learning disabilities and autistic spectrum conditions.

What resources would an SLT suggest to promote communication relevant to BIA work?

Tools that can be useful to aid communication in BIA assessments include Talking Mats and Dementia Care Mapping.

Talking Mats are 'a visual communication framework which supports people with communication difficulties to express their feelings and views. Talking Mats can be carried out physically or in a digital space, for example a tablet, laptop or computer' (Talking Mats, 2022). This provides a method for the person to communicate their views and feelings on subjects represented by pictures that can aid comprehension by breaking down communication into manageable chunks, give time to process information and aid memory.

The pros and cons of Talking Mats can be summarised as follows:

Pros
- It is easy to keep records of conversations as the final result can be photographed and compared with other occasions when the same question is asked.

Cons
- Access to Talking Mats materials can be expensive – some practitioners develop their own materials using similar principles; for example, homemade or printed pictures tailored to the person's choices and circumstances, and a mat to stick them on.
- Practitioners need to be careful about recording the exact question asked and phrasing it precisely to avoid ambiguity or misunderstanding.

Some people with autistic spectrum conditions use other picture-based communication systems, such as the Picture Exchange Communication System (PECS) (Pyramid Educational Consultants, 2016). This is designed to enable the person to ask for what they want or to comment on the world around them. It is of less value when the communication is about making decisions or expressing views and feelings about decisions – in other words, the type of decision-making ability that a BIA will be assessing with the person – so alternative methods of communication may need to be explored in these circumstances.

Dementia Care Mapping (DCM) is a method of observing people with dementia in their environment, in their interactions with others and how they spend their time. It was developed by the late Professor Tom Kitwood at the University of Bradford and is a way for carers to recognise the person's day-to-day experience. It can offer insights into the person's priorities and frustrations relevant to their experience of restrictions and can be used as a tool for improving person-centred care (Alzheimer's Society, 2022).

Kitwood (1997, p 4) described DCM as a 'serious attempt to take the standpoint of the person with dementia, using a combination of empathy and observational skill' and offers a structured approach to observations through noting 'personal detractions' and 'positive events' in communal spaces between the person and staff members. DCM is an approach to person-centred dementia care that can be used as a research or a care planning tool with people with dementia that recognises the fundamental need to maintain understanding of their personhood beyond their diagnosis (Brooker, 2005).

However, the most important resource that is needed to facilitate improved communication with people with mental capacity issues is time. The reality of practice for BIAs under the DoLS is that sufficient time to complete this level of assessment by the BIA, or to wait for an SLT to complete this kind of work before completing the DoLS assessment, is very unlikely to be available.

In such cases, BIAs can take the following steps:

- Learn from what managing authorities already know about the person, their ability to make a range of decisions and preferences in communication approaches when completing their assessment.
- Provide guidance to managing authorities on the work they need to do to support the person to improve their communication, access resources to support this and learn to use these tools to make potentially unfamiliar decisions, for example by including conditions on DoLS authorisation to refer to and working with an SLT on developing the person's communication about the deprivation of liberty attached to a DoLS authorisation. Conditions like this could mean that the person is more able to have their views and wishes heard more clearly in future DoLS assessments. This may include sending information or a form for the care home to complete on areas to be covered by a future assessment, such as asking specifically how the person indicates a choice of drink, whether this method is reliable and whether it is always the same.

How can the support of an SLT be accessed?

The managing authority can refer directly for an SLT communication assessment via the NHS; alternatively, the person and their family could arrange to pay privately for the assistance of an independent SLT. It is worth being aware that SLT availability for work on communication and mental capacity may be difficult to access, with waiting times for NHS SLT services high.

We would like to thank all the professionals who gave their time and expertise to help us complete both the original and this revised chapter. It continues to be an excellent example of multi-professional working.

 KEY MESSAGES

- THE BIA role is not just for social workers – all eligible professions have the core expertise required, as well as distinctive additional knowledge and skills that contribute to the knowledge and skills base of the role as a whole.

- EVERYONE coming to the BIA role has different areas in which they will need to build confidence for effective BIA practice whatever their professional background.

- IT is valuable to recognise what skills and knowledge you can share with your peers.

KNOWLEDGE REVIEW

- **WHAT** unique contribution do the BIA professions make to BIA practice?

- **WHY** is it valuable that the BIA is a multi-professional role?

- **WHAT** challenges might different professions find in acting as BIAs and what support might be useful?

- **WHAT** difference does it make if you practise as a BIA in England or Wales?

- **WHAT** other useful contributions are there to effective BIA practice and how can this support be accessed?

 FURTHER READING

- Further information on Talking Mats, training (including workshops on using the tool in assessing capacity), research and digital versions of the tool are available at: www.talkingmats.com

- Further information on Dementia Care Mapping is available at: www.alzheimers. org.uk/dementia-professionals/dementia-experience-toolkit/research-methods/dementia-care-mapping

- Independent speech and language therapists can be contacted at: https://asltip.com

- Jones, I. and Volkmer, A. (2019) (eds) *Speech and Language Therapists and Mental Capacity*, Havant, J & R Press

4

Working with others

In this chapter we explore the importance of communication and relationship building while the Best Interests Assessor (BIA) engages with relevant stakeholders to effectively undertake their work. The BIA needs to be aware of the range of skills and knowledge required to engage effectively with all those interested in the person's welfare. BIAs need to be able to engage with those below and more:

- the person being assessed, their families, friends and carers
- the Relevant Person's Representative (RPR), those holding Lasting Powers of Attorney (LPAs) and court-appointed deputies
- interpreters
- the Independent Mental Capacity Advocate (IMCA) and other advocates
- the Mental Health Assessor
- the supervisory body
- the managing authority.

This chapter emphasises that in undertaking an assessment, the BIA will need to recognise that they are practising in a diverse world while applying relevant law, policy and guidance.

Introduction

Working together, interprofessional working, joint working and working in collaboration are phrases you will often hear in health and social care settings (Day, 2013). What does this mean for BIA practice and your work with the person, their relatives, carers, friends, professionals and others? The BIA has an important role in working with all the people involved with the person's care, but simultaneously must act autonomously and independently. There is a clear requirement to understand your purpose as a BIA to reach an independent judgement but also to work collectively in gathering information that will inform your decision. The BIA role can, from our experience, feel like a lonely professional position to be in. You have a key function to fulfil and you have a real need to ensure that you have the required capability and professional interrelational boundaries to be effective in achieving your purpose as a BIA. Interprofessional working is key to effective BIA practice (Thomas et al, 2014), as you need to listen, respond and draw on the perspectives and knowledge of others, as well asserting your own judgement.

As we discuss in Chapter 6 in relation to decision-making, you need to be able to coordinate information and opinion that relates to the person you have been commissioned to assess.

During BIA assessments, you are likely to work with:

- the person
- interpreters – British Sign Language, Makaton and other languages
- their family, friends and carers
- the RPR
- the managing authority/paid carers
- those with substitute decision-making powers:
  - attorneys for health and welfare (Lasting Power of Attorney)
  - attorneys for property and affairs (Lasting or Enduring Powers of Attorney)
  - Court of Protection-appointed deputies for health and welfare and/or property and affairs
- IMCAs
- the Mental Health Assessor (Section 12 doctor)
- the supervisory body, including safeguarding
- social workers, social care practitioners or health coordinators.

You will also need to consult relevant documentation and reports, such as:

- urgent and standard authorisation DoLS forms and forms from previous DoLS authorisations, where appropriate
- health and social care records
- advance decisions to refuse treatment, powers of attorney or deputyships.

Introducing your role as a BIA to others

When working with others, there is a clear need to be able to skilfully and articulately communicate the role of the BIA, and the purpose of DoLS, to a wide range of people. The most important, and possibly the most challenging, explanation will be to the person being assessed. However, the most common scenario is likely to be when you will find yourself on the phone, explaining your role to a family member of the person who does not know anything about the BIA role and who may wonder why you are involved with the decision to place their relative in a care home that was made some time ago.

 TOP TIPS

Our top tips for explaining the BIA role are:

- **AVOID** explaining the history of human rights case law and the legislative framework that led to the DoLS.

- **INSTEAD**, start a conversation about the person, their views and wishes and how your assessment will ensure they get the most choice and least restriction necessary that they can in how they are cared for.

- **BEWARE** using jargon – we often use words, phrases and acronyms that are bewildering to anyone outside the health and social care bubble.

- **OFTEN** it can be useful to mention key jargon and acronyms and explain what they are so the person can connect what you are talking about with other conversations or knowledge they have. For example, mentioning the Deprivation of Liberty Safeguards, sometimes called DoLS, or an Independent Mental Capacity Advocate, often called an IMCA, what these are in a simple manner and what purpose they will serve for their family member.

- **AVOID** assuming that the person knows nothing about the BIA role, the Mental Capacity Act (MCA) 2005 or DoLS. Some people will know a bit, others may know nothing and sometimes relatives or carers have not even been informed that their loved one is subject to such legal processes.

- **INSTEAD**, check if relatives or carers have been told their loved one has had a DoLS application made by a care home or hospital and ask if they know what this means. Explain briefly and offer to send them information about the DoLS so they can read it and offer to talk through any questions they might have.

You should be prepared for a range of ways to explain both your role and the purpose of DoLS, to a range of audiences. All those involved depend on you clearly understanding why the BIA role exists and what purpose your involvement serves their loved one. This is particularly important when explaining your involvement to family and friends of a person who is funding their own care, as this may be the first time that a local authority or other official state body has been involved in decisions made about the person's care and relatives may quite rightfully ask why this is the case. You must be clear about the benefits of a check to ensure that the person's rights to freedom from restriction are maintained for as long as necessary. Sensitivity to the circumstances that led the person to be placed in a care home and the feelings of those involved in that process are vital to building the positive relationships you need as a BIA.

Working with the person

The most important person you will work with is the person you are assessing. Because of the nature of the BIA role, you are unlikely to have met or worked with the person before, although you could have assessed them for DoLS in the past. If you are meeting the person for the first time, your view of them is likely to have been formed by reading the application for DoLS from the managing authority, the Mental Health Assessor's report (if it is available when you assess), any IMCA or RPR reports, the case notes and the views of others you may have spoken to in advance, such as the managing authority or family members.

You need to be able to weigh up the information that is presented to you in a non-judgmental manner, keeping an open mind that is neither overly optimistic nor pessimistic but person-centred and contextual. To maintain the principles of the MCA, you must support the person to make the decision themselves and evaluate the most appropriate time and means to communicate and meet with them. Rogers (1980) suggests that if you are to demonstrate effective communication, you should adopt a nonjudgmental attitude, be empathic, show unconditional positive regard in order to build trust, and demonstrate genuine interest. (See also Chapter 3 for information on how an SLT or communication aids might assist you to communicate with the person most effectively.)

The challenges you may encounter when assessing the person include the following:

- The person's capacity and ability or willingness to communicate might fluctuate over time and you may need to be prepared to visit them more than once at different times of the day to give them the best chance to show their ability to make the decision required.
- There are a wide range of communication and capacity issues that you are likely to encounter as a BIA. The person may be chatty and articulate but have an unrealistic view of their capabilities because of their condition (for example in cases of acquired brain injury – see Chapter 6), they may be unwilling to engage with you, or they may be unable to communicate with you at all because of their condition.

Communicating with others in a diverse world

You cannot overestimate the level of communication skills you are going to use when working with others as a BIA. You will be working with a wide range of people from a variety of backgrounds, with various levels of involvement and different needs. You must reflect on your ability to identify communication holistically with an awareness that people are communicating all of the time in many ways (Gast and Bailey, 2014), whether verbally or nonverbally. When reading the DoLS application, you should note if there are identified access needs that can be addressed above and beyond general communication skills. This includes situations where the person may use nonverbal communication, may not be able to communicate at all, or does not wish to be assessed, as well as those where the assessment is causing distress. Maintaining good practice in capacity assessments can be challenging when the BIA assessment timescales do not support endless time for planning and supported decision-making by the person. Nonetheless, you must demonstrate that you have fully engaged in working with the person to support them in reaching a decision. (See Chapter 7 for more detail on the ethical dilemmas involved in working within DoLS timescales.)

It is very easy to assume that families and friends of the person understand the terminology and jargon relating to DoLS and equally to assume that nodding and indications of agreement demonstrates understanding. It is possible that the family member or carer you are talking to believes you are there to decide whether a person should be detained, in a similar way to a decision under the Mental Health Act, rather than to assess whether the restrictions in place are justified, and that you are wanting to ensure that the person has the right to a timely appeal against their liberty being removed. Checking the understanding of all those involved, as you do with a capacity assessment, is key.

Working with interpreters

In your work as a BIA, you may need to involve the services of interpreters. It is unlikely that you will have gained fluent skills in all the languages (verbal and nonverbal) that you could encounter in practice. The interpreter should be provided by the supervisory body, which may have policies on specific agencies, people or companies to be used, and the expertise in the communication mode required. Interpretation may be in person or on the phone, which may present particular challenges.

Conflicts of interest may arise if friends or family members are used as interpreters for assessments as you cannot objectively determine that everything that is being spoken is being translated or is not being interpreted with bias, and friends or relatives may not be familiar with the technical vocabulary needed. Communication translation also needs to engage with differing cultures, ideologies of 'illness' or disability and educational backgrounds (Hsieh, 2016). For instance, does 'deprivation', which can be clearly articulated in English, have the same nuances in other languages and cultures?

There can be a reluctance to work with interpreters in health and social care for a variety of reasons (Gerrish, 2001). However, working with interpreters should not be sidelined and it is an important skill to learn, as it can create a very different dynamic to conversations with which you may not be familiar (Tribe, 2009). It is not possible here to outline every method you should adopt, but we offer some basic points to consider:

- You will need to consider the position of the interpreter, for example whether they have their back to you, or are beside you. It is important that you address the person you are assessing directly and offer eye contact as appropriate, rather than speaking to the interpreter and asking the interpreter to ask questions.
- The interpreter will need to translate everything that is communicated. This means that you cannot retract something you have said as you would not wish another person to do so.

- You should behave as you would if you shared the same language. You do not typically need to speak slower or louder with exaggerated mouth expressions.
- You should consider the amount of information you want to convey to ensure that it can be translated effectively and take into consideration the cognitive abilities of the person you are speaking with.
- With the potential for differing interpretations of your words (because of differing cultural or worldviews), you should check the meaning of what is being said if anything remains unclear.

REFLECTIVE ACTIVITY

Malik, 87, African heritage

Malik has been referred for a DoLS assessment as he has been trying to leave the nursing home where he has been living for six months. Malik often appears to believe that he needs to get to work and although staff are usually able to intervene and distract him, using de-escalating approaches, he is making a clear attempt to leave and if staff cannot prevent him from leaving he is stopped by a locked external door.

Malik has spoken fluent English throughout his working life, except when he is with his family where he speaks Shona. It has become noticeable to staff that when Malik speaks to them in distress he uses a blend of English and Shona, which you know from speaking with his family is not typical for Malik.

Questions
- Which approaches will you adopt to ensure effective communication?
- Who can you work with to assist with communication?
- How will the principles of the MCA and DoLS assist you in understanding which approach to adopt?

We suggest that the following are important when working with this situation:

- It is vital that the BIA ensures that Principle 2 MCA, regarding giving all practicable help, is adhered to so that effective communication can be facilitated with Malik in order that his views and wishes can be understood. As Malik can speak English as well as Shona and can move between these dialects when distressed, you should ensure that a language interpreter is present who can translate Shona for you. It may be appropriate to include a family member in your assessment to aid in reducing his distress as well as assisting in interpreting his communication.

- It is also necessary to ensure that all practicable steps are taken to engage with Malik at the appropriate times and spaces. This includes finding out when and in what circumstances Malik usually believes that he needs to go to work as this may give clues to what is triggering this behaviour, which the home may then be able to alleviate. Understanding when he is usually at his most calm will be useful in terms of planning for your best interests assessment to ensure that any potential distress is minimised. Effective and flexible interpretation will also support the communication element of the functional test for mental capacity so Malik has the best chance of making his views known.

Working with families and their perspectives

Families and professional carers who are caring for the person will have a wealth of knowledge about the person concerned. However, communication with carers has been seen to be consistently lacking among professionals, particularly with family carers (Heron, 1998; DH, 2014), despite the knowledge that, in most cases, the involvement of carers improves the quality and availability of care to the most vulnerable people. It is often reported by families and carers that they are able to detect subtle differences in the person's behaviour and communications that professionals cannot interpret or understand due to their brief involvement with the person. Although a BIA cannot assume that all family members are benevolent, family members and carers are likely to hold a great deal of information that will be beneficial in decision-making. The person may have family and/or friends who have been involved in caring for them for some time who can provide vital information about the person's wishes and preferences during their life.

PERSPECTIVES: FAMILY CARER

Interview with a carer looking after a family member who has a learning disability

As a family carer, please explain what you see as good practice for a BIA.

The best interests assessment needs to be appreciated from a carer's or family perspective, as for some families this would be very daunting. It is important that the process must be explained in layman's terms as most families may never have come across this before.

The best interests assessment needs to bring together the best people that know the person: family, friends, circle of support and professionals, where an open and honest discussion about the best way forward can occur. Having family members present when assessment is undertaken may be helpful.

All discussions with family, friends and professionals are equally valid and together all parties can agree to a balanced approach. Family and friends need to understand the assessment is not about them and their ability to contribute towards the care for the person.

Family members can have a wealth of information to give relating to the person's health and any underlying conditions that may hinder good outcomes, for example phobias that the assessed person may have or any detail that is important.

Valuing the knowledge, views and experience that families and friends have of the person is vital to effective consultation and will enhance your assessment.

Working with the Relevant Person's Representative (RPR)

One key function of the BIA is to identify an appropriate person to act as the RPR, as all those subject to a DoLS authorisation must have this safeguard in place. The purpose of the RPR is to offer additional protective rights to the person who is subject to legal deprivation of liberty under DoLS. The role of the RPR will need to be explained and explored with the families and friends to decide who is most appropriate for the role. Only one person can act as the RPR. It could, but does not have to be, the same person that holds a Lasting Power of Attorney (LPA) or deputyship for the person's health and welfare. It is vital to share detailed information about what the role entails. This needs to be balanced against the potential to scare off possible RPRs when explaining their legal responsibilities following the *Re AJ (DoLS)* [2015] case (summarised later in this section).

ESSENTIAL INFORMATION: PRACTICE GUIDANCE

The Relevant Person's Representative (RPR)

When the DoLS is authorised, a RPR must be appointed by the supervisory body. The RPR must:

- maintain contact with the person;
- represent and support the person in all matters relating to the DoLS, including triggering a review, making a complaint or making an application to the Court of Protection.

> DoLS Code of Practice (Ministry of Justice, 2008, p 76, para 7.2)

Paid RPR

If the BIA is unable to recommend anyone to be the RPR, the supervisory body must identify an eligible person to be appointed as the representative. The supervisory body can pay for a person to be the RPR.

> DoLS Code of Practice (Ministry of Justice, 2008, pp 80–1, paras 7.19–7.21)

Who should identify the need for a representative in the DoLS process?

The BIA must recommend to the supervisory body who they think the RPR should be if they decide that the DoLS should be authorised. They should provide information to the person they think is most eligible for the role.

Who is eligible to be an RPR?

To be eligible to be an RPR, the person must be:

- 18 years of age or over;
- able to keep in regular contact with the person;
- willing to be appointed.

The person must not be:

- financially interested in the person's managing authority (for example, as a partner, director, office holder or shareholder of the managing authority);
- a relative of a person who has an interest in the managing authority;
- employed by, or providing services to, the care home where the person lives;
- employed by the hospital in a role related to the care or treatment of the person;

- employed by the supervisory body in a role that could be related to the person's case.

Who commissions paid RPRs?

Supervisory bodies are responsible for commissioning and funding paid RPR services.

Who provides paid RPRs?

Local authorities must commission paid RPR services for those whose DoLS they have authorised. Paid RPRs do not have to be qualified IMCAs. Many supervisory bodies commission IMCA services to provide paid RPRs but some advocacy services are only able to provide paid RPR services as they do not employ qualified IMCAs.

DoLS Code of Practice (Ministry of Justice, 2008, Ch 7)

Explaining the role of the RPR

As a BIA, you must explain the following to those who might be eligible for the RPR role, considering the eligibility criteria above:

- The DoLS requires that the person has a representative who will be in regular contact with them, will raise any issues and concerns about their care with the managing authority and make sure their views are heard.
- If the person's circumstances change, for example their care becomes more restrictive, the RPR will need to ask the supervisory body to review the person's care.
- If the person objects to their care, the RPR must take the person's appeal to the Court of Protection whether they personally agree with the person's views or not.
- The RPR has a right to help and guidance from an advocate (an IMCA appointed under Section 39D MCA 2005 [2007]), especially if they need help to take the person's appeal to the Court or Protection or to ask for a review.

In our experience, the thought of taking on the responsibility of a Court of Protection appeal, especially where family members may think the person is in the best possible place to be cared for, puts a lot of potential RPRs off. In these circumstances, if a person clearly objects to their care, it is often better for the person that their appeal is supported by an experienced advocate (a paid RPR), paid for by the supervisory body. However, if there is no likelihood of appeal as the person is settled and not showing signs of objection, a family member who is already in regular contact with the person and queries aspects of the person's care as appropriate is likely to be most suitable for the role.

Right to appeal

Article 5(4) of the European Convention on Human Rights (ECHR) (as amended 2010) states that: 'Everyone who is deprived of his liberty by arrest or detention shall be entitled to take proceedings by which the lawfulness of his detention shall be decided speedily by a court.' This offers a significant safeguard to ensure that the person's right to liberty is not removed arbitrarily and their voice of objection is heard directly in the Court of Protection under Section 21A MCA.

When a person lacks capacity because of a medical condition (such as dementia, learning disability or brain injury) that significantly affects their cognitive abilities and their ability to communicate their views, this right may be difficult to exercise. For example, a person with dementia might not want someone to help with their personal care or they might be angry and frustrated because of the life they lead with the condition, but this is not necessarily an objection to where they live. Disentangling what is an expression of frustration and what is a desire to leave a care home is complex, and case law has only recently given guidance on the subject (see *RD and Ors* [2016], summarised later in the chapter). It is debatable as to whether appealing will change the restrictions the person lives with, as there may be no alternative to the current care arrangements, for example where the person's needs are so complex that there are very few providers that can meet them or the home the person wants to return to is no longer available to them. Since the ruling in the *Re AJ (DoLS)* case, the duty on local authorities to identify and support the appeals of those who are objecting to their deprivation of liberty has had a significant impact on practice.

 ESSENTIAL INFORMATION: LAW

Re AJ (DoLS) [2015]

AJ, a woman in her 80s who had been diagnosed with dementia, had been cared for by Mr and Mrs C, her niece and husband, at their home. She signed LPAs for health and welfare and property and affairs to Mr and Mrs C jointly. AJ relied on her niece for support, although she did not acknowledge that she needed any assistance with her day-to-day needs. When Mr and Mrs C were no longer able to cope with caring for her, arrangements were made for her to go into a residential home for respite while Mr and Mrs C went on holiday. The plan was that if AJ settled in the care home, she would remain there permanently.

Mr and Mrs C took AJ to the care home and she said she did not want to stay there and asked to go home. An urgent authorisation for DoLS was completed and the standard authorisation was assessed and authorised for 21 days as the situation was uncertain. Mr C, as LPA for health and welfare, nominated himself as RPR and a Section 39D IMCA was appointed. AJ moved to another home and a succession of DoLS standard authorisations were completed. AJ continued to object to being in the new care home. The IMCA, after a period of time, realised that Mr C was not going to take AJ's appeal to the Court of Protection and made the application to court on her behalf.

Mr Justice Baker noted in his judgment that professionals should consider the person's right to object when planning respite with a view to making a placement permanent, that BIAs should be cautious of recommending family members to be RPRs who may not support the process of taking their objection to court, and that appointing a Section 39D IMCA is not enough to consider that the local authority has done its duty to support the person's right to appeal.

Research on the nature and number of Section 21A appeals to the Court of Protection has noted that 'although the DoLS offers an "enabling framework" to access the COP's welfare jurisdiction in contrast with its main personal welfare route, most detainees under the DoLS are still not exercising rights of appeal in accordance with Article 5(4) ECHR' (Series et al, 2017, p 5). Whether this is because the person's behaviour is not being understood as objecting to their care and treatment, because there are systemic failures in supporting such objections to get as far as court or because there are only a minority of detainees objecting to their care and treatment is not clear. What is clear is that BIAs have a responsibility to ensure that the person is in the best possible position to exercise their rights to question decisions made about their care, and the *Re AJ (DoLS)* [2015] and *RD and Ors* [2016] cases give invaluable guidance on when and how objections should be supported.

Role of the BIA

The cases referenced above make it clear that the BIA is responsible for ensuring that the following are considered when deciding whom to nominate as the person's RPR:

- the need to explain that the role includes the requirement to take the person's appeal to court if the person objects to their care;
- that a family member who feels they have tried all available options before placing their relative in care may not be willing or able to support a court appeal;
- that appointing a Section 39D IMCA is not enough to ensure that there is adequate representation of the person's views available, so appointing a paid RPR in these circumstances may be more appropriate.

As a key safeguard of the person's rights under DoLS, BIAs must prioritise the principle of universal access to appeal as enshrined in Article 5(4) (ECHR). Even where the nature of the person's objection may be unclear, the principle of upholding the person's right to appeal must be paramount. Crucial to this is the principle of access to advocacy to represent the person's views as far as possible where they are unable to represent their own. Bogg (2010) notes that this is essential, as the BIA and doctor involved in DoLS assessments 'are subject to the pre-existing power dynamic between user and worker' (p 118), which may prejudice decisions that are likely to increase the level of restriction the person is subject to. The Section 39D IMCA role that is available to a person detained under DoLS provides 'an external scrutiny and representation that has not previously been afforded to those who may be unable to voice their own concerns and challenges' (pp 118–19). Where there is potential that the person detained under DoLS will object to their care, the BIA should ensure that they have been offered access to a Section 39D IMCA if the RPR is a family member or friend, and that they are willing to pursue an objection to the Court of Protection. Access to a paid RPR will be necessary if there is no family or friend available or those who are available would not support the person's objection.

Following the *Re AJ (DoLS)* [2015] judgment, the number of appeal applications to the Court of Protection has increased and the pressure on advocacy agencies to provide paid RPRs has also increased. It could be argued that by preserving the right of access to appeal for all those whose behaviour suggests they are objecting makes it more difficult for those with genuine objections from having access to the advocacy they are entitled to and having their challenge speedily heard in court. The guidance given in *RD and Ors* [2016] suggests that what the person says about their detention, their emotional response to their deprivation, the frequency and consistency of their objection and their behaviour must all be considered in weighing whether an appeal is necessary or desirable. The guidance suggests that the threshold for appeal is relatively high, which should lower the pressure on the court to hear appeals, thereby increasing access for those who would achieve greater benefit who meet these criteria (Ruck Keene et al, 2016).

It is worth considering Rawls' view that only once all citizens' basic needs are met can they exercise their rights and liberties (Johns, 2016, p 40). Rawls espoused the view that benefits should be distributed to those who are least well off. In these terms, those who are most articulate in their objection to their deprivation of liberty are the most well off, as their views can be clearly heard. It is those who are only able to communicate their objection to their care arrangements by their physical resistance, low mood or begrudged compliance that should be prioritised to have their objections heard in court. The *RD and Ors* [2016] case suggests that where people are more articulate and consistent in their objection, they will be more likely to have their voices heard. Rawls would consider the necessity to distribute resources to those least able to articulate their views of greater weight than to those who can more consistently object.

The *RD and Ors* [2016] case considered the circumstances in which an appeal to the Court of Protection may be appropriate, having examined the applications of five people subject to DoLS authorisations.

ESSENTIAL INFORMATION: LAW

RD and Ors (Duties and Powers of Relevant Person's Representatives and Section 39D IMCAs) [2016] EWCOP 49

In his judgment, Baker J considered:

> When, if at all, does the requirement under Article 5(4) to assist P to exercise his or her right of appeal to the Court of Protection under Section 21A of the MCA arise in cases other than those in which P expresses a clear and consistent objection to the arrangements for his/her care and treatment?

In other words, when should an appeal to the Court of Protection against a DoLS authorisation be made if the person is not clearly expressing an objection to their care arrangements?

Baker J explored this issue, including the role the RPR and Section 39D IMCA play in the appeal process, and gave, in para 86, general guidance for these decisions, including:

1. The RPR must consider whether P wishes, or would wish, to apply to the Court of Protection. This involves the following steps:

    a. Consider whether P has capacity to ask to issue proceedings. This simply requires P to understand that the court has the power to decide that he/she should not be subject to his/her current care arrangements. It is a lower threshold than the capacity to conduct proceedings.

    b. If P does not have such capacity, consider whether P is objecting to the arrangements for his/her care, either verbally or by behaviour, or both, in a way that indicates that he would wish to apply to the Court of Protection if he had the capacity to ask.

2. In considering P's stated preferences, regard should be had to:

    • any statements made by P about his/her wishes and feelings in relation to issuing proceedings;

- any statements made by P about his/her residence in care;
- P's expressions of his/her emotional state;
- the frequency with which he/she objects to the placement or asks to leave;
- the consistency of his/her express wishes or emotional state; and
- the potential alternative reasons for his/her express wishes for emotional state.

3. In considering whether P's behaviour constitutes an objection, regard should be had to:

- the possible reasons for P's behaviour;
- whether P is being medicated for depression or being sedated;
- whether P actively tries to leave the care home;
- whether P takes preparatory steps to leave, eg, packing bags;
- P's demeanour and relationship with staff;
- any records of challenging behaviour and the triggers for such behaviour;
- whether P's behaviour is a response to particular aspects of the care arrangements or to the entirety of those arrangements.

Consulting with the RPR

It is unlikely that all assessments that a BIA completes will be the first DoLS assessment that has been completed about the person. This means that when an existing authorisation comes to an end and the BIA makes an assessment for a reauthorisation, the relevant RPR must be consulted during the assessment process to gather their views on the following matters:

- the current restrictions and whether they remain necessary;
- the person's views about the restrictions;
- whether any conditions have been addressed or whether any further conditions are needed;
- whether or not the person expresses any objections.

The BIA must consider the previous assessor's paperwork to establish what is likely to have changed since the last assessment and will need to consult with previous RPRs and paid RPRs as well as IMCAs to understand the person's current circumstances.

REFLECTIVE ACTIVITY

Jason, 53, White British

Jason has recently been discharged from hospital to a nursing home following a serious car accident that resulted in serious brain trauma. Although Jason can function in day-to-day activities, the brain damage has resulted in flashbacks and fitting, which means that Jason needs to be monitored and supported to avoid injury. Jason has started to run without warning with no regard for his safety on roads or in traffic. The BIA has established that he has a brother who would be eligible to act as his RPR. The brother is not willing to consider any options for Jason's treatment or care other than nursing care provision, as he does not want to contribute towards Jason's ongoing support. His brother is advocating for the current care home as he feels it keeps Jason safe. Jason has repeatedly stated that he wants to go home.

Questions

- What is the purpose of the RPR in Jason's circumstances?
- Who else could the BIA recommend is involved?
- How should the BIA determine whether the appointment of the RPR is appropriate?

We would be considering the following in Jason's situation:

- As the BIA you should be cautious of recommending a person to be an RPR who may not support his stated wish to go home from the nursing home to the extent of supporting his appeal to the Court of Protection under Section 21A MCA.
- His brother is not willing to consider any options for Jason's treatment or care other than nursing care provision even though you consider him to be eligible to be his RPR in terms of willingness to be involved. Although a Section 39D IMCA might be useful to support the brother, it is clear from *Re AJ (DoLS)* [2015] that the Court of Protection would not consider his appointment as RPR to be an adequate safeguard for Jason's rights. Therefore it is likely to be appropriate for the BIA to recommend the supervisory body appoint a paid RPR.

Working with managing authorities

Assessments occur primarily in care homes and hospitals. These locations differ, however, in terms of the professionals who work within them and their physical environment. It is vitally important that the person's dignity and wellbeing is upheld throughout the DoLS process, although this can be challenging; for instance, a person might need assessing for DoLS on an open ward in a general hospital. Such an environment often does not have a space where a person can be comfortably and confidentially interviewed so your BIA assessment may have to take place at the bedside on a busy ward. The focus of staff activity is likely to be the 'nurses' station' and the key nurse may be unavailable to speak to the BIA. A care home may be able to offer the privacy of the person's own bedroom for an assessment, but may not be clear on the role of the BIA and what information they will need to complete their assessment. The BIA must be able to adapt to these settings and work effectively with them, acting proportionately and in a person-centred manner.

As a BIA, it is also essential to consider the roles of those you are consulting. The manager or nurse in charge may have a very different view of the person than a care worker who sees the person every day and understands, on a personal level, their preferences, communication and behaviours. Paid carers will also keep the clinical records and observations that have led them to reach the decision that an urgent and standard assessment is required to safeguard the person. They may hold important information that they do not feel is relevant as they may not appreciate the finer points and minutiae of the details required in assessing a person for DoLS. The BIA's curiosity and investigative questioning will help uncover this often essential information.

BIAs should also consider the varied challenges and complexities of managing a person under the DoLS for managing authorities (such as care homes and hospitals). Lennard (2015) advocates from a managing authority perspective for a greater precautionary approach towards completing DoLS applications, and supports an 'err on the side of caution' maxim for professionals to adopt. Lennard argues that applications for urgent and standard authorisations should be made in most cases where the managing authority is even remotely concerned that restrictions are in place that could amount to a deprivation of liberty occurring and that the person lacks capacity to consent. He also highlights that managing authorities struggle with the variation in decision-making by BIAs (Lennard, 2015). There is concern that precautionary applications for DoLS may not be welcomed by supervisory bodies that are already, since the ruling in the *Cheshire West* case (see Chapter 1), overwhelmed by referrals.

However, the Care Quality Commission (CQC, 2015) continued to report that managing authorities were not making enough DoLS applications even after the significant increase in these applications. Lennard's stance was based on a protection of people's rights approach and was supported by human rights organisations (Liberty, 2013). This need for transparency in decisions about when to apply for DoLS raises practice issues for the managing authority, which, once it has identified that a person may be deprived of their liberty, will know that it will continue to detain the person for some time before the DoLS assessment process is completed and they have the legal authorisation to detain them.

The physical nature of hospital and care home environments offers specific challenges as to how a person's risks are managed and what actions are taken in a proportionate manner. Exploring multi-professional opinions on the person you assess is important, as you may not be familiar with how these environments are managed. Although the BIA's role is not to be confused with managing the person's overall care and treatment, you will need to reach a view on whether the environment makes deprivation of liberty likely. In cases where a person is wrongly placed in a nursing home with a locked external door and the person does not require that degree of restriction, an intervention to lessen the restriction and an urgent review of the person's overall care will be required.

Working with those who have substitute decision-making powers

As a BIA, you should recognise that there may be others who hold legal powers that will affect your powers within DoLS, as well as the powers of the supervisory body, to authorise a person's deprivation of liberty.

Why are these roles important for BIA practice?

As a BIA, you will need to determine when completing the no refusals assessment whether someone has been appointed to hold either:

- LPA for health and welfare, chosen by the person while they had capacity and authorised through the Office of the Public Guardian (OPG, 2020) (MCA Code of Practice, Ch 7) or
- court-appointed deputyship selected by the Court of Protection (MCA Code of Practice, Ch 8) when the person was assessed to lack capacity to make the relevant decisions.

As part of your assessment, you have a duty to consult with anyone who has an appropriate power and to take their views into account. Only LPAs or deputies for health and welfare have powers in the no refusals assessment. LPAs or deputies for property and affairs, or Enduring Powers of Attorney (EPAs) for property and affairs, have no authority within DoLS. It is still useful to record when these powers exist as their views should be gathered and considered for your best interests decision. It is also important to recognise that LPAs and EPAs will have been made by the person when they had capacity to make the relevant decisions, so they represent the views of the person as well as whom they trust to help them make decisions.

It is entirely possible that no such powers exist on behalf of the person being assessed; nonetheless, it is the role of the BIA to find out if such powers exist and to establish any relevant views if they do. The person may also have made an advance decision to refuse treatment prior to losing capacity relating to treatment decisions, and this must also be considered.

How do I find out if these powers or decisions are in place?

BIAs must consider the following key sources of information in order to undertake a no refusals assessment:

- The managing authority; for example, the hospital or care home currently caring for the person, which should have copies of any relevant documents to support them in making decisions about the person's care and treatment.
- Any family or friends interested in the person's welfare; this is particularly important for advance decisions as such individuals are not registered with the Court of Protection.
- If you cannot find any information or there is confusion or disagreement about the powers in place, you can complete form OPG100 (OPG, 2021). Email this to the Office of the Public Guardian (OPG), who will tell you if any EPAs, LPAs or deputyships are registered with them and what decisions they cover.

It is important to check these sources of information even if previous DoLS authorisations have been completed, as circumstances often change. It is also very useful to the supervisory body for BIAs to keep copies of any paperwork relating to powers of attorney, deputyships or advance decisions so that there is clear evidence of the grounds for substitute decision-making.

In our experience, there have been many occasions where people have misunderstood the power they have, often through not understanding the complexity of the law involved. Sometimes, this is the result of people wanting to exercise power they do not have. It is vital that the BIA establishes who has the legal authority to act on the person's behalf, as it is detrimental to the person's ability to exercise their rights if others wrongly assume control of their decision-making. We have experience of the following:

- people who think an EPA, LPA or deputyship for property and affairs gives them the power to make health and welfare decisions;
- people who claim to have LPAs but refuse to supply paperwork and whom the OPG says were turned down for the role on the grounds of being unsuitable;
- more than one family member claiming to have an LPA for a person in a care home. In this case, the care home had no copies of any such paperwork but acted on family members' decisions. No one had registered any powers with the OPG.

It is an essential safeguard to ensure that only those with the legal authority to do so make decisions on behalf of people who lack capacity to make decisions for themselves. It is also important that those with decision-making powers, such as LPAs or deputies, act in the person's best interests. As the case of *Mrs P v Rochdale Borough Council and others* [2016] demonstrates, solicitors with these powers cannot ignore the wishes and feelings of those in whose best interests they should act, even if they judge the person's views unwise.

Advance statements and/or decisions

An important legislative provision within mental capacity law is the recognition and weight that is given to an advance decision or statement of wishes. Advance statements can contribute to best interests decision-making relating to the treatment and care of the person as they include expressed preferences and wishes towards important aspects of the person's life and the everyday choices they would have made. They play a vital role in maintaining the person's voice in decisions made about their life once that person is unable to do so themselves.

An advance decision to refuse treatment, which can accompany an advance statement of wishes, has the potential to have greater impact. It can have the effect, if found to be valid and applicable, of refusing particular treatments or interventions. For an advance decision to be valid, proof is needed that it was made at the point when the person had capacity to make that decision. An advance decision must also demonstrate that it is applicable, as there can be no ambiguity in the wording about the treatment the person has decided to refuse. If there is doubt, especially where the decision is to refuse life-sustaining treatment, the advance decision may need to be taken to the Court of Protection to decide whether it has legal weight and should be upheld. As a BIA, if you are told that the person has made an advance decision to refuse life-sustaining treatment, you will need to see documentation and check that it is valid and applicable to the care and treatment amounting to the deprivation of liberty you are considering. For other decisions, the advance decision can be given verbally.

Some see the use of advance decisions as extending autonomy, as they offer a steer as to what the person's decision-making would have been had they had capacity (Bisson et al, 2009). Although advance decisions can be seen to extend a person's autonomy when anticipating the point where capacity may be lost (Wilson et al, 2010), it will still raise ethical issues for the person and professionals concerned (Manthorpe et al, 2009). For instance, for an advance decision to be upheld, it must be valid and applicable; however, if the person amended their view after the advance decision had been written, evidenced by a discussion with a family member, or by the evidence of the person's conduct leading up to their lack of capacity, it may no longer be applicable. This is where supported decision-making can gain traction, as it is a person-centred approach that recognises that only in exceptional circumstances can a person truly lack capacity in relation to their treatment and care decisions. Caution should therefore be exercised around decision-making where an advance decision is concerned.

Powers within the MCA have been criticised as they focus on a person or professional taking on a substitute decision-maker role on behalf of the person who lacks capacity to decide, rather than focusing on increasing the support available to help the person decide for themselves. The UN Convention on the Rights of Persons with Disabilities (CRPD, 2006) made this distinction in Article 12(4) regarding the right to equal recognition before the law where the person may need support with decision-making as a result of their mental capacity status. *The Essex Autonomy Project Three Jurisdictions Report* (Martin et al, 2016) explored whether the provision for substitute decision-making powers in the MCA 2005 (such as LPAs and court-appointed deputies) had fully met the expectation in the CRPD that supported greater priority for supporting the person's own decision-making, rather than substituting that of others. Although the CRPD has not been incorporated into UK law, judges have used it as an aid to interpretation when making judgments on individual decision-making (see *Cornwall Council v NP and BKP* [2020] summary in Chapter 5).

Working with the IMCA

The IMCA roles in the DoLS, as in Sections 39A, 39C and 39D IMCAs, are safeguards built into the DoLS process from the point of assessment to ongoing review and challenge once an authorisation has been agreed.

The Social Care Institute for Excellence (SCIE) offers guidance on the roles of IMCAs within DoLS (SCIE, 2017), including how the BIA and IMCA can work together. The IMCA role is complementary to the role and work of the BIA, as the BIA is also there to uphold the assessed person's rights. However, the BIA's decision as to whether a deprivation of liberty is warranted is signed off by a supervisory body, which may make the BIA less independent of the ongoing decisions being made about the person's care, as shown in the *Hillingdon v Neary* case (see Chapter 8).

 ESSENTIAL INFORMATION: PRACTICE GUIDANCE

Roles of the IMCA

There is a range of IMCA roles in the MCA and DoLS and it is important that BIAs understand the different roles, when they apply and what they should do.

Section 37 IMCA (MCA)

Must be instructed and consulted where serious medical treatment or accommodation decisions are being made (can also be instructed regarding care reviews and safeguarding adults concerns) and the person lacks capacity, decisions are being made in their best interests and they have no one else to support them (other than paid staff; in other words, they are 'unbefriended').

Summarised from the MCA Code of Practice (DCA, 2007, pp 178–9)

Section 39A IMCA (DoLS)

Must be instructed and consulted when an application for the DoLS has been made and there is no one appropriate, as Section 37 IMCA (other than paid staff; in other words, they are 'unbefriended') for the BIA to consult.

Summarised from the DoLS Code of Practice (Ministry of Justice, 2008, p 36, para 3.22)

Section 39C IMCA (DoLS)

If there is a gap in the availability of an RPR, an IMCA can be appointed to act in the role for the person until a new RPR can be appointed.

Summarised from the DoLS Code of Practice (Ministry of Justice, 2008, p 84, paras 7.34–7.36)

Section 39D IMCA (DoLS)

When a DoLS authorisation is in place, both the person and their representative have a statutory right of access to an IMCA. This role is designed to:

- provide support to the person or their representative;
- assist them to call a review; and
- access appeal processes via the Court of Protection.

If the person has a paid RPR, they should not need an IMCA in this role.

Summarised from the DoLS Code of Practice (Ministry of Justice, 2008, pp 84–5, paras 7.37–7.41)

Who should identify the need for an IMCA in the DoLS process?

The assessing BIA should identify whether any of the DoLS IMCA roles are required during their assessment or when the DoLS is authorised. The care home or hospital should note the need for a Section 39A IMCA on its application if it is aware that the person has no one to consult. The supervisory body will also check to ensure that the request for an IMCA has not been missed.

Who commissions IMCAs?

Supervisory bodies are responsible for commissioning and funding IMCA services.

Who provides IMCA services?

Local authorities have a statutory duty to commission IMCA services for those whom they have responsibility to assess and authorise for the DoLS. IMCA services are usually voluntary agencies or charities, and adhere to guidance that says they should commission trained IMCAs.

> DoLS Code of Practice (Ministry of Justice, 2008);
> MCA Code of Practice (DCA, 2007)

PERSPECTIVES: PROFESSIONAL

Interview with a DoLS IMCA working in England

What makes a good BIA in your experience?

As a starting point, qualities including character, understanding the importance of the role, thoroughness, maintaining freshness, courage, curiosity, the willingness to request data collection, foresight and an overview of services.

- I think that *character* attributes are essential and at the foundation of what makes a good BIA. Honesty, integrity, humility, being respectful to the person and having a person-centred approach are all vital.
- An *appreciation* of the importance of their role as part of DoLS. BIAs are the lynchpin of DoLS. Without the BIA, there would be no DoLS.
- *Thoroughness:* The desire to do a good job for the person. This links with the approach different local authorities take to DoLS. Some have an ethos of consistent thoroughness. Others are more focused on getting through the numbers of assessments needed and potentially lose sight of the people they are working with or come to the assessment with a pre-existing view of the outcome.

- *Freshness:* This is important, and a challenge to all professionals with high workloads. The more BIAs churn through assessments, the less thoughtful and helpful they will be. Some local authorities rotate BIAs regularly into their role from a social work role, which can help maintain a consistently fresh approach to each case.
- *Courage:* BIAs present their professional view and decision. They need to be confident in presenting this. Often, BIAs will assess capacity. When they do, it is important that they do not bring preconceptions to this task and have the courage to walk the line of unwise decision and lack of capacity.
- *Curiosity:* BIAs can question care home practice and suggest changes. They have the potential to be a catalyst for the improvement of services for the person. They can recommend conditions (which are usually accepted by the supervisory body) and make recommendations. However, I find a wide variation between supervisory bodies (and therefore in BIA practice) in imposing conditions. Some supervisory bodies' authorisations rarely have any conditions, others regularly have many. The balance to be struck is choosing conditions that are necessary and specific to the person, rather than generic conditions. They need also to be helpful to the managing authority that are looking after the person.
- *Foresight:* The BIA role is episodic; this carries its challenges. One failure of the DoLS system is the lack of adequate communication between DoLS teams and managing authorities, who I think routinely do not understand the paperwork and conditions. It would be helpful if BIAs could inform managing authorities of conditions they are likely to recommend and where to find these.
- *Data:* Often a BIA is confronted by anecdotal evidence but without recording to back this up. There may be a question whether the person's behaviour and verbal statements amount to a wish to apply to court to challenge the DoLS authorisation. It is useful to me to have managing authorities gathering objective data collection as required, which the BIA can also prompt.
- *Overview:* It is important for the BIA to see how their role fits within the statutory framework of other local authority and health obligations, such as care provision.

What do you think is essential for a positive working relationship between a BIA and an IMCA?

I think that a collaborative approach where we are both are working to establish the person's wishes and best interests with mutual respect is essential. I find it helpful when BIAs make timely contact with the IMCA or paid rep involved as it is rarely sensible to do this when they finalising their report. I appreciate it when BIAs are open to joint working as IMCAs may suggest conditions and recommendations to BIAs to consider. BIAs are required to consult IMCAs and paid reps and consider any reports they submit.

Joint working where there may be objections is particularly important. BIAs will be aware that the presence of verbal or behavioural objections might indicate that the person wishes to challenge their DoLS authorisation and that case law requires that an application be made to the Court of Protection. Most supervisory bodies expect the IMCA service to initiate such applications; however, as considered above, there can be an absence of recorded evidence. Where BIAs recommend conditions for the managing authority to record when the person objects to their deprivation of liberty it is extremely helpful to the IMCA or paid rep that needs to act on that.

Working with the Mental Health Assessor

The Mental Health Assessor will also be undertaking assessments under DoLS and forming a view that the BIA must take into account in their assessment. It is a legal requirement for the BIA to consult the Mental Health Assessor and take their views into account. The BIA should be able to anticipate what information they expect to get from them, and challenge the Mental Health Assessor where this is not forthcoming. It is important to recognise that the period of time it takes for you and the Mental Health Assessor to complete the assessment may be lengthy and their information may lose currency during this time; for example, if there is an objective improvement in the person's mental health, this should be discussed with the supervisory body.

DoLS assessments are undertaken by you as a BIA and by the assessing doctor. It varies across supervisory bodies as to whether you undertake these assessments together or at similar times. It is most likely that assessments will be sequential, with differing amounts of time between them. Given the impact of the *Cheshire West* judgment on the number of DoLS applications waiting for assessment, there may be months between the BIA and assessing doctor's assessments. Assessments lose their validity over time, especially capacity assessments, of which supervisory bodies should be aware. If you think that the conclusions drawn by the Mental Health Assessor are no longer valid when you make your assessment, you should let the supervisory body know, as it may need to commission a further assessment by a Mental Health Assessor.

Information that Mental Health Assessors can usefully provide to BIAs includes the following:

- details of how the person's mental disorder affects their day-to-day functioning;
- information on whether sedating, behaviour- or mood-altering medication is appropriate, necessary or at the correct dose for the person and whether a medication review should be recommended;
- the impact of the deprivation of liberty on the person and suggestions of ways in which this impact could be alleviated that should be considered when drawing up conditions.

Working with the supervisory body

BIAs should consider the role of the supervisory body and the pressures and challenges it faces. As a BIA, you need to work effectively with the supervisory body as it commissions you to carry out DoLS assessments. BIAs can be employed directly by local authorities (or health boards in Wales) or work as an independent practitioner (see Chapter 2 for more information).

As in all areas of practice, maintaining working relationships is an essential part of an effective working environment. Supervisory bodies are also responsible for scrutinising the quality of evidence contained in the assessments that the Mental Health Assessor and BIA produce. This can lead to tensions, as supervisory bodies may be looking for a standard of writing that you are unfamiliar with.

You will need to liaise with your supervisory body to establish an understanding of its expectations for recording your decisions and it may need to negotiate changes, additions or reductions in the information provided. BIAs should not see this as a process requiring defensiveness on their part, as supervisory bodies have a responsibility to maintain the quality of the DoLS decisions they sign off in the interests of the person being assessed.

The supervisory body should offer advice and support to BIAs to assist them in completing their assessments and to ensure that the BIA's skills and knowledge are focused on what the supervisory body signatory requires (see Chapter 8 for further guidance on BIA recording).

It is essential to keep your professional ethics and values in mind regarding pace of work and workload for BIA work. Supervisory bodies are facing increasing censure from courts, the Local Government Ombudsman (LGO) and soon, the Care Quality Commission (CQC). You will need to balance your diligence regarding good assessment and decision-making practice with the rights of those still waiting for the DoLS assessment they have a legal right to. (See Chapter 2 for discussion of the pressures facing supervisory bodies regarding completion of DoLS assessments.)

Working with social workers, social care practitioners and health coordinators

It is vital to recognise that before, during and after your BIA assessment there are likely to be other professionals involved in the person's care whose views, past decisions and plans you must consider in your assessment and you may be making recommendations to for the future. This may not be the case for a self-funding resident in a care home, but in most other circumstances the following steps are essential:

- You must consult with social care and health professionals with prior or current responsibility for decisions made about the person's care.
- You will need to know how the decision was made that brought the person to where you are assessing them, what other, if any, less restrictive options have been tried or whether they are available, and who is responsible for funding the person's care.
- Because of your assessment, you may recommend that conditions are attached to the DoLS authorisation for the managing authority or to recommendations for social care and health professionals. Either of these may require an exploration of new resources or assessments to be undertaken under care and support legislation, such as the Care Act 2014 in England, or the Social Services and Well-being (Wales) Act 2014 in Wales, requiring the involvement of those with ongoing responsibility for care planning.
- You will also find it useful to have already discussed potential options for less restrictive care that are being considered by those who are funding the person's care, so you can weigh them up as part of your best interests balance sheet decision.
- The plans made by those responsible for decisions about the person's long-term care may also influence the length of authorisation you recommend; for example, if there are already plans for the person to move soon, a lengthy authorisation would not be appropriate.

Without such consultation, your assessment will lack the understanding of the context that brought the person to where they are today and what options are available to explore for the future, both of which are essential for a thorough and relevant BIA assessment.

KEY MESSAGES

- **PRIORITISE** the views and wishes of the person and those who can facilitate these.

- **KNOW** who you need to speak to and document clearly and concisely the information they have given you.

- **DEVELOP** a communication strategy and involve interpreters, as appropriate.

- **INVESTIGATE** and gather evidence to verify those who have legal powers and ensure that they are acting in the person's best interests.

- **ENSURE** that you know why the person is in their current care home or hospital, what decisions have already been made about the options available to them and what plans there are for their future.

 KNOWLEDGE REVIEW

- **WHAT** do you need to bear in mind when explaining why you are undertaking a DoLS assessment?

- **WHAT** resources or support might you need to communicate effectively with the person you are assessing?

- **WHAT** contribution should families, friends and carers make to your assessment?

- **WHAT** information are you looking for from the following roles that may be involved with the person you are assessing:
  - RPR
  - IMCA
  - LPA or deputy
  - Managing authority, including manager and care workers
  - Social worker or health professional?

- **WHAT** expectations will supervisory bodies have of your practice?

FURTHER READING

For more information on DoLS IMCAs and representatives, see:

- Social Care Institute for Excellence (2017) *IMCA and Paid Relevant Person's Representative Roles in the Mental Capacity Act Deprivation of Liberty Safeguards: SCIE Guide 41*, which can be accessed via their MCA resource hub

To search the Office of the Public Guardian's registers of powers of attorney and deputyships using the OPG100 form, see:

- Office of the Public Guardian (2021) 'Find out if someone has a registered attorney or deputy'

For more information on the role of the RPR, see:

- Department of Health/Office of the Public Guardian (2009) *Deprivation of Liberty Safeguards: Guide for Relevant Person's Representatives*

- Age UK (2022) *Factsheet 62, Deprivation of Liberty Standards*, which includes guidance on the role of the RPR

Part 2
Assessments, challenges and dilemmas

5

Making Deprivation of Liberty Safeguards decisions

Introduction

This chapter explores the various decisions you will make during your Deprivation of Liberty Safeguards (DoLS) assessment when acting as a Best Interests Assessor (BIA). BIAs make the following key decisions:

- whether the person is eligible for DoLS because they are over 18;
- whether there is no relevant power in place that refuses;
- whether the person has capacity to decide to consent to their care or treatment in a care home or hospital, sometimes called 'capacity for residence decisions';
- whether the person's care arrangements do, or will, amount to a deprivation of their liberty;
- whether the care in place is necessary to prevent harm coming to them;
- whether the care arrangements are proportionate to the risk of the harm identified occurring;
- whether the care is in the person's best interests, including whether they object to the care and treatment;
- in cases where a recommendation is made to authorise deprivation of liberty:
  - who should act as the Relevant Person's Representative (RPR);
  - what conditions apply to the managing authority, or what recommendations are made to the social worker or healthcare professionals involved;
  - for how long the DoLS should be authorised.

BIAs need to be clear about the scope and focus of the decisions they make. You are not being asked to make long-term care and treatment decisions. You are being asked to look at where the person is currently living, or where they will move to very soon, and whether they can decide to be there, consent to the restrictions that are in place there and whether these are appropriate to their needs or not. As noted by Dalrymple and Burke (2006, p 290):

> Legislation can be used to deny rights but we need to be aware of our role in minimising the oppressive aspects of practice and the law and

we must endeavour to maximise the rights to which all people are entitled. It is for that reason that we see the law as an instrument to protect people's rights. It is a powerful instrument but it is one that we can control and we should therefore not become subservient to it.

Assessment and decision-making

The fundamental purpose of the BIA's role is to reach a decision that either justifies or challenges a person's liberty being deprived within hospital or care home settings. These BIA decisions are located in a legal, ethical and practice context. The most important person in the assessment process is the person being assessed.

However, each assessment involves many individuals, each with their own potential to contribute information related to the person being assessed. This can include the person's background, their previously expressed wishes and values, as well as the consulted person's views on what has been occurring and what needs to happen next. (See Chapter 4 for an exploration of working with others during the BIA assessment.)

To reach any decision, the BIA needs to be a 'curious investigator' – gathering evidence, scrutinising it and reaching considered conclusions – rather than a passive observer. To achieve this, you will review the person's case notes as maintained by the managing authority, and any relevant health and social care records, speak with interested people, and negotiate the difference between fact and opinion in what these tell you. This is not an easy task, as looking at a situation through the magnifying lens of the BIA can reveal approaches by health and care staff that may be enabling or limiting to the person being assessed. It will identify where positive risk taking (Langan and Lindow, 2004) is being deployed or not and may highlight any restrictions that are disproportionate and will need to be challenged by the BIA. Public bodies such as hospitals or care homes that are acting beyond their jurisdiction should be challenged by the BIA through their DoLS decision-making and recording, or via adult safeguarding procedures where relevant, if they are aware that disproportionate restrictions are in place.

The question then is, how to conduct a BIA assessment? What do you actually do? All the legal frameworks, case law and guidance in the world will not answer the question 'what do BIAs actually do?' Below is a personal insight into how one of the authors approaches BIA assessments.

REFLECTIVE ACCOUNT

Doing BIA assessments

My starting point when asked to complete a BIA assessment is always to find out the person's story. There is so much insight into best interests decisions, especially least restrictive options that are available and could be tried or have already been eliminated, to be had from establishing the path to the person's current residence and care. This can be identified through some simple questions that can guide your assessment overall:

- How did the person get here?
- Why here?
- Who decided?
- How much control did the person have over this decision?
- Was this planned to be permanent or temporary?
- Has this decision been revisited and what are the person's views now?

The narrative thread that can be established from these questions allows the BIA to consider in a person-centred way what deprivation of liberty, necessity, proportionality and best interests mean to them. For example, here are two contrasting narratives that the authors have encountered in practice that lead to different perspectives on restrictions and best interests. Neither sets of restrictions were considered to be unnecessary.

1. James is a man in his 60s with a lifelong condition (learning disability) who moved into a long-stay hospital when he was a teenager as his mother was not able to care for him at home. He moved into a large residential home in the 1990s when the hospital was closed as a result of community care reforms. He has moved various times and now resides in a small care home where he has lived for eight years. He has his own room, and is active in decisions made about the home that he shares with others he considers his friends. James is free to come and go with supervision, and support workers assist him to go shopping, meet other friends and be active in the local community every day.

2. Freida is an older woman with dementia who was admitted to a nursing home two years ago. Her family tells you that her home has been sold to pay for her care and she is unaware. They would rather you did not tell her as this would distress her. When you speak to the social worker, they tell you that she was originally discharged to the home as a temporary measure as the hospital needed the bed. She was moved there in her best interests without her consent and, once there, her family, who have LPA for her property and finances, sold her home. She continues to ask to go home.

By identifying and better understanding these narratives, the BIA would be in a position to consider whether less restrictive options are available and what impact the restrictions are having on the person's wellbeing in terms of their proportionality.

How can you gain access to this narrative?

The story of how the person came to be where they are now, and why, is often not explicitly written in DoLS referral forms or current care plans, although decision-making about what current care looks like for the person and what reviews have taken place should be.

The story of the person's admission could be available from the person themselves if they are able to communicate this. If not, talking to friends, family and/or their key worker in the care home or hospital can be illuminating. If they were placed in a care home by a local authority, then their care management records should hold this information. If you are able to speak to the social worker who placed them, this can be invaluable and uncover the motivation for decisions and alternative options explored that may not have been explained explicitly in the case notes.

This decision-making process for entering the care home or hospital is likely to be much easier to access in Freida's case than in James's, considering the time that has lapsed since the original decision to admit James into institutional care. It may only be possible to find out the story of his most recent placement, but this is still a useful starting point to understanding both that decision-making process and the person's agency within it.

All this means a lot of time spent examining care records, talking to those involved with the person's care, whether in a personal or professional capacity, often before you meet the person and find out how they are and what they want at the moment of your assessment. You will also need to keep your own clear record of what information you found where or from whom.

Article 8 and care decision-making

One of the issues that may arise when a BIA is identifying the decision-making that lead to the person you are assessing being placed in a care home might highlight is whether their Article 8 right to privacy and family life was breached in the process. Placement decision-making, especially where a person has impaired mental capacity, may be unlawful if these essential legal steps have not been considered:

- If the person had mental capacity and consented to the placement, this is not a breach of Article 8.
- If the person was assessed to lack mental capacity to make the decision about admission to a care home and a fully evidenced best interests decision was made on their behalf, this is not a breach of Article 8.
- If the person was assessed to lack mental capacity to make the decision about admission to a care home and they or their family objected to this decision and the Court of Protection ordered that placement in a care home was in their best interests, this is not a breach of Article 8.

A placement in a care home in any other circumstances could be a breach of the person's Article 8 rights. For example, where the person was coerced into placement despite their objections, their consent was not obtained or a mental capacity assessment and best interests decision were not made. If this is something you identify through your BIA assessment as having occurred it is recommended you discuss what steps may need to be taken with the supervisory body that commissioned you to assess the person.

The six DoLS assessment decisions

As a BIA, your involvement with a case begins with the decision to accept the assessment commissioned by the supervisory body. The supervisory body will explain which assessments you are being commissioned to complete. Of the six assessments required by the supervisory body to be completed for a DoLS authorisation, up to five (all bar the mental health assessment) could potentially be undertaken by the BIA, so it is essential from the start to be clear which assessments you will be required to focus on.

The DoLS Form 3 that BIAs complete (Welsh Assembly Government, 2015; DHSC, 2018) includes the following assessments:

- Age
- Mental capacity
- No refusals
- Best interests (including deprivation of liberty, necessary, proportionate and best interests).

Age assessment

All BIAs are expected to complete the age assessment and it is typically the most straightforward. This requires you to use verification skills, such as reviewing relevant paperwork in the person's health and social care records and observing the person you are assessing. In cases where the person is evidently much older than 18, this will not require much investigation.

This assessment can be challenging when a person's status and origin are unknown and they appear close to the age of 18. This can occur with unaccompanied minors, for example asylum-seekers who appear older, but have no supporting identification documents to corroborate their age. Age assessments in these circumstances are typically difficult to undertake and require experienced practitioners who are familiar with age assessment work. In these situations, the compliance criteria for undertaking age assessments established in the case of *B v Mayor and Burgesses of the London Borough of Merton* [2003] should be followed. These stipulate pragmatically that the age assessment must be conducted by two fully qualified social workers, one of whom must be specifically trained in age assessment, who are accompanied by an appropriate adult and an interpreter as required.

Age assessments of this nature should not be undertaken by the BIA, but referred to the appropriate children's and young people's services for joint working to establish whether or not the assessed person is over 18. As a BIA, however, you are merely asked in these cases to reach a decision based on your professional judgement. If you are still uncertain, a short DoLS authorisation with a condition asking for evidence of age to be explored may be an appropriate conclusion.

Mental capacity assessment

The mental capacity assessment is key to the BIA assessment, as DoLS can only be used when the person lacks capacity to decide to consent to their care arrangements. It is common to hear that a person 'lacks capacity' in health and social care discussions, but, as Graham and Cowley (2015, p 61) point out, 'it is important that you consider this statement critically … [and] ask two questions.

1. What for?
2. What evidence do you have?'

The DoLS mental capacity assessment is the evidence you have that the person lacks capacity to make the deprivation of liberty decision at the time you assessed, that is, can the person consent to the residence for care and/or treatment that amounts to a deprivation of their liberty? In the early years of DoLS implementation, the main reason that DoLS assessments found the person ineligible was because the person had the capacity to make the decision themselves – 90 per cent of DoLS applications in England in 2015–16 where the person was assessed were not granted (NHS Digital, 2016, p 34). Long waiting lists for DoLS assessments has shifted the balance to changes in circumstances being the main reason DoLS assessments are not authorised, but having mental capacity remains a significant reason for finding a DoLS authorisation is not appropriate.

The DoLS mental capacity assessment must provide sufficient evidence to show the threshold has been reached to interfere with the person's right to make this decision themselves. Richards (2016, pp 1–2) highlighted the beneficial impact on the person that can arise from the BIA finding that the person has the capacity to make this decision themselves.

You may or may not be asked to carry out the mental capacity assessment, depending on the local practice of your supervisory body. Some ask the Mental Health Assessor to do this as routine, so you may be considering and scrutinising the decision they have reached as part of your overall BIA assessment. You may agree with the conclusion they reach but it is also possible that you may not from your wider assessment. If so, consult with your supervisory body about what you should do next.

The focus of the DoLS mental capacity assessment should always be on whether the assessed person can consent to remain resident in the care home or hospital for the purpose of care and treatment. If they can consent themselves, the DoLS assessment will cease and the person can choose whether they stay or leave. The DoLS capacity assessment is on both Forms 3 and 4 (completed by the Mental Health Assessor), so either the BIA or Mental Health Assessor can record their decision in the same format.

The capacity assessment on Forms 3 and 4 (Welsh Government, 2015; DHSC, 2018) is set out in four sections to enable assessors to complete it in a legally compliant manner: practicable steps; mental disorder; ability to decide; and causative nexus.

Practicable steps

Principle 2 of the Mental Capacity Act (MCA) 2005 is clear that support must be offered or adopted to enable the person to be supported to make their own decision before any action is taken to act on their behalf. BIAs must evidence what actions they have taken to help the person demonstrate their ability to make the decision. BIAs must show they have considered the following:

- the time of day the assessment was carried out to ensure that the person was at their most alert;
- any communication tools or resources, such as aids, equipment, or interpreter, required to help the person understand, and any other special arrangements relating, for example, to location of assessment, removal of distractions and background noise, privacy and so on;
- access to people who know the person well and can support them to communicate, bearing in mind the possibility that this person may distract or prevent the person from expressing their own views;
- use of specialist assistance, for example input from a speech and language therapist (see Chapter 3).

The BIA must also decide what they think are the salient points that the person needs to show that they understand about the decision to be made and use these points to decide what and how information will be presented to the person.

The case of *CC v KK and STCC* [2012] introduced the idea of the 'salient points'. In his judgment, Baker J highlighted that 'it is inappropriate to start with a blank canvas. The person under evaluation must be presented with detailed options so that their capacity to weigh these options can be evaluated' (p 18). Baker J went on to say that 'it is not necessary for a person to demonstrate a capacity to understand and weigh up every detail of the respective options, but merely the salient factors' (p 19). Therefore, the information the assessor provides to the person and their judgement of the responses they get to their questions about these must focus solely on the key elements of the decision about where they currently reside for the purpose of care and treatment. This is termed 'capacity for residence' and further cases have followed *CC v KK and STCC* to establish more clearly what the salient points for capacity for residence are.

The case of *LBX v K, L and M* [2013] identified a number of salient points for care and residence that have been developed and supported in other judgments, including *Derbyshire County Council v AC, EC and LC* [2014].

Hilder J in *London Borough of Tower Hamlets v A and KF* [2020] confirmed the primacy of the approach used in *LBX v K, L and M* [2013] in relation to the salient points regarding care and residence. This case noted different approaches to assessment of care and residence in relation to this Section 21A DoLS appeal and the efforts made to assess the person's mental capacity in relation to each decision (care and residence) separately. The judge suggested that these decisions could not so easily be separated into 'silos' as the actual decision to be made overall regarding a DoLS authorisation is about residence in order to receive care. The options for A were regarding options to live in a care home or receive care in her own home. There may be other occasions where salient points for residence decisions might be different to salient points for care decisions, but in DoLS mental capacity assessments these need to be considered together as the decisions are interrelated.

39 Essex Chambers (2020) summarised the issue in this case as regarding the difference in the kind of care that A was going to receive between the two options – her own flat and the care home – and this being likely to impact on her functioning and wellbeing. The court accepted that the care she would receive in both places was relevant information that A needed to understand as part of her residence decision and that A lacked capacity to make decisions about her care needs. This exploration of the different factors needing to be considered and their need to be assessed together offers useful guidance for BIAs unpicking the information that people need to understand within DoLS mental capacity assessments.

The *salient points for residence* identified from *LBX v K, L and M* [2013] are:

- what the two (or more options) for living are, including the type of property and facilities available;
- broad information about the area and potential risks there;

- the difference between living somewhere and just visiting;
- the activities available were the person to live there;
- ability to see friends and family or not;
- that rent and/or bills will need to be paid for staying there – it is not considered relevant that the person understands how much the placement would cost or how this would be paid;
- rules and obligations;
- who the person would be living with;
- the sort of care available at each placement broadly.

The *salient points for care* identified from *LBX v K, L and M* [2013] are:

- what areas the person needs support with;
- what sort of support they need;
- who will be providing them with support;
- what would happen if they did not have any support or they refused it;
- that carers might not always treat them properly and they can complain if they are not happy about their care.

In neither instance were the funding for residence or care considered relevant to the information the person needed to understand.

To create person-centred salient points for your assessments, you will need to consider the person's circumstances based on the information you have gathered about their care and why they are where they are from the managing authority and those involved in managing their care.

From this, you can plan what information you will present and the questions you will ask about the following:

- where the person currently resides, for example a care home or a hospital;
- why they are there, for example what care and support needs they have;
- the care and treatment they receive there from health and care staff, for example the care plan in place;
- the risks associated with not receiving this care and treatment;
- the pros and cons of other available options, for example the risks and benefits of being at home, if that option exists, or in another care placement.

You will then need to think about what the person needs to know when you present these points, for example available options and how you will present them. You will also need to plan how you will record and evidence their responses; for example, will someone be with you and the person during the assessment to record their responses, will you be taking notes yourself, or will you write up your notes afterwards? If you use a pictorial format such as Talking Mats for communicating with the person, you could take photographs of the person's responses.

Mental disorder (diagnostic test)

Your decision here should be based on the diagnosis of mental disorder identified by the Mental Health Assessor and you should refer directly to the diagnosis they give in their assessment. If this is not clear, or a formal diagnosis was not available to the Mental Health Assessor, you may want to ask them to clarify or ask for a formal diagnosis to be explored as a condition or recommendation of your authorisation, if appropriate.

Ability to decide (functional test)

a) The person is unable to understand the information relevant to the decision
Here you will need to explain the information you presented to the person, how they responded and why their responses suggested to you that they did, or did not, understand the information you presented. It is vital to ensure that you have provided the person with information directly related to the decision (that is, the salient points), rather than making your assessment of their understanding more general, so that you can reach a decision-specific conclusion about their understanding. It can be useful to note down at the time exactly what the person says during the assessment, or as soon as possible afterwards, so you can consider their exact response in coming to your conclusion.

b) The person is unable to retain the information relevant to the decision
You will need to consider how the person responded to the information at the time of your assessment and whether they responded in a coherent way that suggested they could explain the information and reach a decision. Were they able to engage in the conversation about their care and where they lived long enough to answer questions or give reasons for their decision? The person is not expected to retain the information for any longer than is required to reach their decision, for example they do not have to be able to recall your conversation later.

c) The person is unable to use or weigh that information as part of the process of making the decision
This section asks the assessor to focus on the restrictions identified in the care plan, for example the nature of the placement, that have been designed to reduce potential risks. Can the person understand what harm they would come to if the care were not available? Do they have a plan to deal with that risk of harm if they were responsible for caring for themselves? Does the person acknowledge that they need the care they receive? Do they deny that they need the care the managing authority is providing? Do they forget or are they overly optimistic about the support they need? If you are not confident that the person recognises and can mitigate the risks in their situation that lead to residence in a care home or hospital for care and treatment their answers may indicate that they cannot use or weigh the information about the decision.

d) The person is unable to communicate their decision (whether by talking, using sign language or any other means)

The assessor needs to consider both whether the person is able to communicate their views by any means and whether they have communicated their decision about their residence for care and treatment. If the person is able to communicate their view on the decision, the assessor must record it. This is essential information, as it will be required when considering whether the person is expressing an objection to their deprivation of liberty, which would require their case to be taken to the Court of Protection. If the person *cannot* communicate their decision by whatever means, you should indicate this on the form by leaving the relevant tick box blank.

Causative nexus

The case of *PC v City of York Council* [2013] defined the importance of establishing the 'causative nexus' between the diagnostic and functional test of the mental capacity assessment. In this Court of Appeal judgment, the three judges held that the original judge had failed to establish the link between the mental impairment causing the ability to decide and the decision itself. The assessor must make it clear in this section that they think the person's inability to make this decision is caused by the mental disorder (as identified by the Mental Health Assessor) not by another factor. Other factors that could impact on the person's ability to make decisions could be the nature and complexity of the decision itself or coercion and control by another or others about how they believe the person should decide. It is your responsibility as a BIA to weigh the evidence you have regarding the person's decision-making ability to come to a professional judgement as to whether the person's cognitive impairment or mental health condition is affecting their decision-making or if something else is impacting this.

The judgment in *NCC v TB and PB* [2014] referenced the *PC v City of York* judgment, making it clear that the diagnosis of mental impairment needed to be established *before* concluding whether the person's inability to decide stemmed from their mental impairment. This case involved deciding whether a coercive relationship with the person's partner was influencing them or whether it was their mental impairment that was particularly impacting on their ability to use and weigh risk.

Fluctuating capacity

One of the circumstances that practitioners often find challenging when conducting mental capacity assessments is when the person's mental state fluctuates, changing the person's ability to make decisions over time, whether over the course of days, hours or minutes. Many conditions can affect this, including the nature of the person's mental impairment. For example, bipolar conditions can cause cycles of depression and mania over days and weeks, and dementia can cause greater cognitive impairment within the cycle of the day, for example when 'sundowning' occurs. The use or withdrawal of prescription medication, drugs or alcohol, or physical health conditions, including infections that can cause states of delirium (OFH, 2020; Mental Health and Justice/Wellcome, 2022) can cause short-term effects on cognition.

It can be difficult to have confidence in a decision regarding mental capacity where the person's ability to engage with the functional test of capacity may vary over months, weeks, days or even during the course of a day. Mental Health and Justice/Wellcome (2022) suggest considering whether decisions are one-offs or repeated decisions. A one-off decision may be possible to put off until the person's cognition improves, for example until after an infection can be treated, but immediate decisions may need to be made in the person's best interests in the short term to ensure decisions about care and treatment are made lawfully. Longer term decisions will need more considered responses regarding the person's mental capacity to consent or not with regard to the longer term implications of a decision, such as whether to move into a care home or not.

Guidance around repeated decisions or decisions with longer term impacts are likely to be more relevant to DoLS than the wider MCA. The concept of *micro* (small, everyday decisions about the person's care, health and wellbeing) and *macro* (big, life-changing decisions like serious medical treatment and residence) decisions in this context can be helpful where:

> the management of a physical or mental health condition which requires a multitude of 'micro-decisions' over the course of each day or week. Although capacity is time-specific, in such a case, it will usually be appropriate for you to take a broad view as to the 'material time' during which the person must be able to take the decisions in question. If the reality is that there are only limited periods during the course of each day or week that the person is able to take their own decisions, and the decision-making is not 'macro', then it will usually be appropriate for you to proceed on the basis that, in fact, they lack capacity to decide. (Mental Health and Justice/Wellcome, 2022)

This unpicking of types of decisions and fluctuating capacity was used by Newton J in *Royal Borough of Greenwich v CDM* [2019]. This case concerned whether CDM had capacity to make decisions regarding the management of her diabetes, which was the main risk factor leading to her deprivation of liberty in a care home. The judge focused on whether the assessment of her mental capacity concerned her overall capacity to make decisions about her diabetes management or if:

> 'the matter' in relation to which CDM is being assessed is one macro-decision which encompasses all of the many micro-decisions that CDM is required to make when managing her diabetes, or, whether

CDM's capacity should be assessed in respect of each micro-decision or group of micro-decisions.

Unpicking the micro-decisions could allow space for CDM to make individual, smaller decisions autonomously where possible in the spirit of supporting her autonomy, and there were times that were identified that she could do this. However, the judge's view was that the nature of diabetes management was too interrelated and her ability to make decisions too unpredictable and changeable to allow for this to affect the fact that overall, on the macro-level, she was unable to use and weight risk in relation to managing her diabetes. This case was not definitive, although the concepts of 'one-off/regular', 'short/long term' and 'micro/macro-decisions' all offer useful frameworks for decision-making in other contexts where a person's mental impairment causes fluctuating capacity.

It is important to keep decision-making where fluctuating capacity is identified under regular review so a shorter DoLS authorisation may be indicated to ensure the person's mental capacity, views and wishes are regularly checked so changes to decisions can be made, as appropriate.

The concept of executive capacity is also valuable to consider and is explored in more depth in Chapter 6 in relation to conditions where more than functional capacity needs consideration.

A brief aside on language

The frequently used phrase 'the person has been *deemed* to lack capacity' (our emphasis) causes us some unease. 'Deemed' suggests to us that an unchangeable and fixed decision has been made by an unnamed and unquestionable power. It disguises the fact that a professional should have completed an assessment and reached a legally compliant decision based on their knowledge of the person at a particular time that can be questioned and scrutinised by others. A person 'deemed' to lack capacity begs the questions: 'Who decided that? and Why?' We prefer to talk about a *decision* having been made that the person lacked capacity to make the decision at the time. This gives those assessing the power to scrutinise and possibly revise that decision, allowing for professional accountability for decision-making and change, as appropriate.

No refusals assessment

For the no refusals assessment, you will need to establish two things:

1. Are there people with relevant decision-making powers or arrangements in place, such as Lasting Powers of Attorney (LPAs) or Court of Protection-appointed deputies, or a relevant advance decision to refuse treatment? (See Chapter 4 for more information on these roles, how to establish whether they exist and what issues there may be in working with these powers.)

2. If such a power or decision does exist, does it conflict with the planned deprivation of liberty? In other words, if there is a person with a health and welfare LPA, what is their view of the placement or the person's stay in hospital? If they support it, there is a finding of no refusals, and the other assessments can proceed. If they disagree with it, the DoLS cannot be authorised and alternative arrangements for the person's care should be considered.

REFLECTIVE ACTIVITY

Oscar, 65, White British

You are requested by the supervisory body to complete age, no refusals, mental capacity and best interests assessments for a DoLS authorisation for Oscar, who has suffered a stroke and subsequent cognitive impairment, which has resulted in a care home placement. During the no refusals assessment, you discover that Oscar's husband, Andrew, has an LPA for property and financial affairs and health and welfare for Oscar. Oscar owns his own home and lived there with Andrew prior to his stroke. Andrew is not happy about Oscar staying in the nursing home to which he was discharged from hospital, as Oscar has told him that he wants to leave, and would prefer to care for him there.

Questions
- What will you need to verify? How can you check this?
- What power does Andrew have to change the decision about how Oscar is being cared for?

Our approach to Oscar and Andrew's situation would be to ask Andrew for documentary evidence of the LPA, save a copy of the LPA with Oscar's DoLS assessment records and check these to ensure that they have been enacted by the Court of Protection. If Andrew is making a valid refusal of the DoLS authorisation, then this will need to be documented on Form 3 and sent to the supervisory body for action.

We would include Andrew's views on what alternative options for care may be available and discuss with the social worker who was involved in placing Oscar in the care home, if there was one, to see what alternative options to the care home could still be explored. We would expect the supervisory body to pass the need to explore alternative care options over for an urgent care review, since without a DoLS authorisation, it is likely that Oscar is being unlawfully deprived of his liberty.

Best interests assessment

The best interests assessment requires you to decide whether each of four criteria apply:

1. whether a deprivation of liberty is or will be occurring;
2. if that deprivation of liberty is necessary to prevent harm coming to the person;
3. if the restrictions amounting to that deprivation of liberty are proportionate to the risk of that harm occurring; and
4. if so, whether the deprivation of liberty is in the person's best interests.

These four questions are set out in a different order in the DoLS Code of Practice (Ministry of Justice, 2008, para 4.58), but considering these questions in the order outlined in this chapter allows us to consider the necessity to prevent harm and proportionality questions before summing up the person's best interests overall. This is also the order used in the English and Welsh DoLS forms (Welsh Government, 2015; DHSC, 2018).

1. Deprivation of liberty

When deciding whether the restrictions the person is experiencing amount to a deprivation of their liberty, you must consider the case law that informs the current definition of deprivation of liberty, especially the subjective, objective and imputable to the state elements from *Storck v Germany* [2005]:

- *Subjective*: assessment has been made that the person lacks capacity to consent to the restrictions.
- *Objective*: that the person is confined to a certain place for a not negligible period of time as judged using the 'acid test' of 'under continuous supervision and control and not free to leave' (from the *HL v The United Kingdom* and *Cheshire West* judgments; see Chapter 1), evidenced using the framework identified in *Guzzardi v Italy* [1980] (see Figure 5.1).
- *Imputable to the state*: that the state is responsible for the decisions requiring the person to be deprived of their liberty; for example, because the NHS or a local authority has decided they should reside in a care home or hospital, because their care is funded by the NHS or a local authority, or because the managing authority is regulated by the Care Quality Commission, Care Inspectorate Wales or Healthcare Inspectorate Wales.

This is the key decision of the BIA assessment. You are being asked to decide whether you think that the person's human right to liberty and security is being restricted. It might feel like you are overwhelmed by legal principles and guidance on this issue, but it is essential to step back from the decision and think about the impact of what you are deciding. Is the person experiencing restrictions as

Figure 5.1: Deprivation of liberty definition case law

> **'The person is deprived of their liberty'** (Storck v Germany, 2005) by *three* elements
> 1. **Objective** element: detention for a 'not negligible' period of time eg, the 'acid test' **AND**
> 2. **Subjective** element: consent eg, capacity to consent to the deprivation of liberty **AND**
> 3. **Imputable to the State** element: State responsibility for the care or treatment or monitoring of the care setting

The 'acid test' (Supreme Court Cheshire West, 2014)

1. 'Continuous supervision and control...'

Type (Guzzardi v Italy, 1980): eg, list of restrictions in place including nature of the environment (hospital or care home) and physical restrictions in place, supervision and monitoring by staff including amount and nature of personal care given, restrictions on autonomy access to activities and community medication designed to manage behaviour or mood, including if given covertly

Duration: eg, how long have the restrictions been in place and how long planned in future?

Effect: eg, what impact are the restrictions having on the person (positive or negative)?

Manner: eg, how is care given or restrictions applied? Is coercion, medication or force used to keep the person in the care setting or to manage their behaviour?

Degree and intensity: eg, what impact is living with restrictions having on the person? Are they agitated or distressed by them? Is their physical/mental health improving? Are they aware of the restrictions they live with?

The 'acid test' (Supreme Court Cheshire West, 2014)

2. '... and not free to leave'

Short term: eg, can the person go out and come back when they want? Would staff prevent or dissuade them from leaving whether on their own or with family/friends? Would staff try to bring the person back if they left?

Long term: eg, does the person have freedom to choose to live elsewhere? Would their family/friends be allowed to take them to live elsewhere?

Not relevant

The person's compliance or lack of objection

The 'relative normality' of the placement, eg, that it is a usual setting for the person to live considering their condition

The purpose of the placement, eg, to provide care to meet their needs

a result of their care and treatment that are having an impact on their ability to move freely and live their life as they choose without interference? Are these short- or long-term restrictions? If there are restrictions or interference, what impact do they have on the person? How does the person react to these restrictions? Are they causing distress or anger, or are they accepted and seen to be improving their physical and emotional wellbeing? The answers to these fundamental questions should help you decide whether the person is being deprived of their liberty.

When thinking about the details of whether the person is deprived of their liberty, the *Re NRA and others* [2015] judgment made it clear that 'it is well-established that the approach to the existence of a deprivation of liberty is governed by the Guzzardi principle'. Some supervisory bodies ask BIAs to set out a list of the restrictions that the person is subject to under headings from the *Guzzardi* judgment in their Form 3 to show that they have considered each of these elements when concluding whether the person has been deprived of their liberty or not. This shows that the BIA has explored the potential range of types of restriction the person might be subject to as well as the person's experience of, and responses to, these. This should be followed by a summary of why you think the person meets the criteria of deprivation of liberty.

Cheshire West and unforeseen consequences: DoLS and death in state detention

One of the unforeseen consequences of the *Cheshire West* [2014] judgment's revision of the definition of deprivation of liberty was to include those in unconscious states where the person's lack of mental capacity to consent to treatment was evident and their state of consciousness and loss of freedom of movement brought them within the 'acid test' definition of deprivation of liberty. The legal necessity for a coroner's inquest where a person has died in state detention under Sections 7 and 48 of the Coroners and Justice Act 2009 was initially interpreted to include those who died while subject to a DoLS authorisation. This brought significant numbers of people whose care and treatment was not in question at the end of their life into the scope of a legal measure designed to ensure that unlawful death in detention settings, such as prisons, police custody and psychiatric hospitals, was subject to scrutiny.

The case of Maria Ferriera, a woman with learning disabilities who died in intensive care, brought this issue to the attention of the court, as her sister objected to the requirement for a coroners' inquest. The Court of Appeal in *R (Ferreira) v HM Senior Coroner for Inner South London* [2017] ruled that Maria was:

> not deprived of her liberty at the date of her death because she was being treated for a physical illness and her treatment was that which it appeared to all intents would have been administered to a person who did not have her mental impairment. She was physically restricted in her movements by her physical infirmities and by the treatment she received (which for example included sedation) but the root cause of any loss of liberty was her physical condition, not any restrictions imposed by the hospital. (para 10)

This judgment essentially ruled that where a person is receiving treatment for a physical health condition that affects their consciousness and is in line with the freedom of movement expected in the circumstances, this is not to be considered as a deprivation of liberty in the same manner as would be relevant for someone of unsound mind and therefore a coroner's inquest is not required. The Coroners and Justice Act 2009 was amended from April 2017 to state that 'a person is not in state detention at any time when he or she is deprived of liberty under section 4A(3) or (5) or 4B of the Mental Capacity Act 2005' (Policing and Crime

Act 2017, Section 178). This meant that deaths considered to be natural where the person is subject to a DoLS authorisation, Court of Protection order under Section 16 MCA 2005 or while the court application is being made will not need to be reported to the coroner, although those where a deprivation of liberty has not yet been authorised will need to be (39 Essex Chambers, 2017).

The government referenced the *Ferriera* judgment to emphasise during the COVID-19 pandemic that 'where life-saving treatment is being provided in care homes or hospitals, including for the treatment of COVID-19, then this will not amount to a deprivation of liberty, as long as the treatment is the same as would normally be given to any patient without a mental disorder' (DHSC, 2021). (For further information on vital acts with LPS, see Chapter 10.)

2. Necessary to prevent harm

The best interests section of Form 3 then asks the BIA whether it is necessary to deprive the person of their liberty under DoLS because of the harm that might come to the person if those restrictions were not in place.

The BIA must consider both the *actual* risks of harm (for example, those events that will occur if the restrictions were not in place and that have occurred before) and the *potential* risks (the harm that those making decisions about the person's care believe will occur because of their experience and knowledge of the person or how their mental health condition may develop). The BIA should also consider how *severe* the harm may be (whether it will cause significant injury or have a great impact on the person's wellbeing) and how *likely* the harm is (whether the harm will probably occur immediately or it would take time for the harm to affect the person).

This section is essential to ensure that restrictions are only in place because of a genuine, identified risk of harm to the person, not because of assumptions made about the person because of their condition, for example dementia or a learning disability, or any associated risk aversion on behalf of the managing authority.

The BIA is considering here how risks to the person are managed in their care plan, which is as much about minimising risks as it is taking risks (Davies, 1996). Understanding the nature of the person being assessed is key in this decision. Were they a person who usually took risks in their life? Did they resist authority and control, like Manuela Sykes (*Westminster City Council v Manuela Sykes* [2014]), or did they seek a life of safety and security? Is the BIA assessment going to sanction an unnecessarily paternalistic approach by the managing authority or are the restrictive measures justified for the person? The BIA needs to identify the link between the risks identified to the person, their potential harmful impact and the restrictions in place that are designed to prevent them. Theory and research can help the BIA to better respond to the current risks, as the risks will then be better understood, and therefore offer a proportionate response. In this way, the BIA understands what is necessary to prevent actual rather than perceived harm and demonstrate defensible decision-making.

An example of this could be through understanding the benefit of assistive technology. For instance, if a person with dementia tends to get out of bed during the night and walk into other people's rooms in the care setting, an alarm on the person's door could be used to alert staff when they are awake. Staff members can then monitor and distract them, rather than using a disproportionate response such as night sedation and bed rails. Another example could be the BIA recognising how the impact of unfamiliar surroundings can be disorientating for a person with dementia and how this can escalate uncharacteristic behaviour. In these situations, the BIA could consider alternative plans rather than seeing care in a residential setting as always the most appropriate response.

The BIA's decision in this area must aim towards the examination and implementation of less restrictive options for care (Principle 5 MCA) and evidence why the restrictions in place for the person listed in the deprivation of liberty section are needed to prevent the harm that the BIA has identified. There should be an explicit link between the restrictions in place and the harm they are designed to prevent.

3. Proportionate to the risk of harm

It is essential that the BIA considers whether the restrictions identified in the person's care plan are proportionate to the risk of harm identified in the previous section. *Proportionality* is a key legal principle when considering how much intervention is necessary to ensure a person's safety. This legal principle directs BIAs to the minimum restriction necessary for the minimum period of time.

BIAs often struggle with the idea of proportionality, but this question is key to ensuring that the restrictions in place match the level of risk. It is essential to recognise that it is impossible to eliminate all risk, although families and managing authorities may feel that they must try to do this to keep the person safe. Part of the challenge of the BIA role is the dilemma of a trade-off between two competing rights and resulting risks. For example, a person who uses a walking aid may become aggressive because of their mental disorder and risk injuring themselves or others with the aid. Removing the aid limits their mobility and affects their dignity, but failing to remove it puts them at risk from retaliation from others. The BIA must consider whether removing the ability of the person to move freely in their environment is a proportionate response to the likelihood and severity of the risk that another resident might hurt them.

Practice as a BIA requires a balanced and pragmatic approach, as risks may vary according to situations and responses must be individual, rather than routine. For example, in deciding that a care home placement is proportionate to the risk of harm, you must consider that depriving a person of their liberty may create new risks that did not exist in their previous home. Institutional settings, such as care homes and hospitals, bring a range of new risks that should be acknowledged when comparing options. These can include the impact of a change of environment on a person with a cognitive impairment, as well as the impact that other residents may have on the person's wellbeing if there are difficulties in forming relationships or if the person's behaviour is not tolerated by others, as well as risks to the person's emotional and physical wellbeing.

4. Best interests

It is vital to note that what is in a person's best interests differs from person to person. To make your best interests decision, you will need to gather as much information as possible from family, friends and others to establish what the person's view of their best interests would have been, as well as their views on what is in the person's best interests now. The detail that is offered or that you can gain through questioning will be invaluable in understanding the person's past wishes and feelings, and contextualising their current circumstances within them.

REFLECTIVE ACTIVITY

Terry, 81

Terry worked as an engineer in a mechanics shop around the corner from the family home where he lived with his wife Margaret. Through years of attending the same place of work, Terry had a routine that he stuck to religiously as it kept him organised. This routine continued after his retirement. Terry had been a frequent smoker all his life, and showed no sign of giving up despite health warnings. He also enjoyed a social drink at the local pub near to his place of work. Terry has been in a dementia care home for three years as Margaret could no longer act as his carer.

While at the care home, Terry has continued to want to smoke, go to work and drink at his local pub. However, the disorientation caused by his dementia has resulted in him becoming angry, not recognising his surroundings and trying to leave the nursing home to smoke, or go to work. Staff have had to intervene with restraint and medication. Terry does not understand or agree with their behaviour, so he has not been leaving the care home at all. When staff previously took him to the pub, Terry responded well but then wanted to return to his former home with Margaret rather than to the care home.

Questions
– What is in Terry's best interests?
– What harm are the staff trying to prevent?
– Is their response proportionate?

> We think that adopting a person-centred approach is vital here so as to establish what is in Terry's best interests in this situation. You already have some vital information about how Terry chose to live his life previously, have some understanding of what he enjoyed and his attitude to risk and harm prior to losing mental capacity to make decisions like this.
>
> We would want to explore with the care home ways to ensure that his main pleasures in life, smoking and drinking socially, could be facilitated rather than being opposed. Consultation with others including the care home staff and his wife as part of the best interests process could highlight key ways that his views and wishes could be better incorporated into his care. Less restrictive care in his current placement can be included as an option on the Form 3 balance sheet to reflect the need to explore alternative options.
>
> Preventing Terry from smoking, having a drink and not visiting his home by using restraint and medication appears disproportionate to us. Care homes have, in some instances, invested in environmental reminiscence, which could offer the opportunity for a pub-like space in the home that he and other residents might choose to use. Supporting Terry to go to a local pub at quiet times with the understanding of the publican, to visit his workplace and visits home to his wife are also suitable alternatives to explore.

As Ruck Keene et al (2021a, p 2) note:

> it cannot be emphasised enough that all practicable steps must be taken to support a person to take their own decisions before any question of best interests arise. In other words, the better the application of the MCA, the fewer best interests decisions will be required. In many respects, having to determine someone's best interests should be seen as a failure: a failure to enable the person to decide for themselves.

In this context, efforts made to engage with the person, understand the decisions that brought them to their current circumstances, identify how they would have chosen to live and look after themselves all feed into the point where, if necessary – and only, if necessary – a best interests decision must be made regarding the care that amounts to a deprivation of liberty where they reside.

A best interests decision remains the crucial point at which the person's views and wishes should be considered when reaching a conclusion in the BIA's assessment, considering everything else that has been identified during the course of the assessment. This decision should be considered, thoughtful and never routine, taking into account the legal weight of the person's human rights and the direction of their life that BIAs hold in their power.

In *Cornwall Council v NP and BKP* [2020], the judge weighed alternative plans of care following NP's inpatient admission for a neurological condition in either a care home or the home he had lived in with his wife of 35 years. It was not in question that he lacked mental capacity to make the decision about where to be cared for and would have chosen to go home if he had been able to choose to do so. The social worker suggested that NP's aggression made going home a risky option and recommended a placement in a care home instead.

The judge considered 'the leading case as to the application of the best interests criteria' – the decision of the Supreme Court in *Aintree University Hospitals NHS Foundation Trust v James* [2013], where Baroness Hale observed:

> 39. The most that can be said, therefore, is that in considering the best interests of this particular patient at this particular time, decision-makers must look at his welfare in the widest sense, not just medical but social and psychological … they must try and put themselves in the place of the individual patient and ask what his attitude to the treatment is or would be likely to be; and they must consult others who are looking after him or interested in his welfare, in particular for their view of what his attitude would be.

> 45. The purpose of the best interests test is to consider matters from the patient's point of view. That is not to say that his wishes must prevail, any more than those of a fully capable patient must prevail. We cannot always have what we want. Nor will it always be possible to ascertain what an incapable patient's wishes are. … But insofar as it is possible to ascertain the patient's wishes and feelings, his beliefs and values or the things which were important to him, it is those which should be taken into account because they are a component in making the choice which is right for him as an individual human being.

In *Cornwall Council v NP and BKP* [2020], NP's wife, BKP, submitted that she was willing to care for him, understood the risks and had:

> cared for NP's mother, who had Parkinson's disease and dementia, at their home for ten years. She explained that before the Covid-19 lockdown, she used to visit her husband in the X rehabilitation unit every day, but since lockdown she has been shielding and the ward has been unable to accommodate visitors. NP and BKP have therefore not seen each other for six months. BKP explained the very close relationship that she has enjoyed with her husband over many years. In setting out her view that it would be in NP's best interests to return

home, she said that the time at home would: 'Give [NP] and I time together, some of which would be private, which I believe would be overall good for both our mental health' and 'enable us to have privacy of our relationship, a hug, a kiss goodnight and experience most of the lucid moments he has together'. (para 12)

The judge noted that this might be NP's last chance to live a non-institutional life and unusually included consideration of CRPD (2006) 'Article 19 – Living independently and being included in the community'. This recognises that people with disabilities have equal rights to:

live in the community, with choices equal to others, and shall take effective and appropriate measures to facilitate full enjoyment by persons with disabilities of this right and their full inclusion and participation in the community, including by ensuring that:

a) Persons with disabilities have the opportunity to choose their place of residence and where and with whom they live on an equal basis with others and are not obliged to live in a particular living arrangement.

The importance of enabling the person to experience a trial period of care at home where there is a possibility of experiencing the care of loved ones and home should not be underestimated when planning discharge from hospital where the alternative is likely to be permanent institutional care.

Tools to aid best interests decision-making

Establishing what is in a person's best interests can be challenging. Tools such as the statutory best interests checklist (MCA Code of Practice, DCA, 2007, pp 65–6) and balance sheets are designed to ensure person-centred rather than routine decision-making.

Methods such as these are needed so BIAs can show that they have considered the full range of criteria, safeguards and risks and benefits of options in order to reach well-evidenced best interests decisions and how each piece of evidence has been weighed up in reaching their conclusion. Ruck Keene et al (2017, p 2; original emphasis) state that 'it is *extremely* important to understand that the MCA does not specify what is in the person's best interests – it sets down the process to apply'. By giving structures to those making best interests decisions, the law does not set out rigid answers to the question of what is in the person's best interests; rather, it sets out the way that these decisions must be made, which also means that different people may come to different conclusions in the same circumstances. What is important is that there is sound proof of the evidence weighed and professional reasoning that led to the decision.

Best interests checklist

The checklist (see Chapter 1) for all those, including BIAs, to follow when making best interests decisions under the MCA is one 'that recognises that a conclusion that a person lacks decision-making capacity is not an "off-switch" for their rights and freedoms' (Ruck Keene et al, 2017, pp 2–3). The checklist is designed to prompt decision-makers to respect the views of the person and not discriminate against their rights and freedoms just because they are unable to make the decision themselves at the time. It is important to recognise the obligation that BIAs have to ensure that their best interests decision meets the requirements of the Equality Act 2010 by not making assumptions about the person's best interests based on any of the nine protected characteristics that the person might exhibit (see Chapter 6 regarding discrimination and BIA decisions).

Some supervisory bodies ask BIAs to structure their recording of their best interests decision using the best interests checklist as a way to ensure that all features of the checklist have informed the BIA's decision-making process. The DoLS Code of Practice (Ministry of Justice, 2008) notes the following issues that also need to be considered when making deprivation of liberty best interests decisions:

- whether any harm to the person could arise if the deprivation of liberty does not take place
- what that harm would be
- how likely that harm is to arise (i.e. is the level of risk sufficient to justify a step as serious as depriving a person of liberty?)
- what other care options there are which could avoid deprivation of liberty, and
- if deprivation of liberty is currently unavoidable, what action could be taken to avoid it in future. (p 52, para 4.61)

Balance sheet

This method allows best interests decision-makers to set out the options that are available to the person, offer the evidence for and against each decision and explain why a particular option was chosen. The balance sheet was first used in *Re A (Male Sterilisation)* [2000] as an 'informal standard of best interests deliberation' (Kong et al, 2020, p 755) that enabled explicit exploration and reflection around the best interests options available.

It is important to be aware that this approach has its critics. Kong et al (2020, p 756) note that 'guidelines for legal, social, and health care practitioners … recommend and endorse the balance sheet approach as a structured deliberative tool that is an essential part of the section 4 best interests checklist'. The adoption of the balance sheet approach has allowed practitioners to 'to see what the best interests decision-maker has considered to be relevant, and that they have considered relevant factors' (Kong et al, 2020, p 779). The difficulty is that balance sheets can create the illusion that it is possible to mechanistically calculate the best interests of a person through weighing the risks and benefits of options rather than as an activity that demands a reflective account of the various options, risks, views, wishes, complexities and nuances of a person's circumstances in order to come to a conclusion.

Kong et al (2020) highlight in particular the need to apply ethical reasoning to what could otherwise be reduced to a numerical exercise: 'Whether a person's emotional or physical well-being takes priority, whether her autonomy trumps her safety – these fraught issues resist the language of trade-offs and demand an orientation of valuing in ways that recognise their nature as intrinsic goods' (p 780).

BIAs should be cautious to ensure that their use of the balance sheet takes account of the person's circumstances and is driven by person-centred values rather than an accountant's eye to numerical value and cost.

It is vital that the options available to the person are set out and explored in turn. Sometimes, BIAs leave out potential options from the balance sheet, such as the person returning to their home from residential care, where there is little appetite for that option even though the person still has a home to return to. It is not clear then whether that option has been considered when, in fact, there are factors both for and against it. It is important to show that the BIA has considered all options that are available, especially if the option of going home is requested by the person themselves.

In Terry's case in the earlier Reflective Activity, it is worth including the option of Terry returning to his home, but in this case the views of his wife about whether this would be something she could cope with must form part of the evidence considered for that option, which may differ from the views expressed in *Cornwall Council v NP and BKP* [2020].

Available options

The *North Yorkshire County Council and A Clinical Commissioning Group v MAG* [2016] case in the Court of Appeal explored best interests decision-making in deprivation of liberty cases and focused on the extent to which public bodies with responsibility for funding care have to make resources available. Generally, the response has been that if an alternative package of care to the one the person currently has is not something that the local authority is likely to be able to provide (financially or in terms of the resource required being actually within their power to provide), the court is unlikely to rule that the alternative must be available. This view was supported by the Supreme Court's decision in *N v ACCG and others* [2017] (known as *Re MN* in the Court of Appeal and *Re M* [2013] in the Court of Protection), which concluded that there was no useful purpose to continuing the hearing as the court had no power to choose between any more than the 'available options'.

It is recognised that local authorities do not have the resources to provide all care possible to all those it is responsible for. The Care Act 2014 allows for care and support to be rationed via the use of eligibility criteria for local authority-funded care. However, they have a legal duty to plan care that meets the person's eligible assessed needs under the Care Act 2014, and it is not in the Court of Protection's power to compel local authorities to do otherwise. This may be more appropriate a decision to consider via judicial review, as suggested in *A Local Authority v X* [2016]. Fundamentally, BIAs cannot invent or wish for options to consider that are purely hypothetical. Rather, they must look at the options that the local authority or NHS body could provide and would be *likely* to be available to them.

As a BIA, you are ultimately accountable for the decisions you make – to the person whose life may change significantly because of your decision, to family and friends who care for that person, to your supervisory body, which is responsible for approving your BIA decision, and to the courts, which may choose to scrutinise your decision. Your decision must be well considered and your report should give a clear, reasoned statement of why you reached the decisions you have.

DoLS Form 4

Form 4 (Welsh Government, 2015; DHSC, 2018) is completed by the Mental Health Assessor. As a BIA, you are required to consider the Mental Health Assessor's decisions and recommendations as part of your own assessment, so it is important that you know what information you should expect from the Mental Health Assessor.

Mental capacity assessment

If the supervisory body you are working for asks the Mental Health Assessor to complete a mental capacity assessment, you must ensure that you have considered their assessment. Capacity assessments are time-specific, so if the assessment was completed some time ago, you will need to consider whether you think it is still valid. If you think it is out of date, ask the supervisory body to consider commissioning another assessment. Alternatively, the supervisory body may ask you to complete the assessment. If you assess the person and believe that your findings contradict what the Mental Health Assessor has said, you should contact the supervisory body so it can consider whether it wants you to complete a second capacity assessment. Doctors, as well as BIAs, are guided to 'balance the risks of doing harm against the possible advantages of intervention, including in clinical assessments of capacity' (Ruck Keene, 2015, p 202).

Mental health assessment

It is the Mental Health Assessor's responsibility to decide whether the person has a diagnosis of mental disorder that meets the definition of the Mental Health

Act (MHA) 1983 (2007). The Mental Health Assessor may give details about how they reached their decision, including, for example, the person's responses to any tests and how the mental disorder is affecting the person's ability to make decisions. They may also give information on what prescribed medication may be acting as a restriction, whether the medication is appropriate for the person, whether the dose is suitable and whether the medication needs reviewing. It is also their responsibility to state what impact the deprivation of liberty is having on the person's mental health, whether positive or negative. This can also include recommendations on what changes could improve the person's mental health. BIAs can consider these for inclusion as conditions or recommendations in their own assessment.

Eligibility assessment

The Mental Health Assessor will decide whether the person is eligible for detention under the MHA, which would therefore make them ineligible for DoLS. BIAs who are also qualified as Approved Mental Health Professionals (AMHPs) may be asked to complete the eligibility assessment on Form 4, but this is unusual, so BIAs are, in practice, unlikely to need to complete this form. The Mental Health Assessor or BIA/AMHP should refer to cases A to E as set out in Schedule 1A MCA to decide whether the person is eligible for DoLS. The MCA asks those assessing eligibility for DoLS to explore the following:

- whether inpatient or forensic sections of the MHA already apply;
- whether the community provisions of the MHA (Section 7 Guardianship, Section 17 Leave or Section 17A Community Treatment Order) would conflict with a DoLS authorisation; or
- whether the MHA should be used because the person is eligible for the MHA, they are in hospital for treatment of a mental disorder and are objecting (or have expressed objections in the past) to their care and treatment.

The guidance available to make the eligibility decision was updated as a result of the *AM v South London and Maudsley NHS Foundation Trust* [2013] judgment, which clarified when the MHA or DoLS was most appropriate to be used for detention in a mental health hospital setting, dislodging previous guidance from *GJ v the Foundation Trust* [2009]. The MHA Code of Practice was revised in 2015 to provide guidance to AMHPs and Mental Health Assessors when making these decisions (DH, 2015a, Ch 13).

In the first edition of this book we noted that the Court of Appeal's [2017] judgment in the *Welsh Ministers v PJ* case suggested that, unlike the MHA and DoLS Codes of Practice, the judges considered that a Section 17A Community Treatment Order (CTO) could be used to legally deprive a person of their liberty without requiring other legal measures in place to protect these rights. The Supreme Court (*Welsh Ministers v PJ* [2018]) disagreed and noted:

that there is no power to detain a patient on a CTO, no power to impose medical treatment without consent, and no sanction for failing to comply with the care plan, other than the limited power of recall. The court commented that if the CTO patient cannot be made to take their medication, how can Parliament have intended an even greater interference with their fundamental rights? (Fitzpatrick, 2018)

We welcome this clarity from the Supreme Court that CTO conditions are no substitute for other frameworks for lawful deprivation of liberty (like DoLS or Section 16 COP applications) as this would otherwise have opened the legal measures for deprivation of liberty far wider than the current already complex legislative framework provides.

Other BIA decisions

There is a range of other decisions that BIAs must make if they decide that the person has met all six of the DoLS assessments and recommend the DoLS should be authorised. These include the following:

- Who should act as the RPR? (See Chapter 4.)
- Are there any conditions for the managing authority or recommendations to the social worker or healthcare professionals involved? (See Chapter 8.)
- How long should a DoLS authorisation last? There are some key principles to take into consideration in this respect:
  - Twelve months should not be considered the default duration of an authorisation. A 12-month authorisation should only be applied when care is well established, and there are no disagreements between the person, family members, managing authority and funding body.
  - If any issues have been identified and need addressing (in the conditions or recommendations, for example), the duration of the authorisation should be linked to the amount of time it takes to address these issues.
  - The presence of a care plan involving covert medication in the person's best interests must prompt a timescale for the DoLS authorisation linked to this being regularly reviewed since it presents an interference with the person's Article 8 right (as set out in *Re AG* [2016].
  - If it is evident that the current care plan is not a suitable long-term option and less restrictive options should be considered, then a long authorisation is not desirable. In *P v Surrey County Council and Surrey Downs CCG* [2015] the supervisory body came in for criticism where a placement that was agreed as unsuitable in the long term was the subject of a long DoLS authorisation. The reasoning given was to avoid the distress caused to the person by a further assessment – this argument was not supported by the fact that the person showed no distress during the assessment for the authorisation.

- Think about exactly how long you want the authorisation to last and be specific – with differing month lengths, six months is not necessarily the same time as 26 weeks.

Defensible decision-making

To make a decision that is well evidenced and can bear criticism, you should ensure that your decisions would stand up to the scrutiny of a court. Confidence that your decision, and your record of it, will stand up in court is increasingly becoming an everyday requirement of BIA practice.

Legal competence and capability

Bray and Preston-Shoot (2016, p 4) explain that 'legal literacy can be defined as the ability to connect relevant legal rules with the professional priorities and objectives of ethical practice'. This means that each decision you make should show that you have a confident grasp of how the law guides your practice and that you are able apply it capably and consistently.

The European Convention on Human Rights (ECHR), as incorporated into domestic legislation through the Human Rights Act 1998, gives the opportunity to challenge decision-making by public bodies in the context of human rights. The case of *HL v The United Kingdom* (see Chapter 1) held that those deprived of their liberty must have their rights enshrined in law where their Article 5 right to liberty and security is limited without a legal framework. The subsequent introduction of the DoLS into the MCA (using the MHA in 2007) has formalised a system for assessing and authorising deprivation of liberty, although what amounts to a deprivation of liberty has shifted because of case law such as the *Cheshire West* judgment since this system was implemented in 2009. You need to be able to articulate why the BIA role exists, what case law was influential in bringing this role into existence and how the legal framework guides what you do. It is essential that you understand that the BIA role was created in direct response to the ECHR.

If, as a BIA, you are unsure how to proceed in your decision-making, it is important to consider the three cases of *Bolam v Friern Hospital Management Committee* [1957], *Bolitho v City and Hackney Health Authority* [1997] and *Montgomery v Lanarkshire Health Board* [2015].

The *Bolam* case introduced the 'Bolam test', which sets the legal standard for demonstrating what can be expected from a 'reasonable' competent professional, within their profession. If the professional practice you propose is accepted as proper by a body of responsible and skilled professional opinion, a judge is unlikely to find you negligent in court. The implication of this in practice is to demonstrate that you have held what has commonly become known as a 'Bolam discussion', that is, you have checked that the decision you plan to make is considered reasonable within the limits of current practice by another professional. In this case, it did not matter that there may be a contrary opinion from another body of professional opinion, only that there is one to support your actions.

However, in *Bolitho v City and Hackney Health Authority* [1997], the judge makes it clear that the court must still be satisfied that the body of opinion is reasonable or responsible and that it can withstand logical scrutiny (that is, there is an evidence base to support it), which means the protection that the *Bolam* judgment previously offered is not as generally reliable as it once was. An example of this can be seen in *Montgomery v Lanarkshire Health Board* [2015] in relation to medical negligence and the issue of gaining informed consent from a patient. This case highlights that doctors (and other professions) can no longer rely on Bolam discussions – that is, relying on a body of professional opinion to support and protect their conduct when they have not gained informed consent from the patient. Withholding information about the possible risks of action or no action, however small or protective the professional believes such actions to be, cannot be justified. These judgments must inform your development as a BIA, and we encourage you to read and reflect on them as you make your decisions.

 KEY MESSAGES

- **BIAs** undertake different assessments as commissioned by the supervisory body and all of these require a range of decision-making knowledge and approaches.

- **YOU** are responsible for ensuring that you gather views from as widely as is possible and appropriate, to recognise the person's views and reflect these in the decisions you make.

- **YOU** are responsible for ensuring that the decisions you make are reflective of the person's circumstances at the time you make them and are responsive to the risks and options in the person's situation.

 KNOWLEDGE REVIEW

- **WHICH** DoLS assessments are you likely to be asked to complete?

- **HOW** should you plan for a DoLS mental capacity assessment? What information will you need and what must you do to ensure that you are compliant with Principle 2 MCA?

- **WHICH** two elements are essential for a no refusals assessment?

- **WHAT** case law is relevant to the information you need to gather to decide whether the person is deprived of their liberty?

- **HOW** is risk considered in assessing whether restrictions are necessary and proportionate to the risk of harm?

- **WHAT** process do BIAs use to decide whether the care arrangements are in the person's best interests?

FURTHER READING

- 39 Essex Chambers produce regular case law newsletters and guidance on mental capacity, deprivation of liberty and best interests, available from: www.39essex.com/resources-and-training/mental-capacity-law

- Bournemouth University/Burdett Trust for Nursing (2022) have developed a mental capacity toolkit for health and social care professionals supporting their knowledge and skills regarding applying the MCA and DoLS in practice, available from: https://mentalcapacitytoolkit.co.uk

- Ministry of Justice (2008) *Mental Capacity Act 2005 Deprivation of Liberty Safeguards Code of Practice*

- Mughal, A. and Richards, S. (2021) *Deprivation of Liberty Safeguards Handbook*, 2nd edn, Hounslow, BooksWise

- The Mental Health and Justice/Wellcome (2022) online guide is an excellent resource for health and social care professionals who need to assess and make decisions about mental capacity, available from: https://capacityguide.org.uk

At the time of writing, 39 Essex Chambers had published the following guidance notes drawing on case law:

- Making best interests decisions (Ruck Keene et al, 2021a)

- Relevant information for different categories of decisions (salient points) (Ruck Keene et al, 2021b)

- Assessing and recording mental capacity (Ruck Keene et al, 2022)

- Fluctuating capacity (Scott and Ruck Keene, 2021)

Please note that these guidance notes are regularly updated – go to the 39 Essex Chambers website for the most up to date version: www.39essex.com/tag/mental-capacity-guidance-notes

6

Evidence-informed practice

This chapter aims to explore the evidence base for Best Interests Assessor (BIA) practice that is designed to enable you to reflect, refine and evidence your decision-making in the context of risk, contested viewpoints and the varying contexts of the individuals you will be assessing. It tackles the following key areas:

- Defensible or defensive decision-making: What influences the decisions you make?
- Discrimination in decision-making.
- Bias in decision-making.
- Evidence-based decisions regarding people with dementia, learning disabilities, mental illness and acquired brain injury.
- Key messages, knowledge review and further reading.

Introduction

As BIAs we can demonstrate good practice by reflecting on how and why we reach the decisions that we do. That way, when challenged or asked to account for these decisions, we can feel confident in how these decisions were reached. However, we must always be aware of the possibility that conscious or unconscious bias can affect these decisions.

Defensible or defensive decision-making: What influences the decisions you make?

Many things can influence the decisions you make as a BIA. It could be your professional experience, which might lead you to consider your decisions in light of past positive or negative experiences, or your professional knowledge, which might lead you to take more calculated risks based on your knowledge of the hazards associated with particular decisions. The crucial distinction is between *defensible* decisions (evidence-informed choices made with conscious knowledge of biases and circumstances) and *defensive* decisions (those made to protect yourself from criticism and censure).

REFLECTIVE ACTIVITY

John, 48

John has three children aged 17, 19 and 21, whose education he is funding. He has been married for 20 years and was successfully running his own motorcycle training business. Six months ago, he was involved in a serious motorcycle accident where he sustained a brain injury as his helmet was not sufficiently secured and he was travelling in excess of the speed limit. John now has regular fits and suffers from post-epileptic delirium, where he can become aggressive and verbally abusive. His wife has said on many occasions that this is not normal for her husband, who had formerly been a calm person, although he had been charged with common assault as a teenager.

The family told hospital staff that they did not want John to return home, although John pleaded with them to let him go. The social worker felt that his return home needed to be tested before a residential placement was considered, although the medical team told his wife that she should not be persuaded to consider this obviously risky idea. The social worker had explained to the family that they would have to fund their own care because of their financial resources. John's wife is not willing to engage in any discussions about funding, although according to hospital staff she appears warm and caring towards John.

As a BIA, you are asked to assess John under DoLS, as the ward staff believe they are now depriving him of his liberty through the cumulative effects of the restrictions placed on him to keep him safe because of his impulsive behaviour. When you speak to the ward staff, you are told that there is no doubt he is being deprived of his liberty and needs to be kept safe in his best interests – a view echoed strongly by the ward consultant. You speak to the consultant, who is certain and persuasive in his view that John has no capacity in any respect, as he has been treating John for the past 14 days. He queries why another capacity assessment is needed when he has already reached his view based on his expertise in working with people with brain injuries.

You find the ward a difficult environment to assess in, as you cannot interview John privately. He is agitated when you speak to him, and tells you in a loud and angry voice to leave him alone or take him home. When you ask for assistance, the ward sister remarks that this a busy ward and although the assessment is needed, so is the bed he is occupying. The sister says firmly that John needs to be moved soon, as he is blocking a bed that should be available for someone in greater need and asks: 'How would you feel if your mother was waiting for that bed?'

You are very aware that you are not medically trained and that, when assessing John, you rely on your limited knowledge of brain injury. You check the health and social care records and notice that there are days where there are no running records, but you discover a letter from John's wife begging for help to get John admitted to a care home because she is frightened about him coming home. The ward sister's response to your questions suggests that hospital staff support her request. John reminds you of another case you were involved in, where you decided that the person you were assessing needed to be cared for at home, but the family was unable to cope and you came in for a significant amount of criticism. You know that this makes you more cautious about taking risks, but you don't think your decision-making has been affected. You decide to recommend that the DoLS is authorised in hospital for a short time and that John's social worker should look at residential care options with the wife.

Questions

– What do you need to consider when making DoLS decisions about John?
– What impact might the following have on your decision:
    – the ward staff's views?
    – the family's view?
    – John's brain injury?
    – your experiences of making risky decisions in the past?

We think that the following are important to consider in making these decisions:

– Your assessment needs to be thorough (as they all should be) with explicit noting of the views and evidence from each source you read or speak to. You will need to triangulate what is known and not known and what you are told with all those involved and interested in John's care. Triangulation of what John says he is able to do and the reality of this is very important where John's brain injury may be affecting his executive capacity to carry out risky decisions safely.
– You need to consider and reflect on the potential biases of the professionals on the ward in favour of the outcome they are seeking. You will also need to be alert to how this might influence the decisions and views of the family, while taking seriously the views of those who would need to be involved in his care if he were to return home.

> - You should reflect on your own risk thresholds while also maintaining a person-centred approach, as overidentifying one case with another when the facts and people are different may impact on the decisions that are made. You should also reflect on your own resilience and tolerance for professional disagreement when under pressure.
> - As you are not medically trained, a conversation with the supervisory body and Mental Health Assessor is key here to ensure that bias does not emerge in the assessment regarding the impact of John's condition on his decision-making abilities.
> - Ask the ward for access to the missing notes as these could hold important information. If these are not available, you may want to consider making the ward keeping records of John's views and wishes, as expressed, a condition of any DoLS authorisation you recommend.

When thinking about how you make decisions, it is vital to understand how you know that you have made a 'good' decision. There are various ways of evaluating your decision, whether it is how well it fits the requirements of your decision-making process or by measuring it against the outcome of that decision including whether any negative potential outcome was avoided. You will need to differentiate between the probability of something harmful occurring because of your decision from the actual outcome. This will help you see how probability and likelihood may affect decisions differently and why some decisions go well and others do not. Considering the outcome might also require you to look beyond the individual you are assessing to the impact of the outcome on the wider community and society.

Risky decisions

If the benefit of a person taking a risk outweighs the possible harm that might occur because of taking the risk, it is easy to see why a decision to chance gaining the benefit is taken over the negative outcome that may arise. For instance, a bet of 1:100 in favour of flipping a coin for heads does not make that a bad bet if the coin falls on tails; it was just the outcome you didn't want. The bet was still a good one, given the probability of flipping a head was 50:50. O'Sullivan (2011, p 176) explains this by arguing that an 'effective decision' is where 'sound' decision-making has resulted in a 'good' decision outcome, compared with an 'unsound' decision that results in a 'culpable' decision. O'Sullivan goes on to suggest that between these positions is good or bad fortune (the 1:100 bet). BIAs need to be able to explain the factors and evidence they considered that resulted in that good decision outcome.

The development of practice wisdom (Williams and Tsui, 2008) through experience may help you as a BIA to focus more on likely or potential good outcomes, although this needs to be balanced against the risk that your decisions are guided by the effect of a variety of different kinds of biases. You are asked as a BIA to achieve certainty with people who can be unpredictable, and outcomes are not always foreseeable.

BIA decision–making needs to be dynamic, drawing on a variety of information and opinion before coming to a conclusion. You need to weigh up probability, severity and likelihood of risk based on the information you gather during your assessment.

Reflection

Social workers like to talk about being reflective. Reflective practice is about being critical and thoughtful by evaluating your own decision-making. Reflective practice is a formal way of saying that we should think about our actions, what impact they have and whether anything can be done better. If you think about reflective practice in this way, it clearly has a place in BIA practice because of the impact BIA decisions have on the lives of vulnerable adults. Reflection can take place on an individual level, with a peer, a supervisor or a group. The important thing is to ensure that reflection takes place and that it has a positive impact on your practice.

There are many models of reflection available to BIAs to aid their critical thinking – Maclean (2010) summarises many of them in an easily usable format. Schön (1983) suggests that as practitioners we should be undertaking 'reflection–in–action' (thinking about what we are doing while we are doing it) and 'reflection–on–action' (thinking about what we did afterwards and planning how we can improve it). BIAs must think on their feet, as DoLS assessments often take place in complex situations. Schön asks practitioners to connect with their thoughts, feelings and emotions, drawing on practice wisdom to address the situations encountered in practice and exploring afterwards how effective these have been.

Reflective practice also asks you to think about your level of competence and skill, and whether or not you are aware of how you apply your skills and knowledge. The original Gordon Training International conscious/competence model has been revised (2021) to include skills instead of competence:

- Unconsciously unskilled: 'I am not aware of what I cannot do.'
- Consciously unskilled: 'I know there are things I cannot do.'
- Consciously skilled: 'I know how to do this but I need to concentrate to get it right.'
- Unconsciously skilled: 'I am doing this right and I don't need to think about it too much.'

Thinking about John's case, how consciously are the BIA's decisions in that situation being influenced by their knowledge and experiences? Do you think they are aware of their own level of skill in this situation?

Talking to others to explore your knowledge is an important strategy for well-informed and reasoned professional judgement. Reflective supervision in whatever form you can access it offers the opportunity for feedback and practice evaluation that is vital for robust BIA assessment and decision-making. As a BIA, it is unlikely that you will move through these different stages in a linear fashion, as adverse incidents or unwanted outcomes may challenge your confidence. In John's case study, the BIA reflected on a past case and the impact of making an unpopular decision. This may have influenced the BIA's decision to go along with the views of the ward professionals and the wife rather than John's views. A supervisor could have assisted the BIA to explore whether this was a decision based purely on John's best interests or whether their previous experience had made them more risk-averse.

A supervisor can assist the BIA in differentiating between their subjective view of their own skills, the subjective views of others and a more objective reflection on the reality of their practice. The supervisor needs the expertise to enable the BIA to move from an unconscious to a conscious assessment of their own skills and abilities. BIAs, like other professional practitioners, often move between states of consciousness when they acquire new skills and apply them, becoming skilled or complacent, and requiring conscious ways to ensure they remain skilled. An experienced supervisor should be able to support a BIA to tackle the impact of adverse incidents when an assessment causes stress or fear, resulting in a loss of confidence. Active work on addressing the sources of stress to build defensible responses are essential to ensure that BIAs do not react by becoming more risk averse than necessary.

The Dunning–Kruger effect (Dunning, 2011) is also worth considering here. This unconscious bias recognises that

> poor performers in many social and intellectual domains seem largely unaware of just how deficient their expertise is [and] not only does their incomplete and misguided knowledge lead them to make mistakes but those exact same deficits also prevent them from recognizing when they are making mistakes and other people choosing more wisely. (p 247)

In John's case, the consultant may be expert in working with people with brain injury but his expertise in assessing mental capacity may be more limited, leading to an overestimation of his skills in this area. The effect also notes that those with expertise often underestimate their own abilities, which could account for the BIA's lack of confidence in their skills and abilities in this situation.

It is important to recognise whether you may be overidentifying with the person you are assessing. This could result in your decisions being oppressive or overly empowering, and feelings and emotions distorting your decision-making. It can be challenging to recognise and distance yourself from your emotions, as you need to demonstrate compassion and empathy as a BIA while not overidentifying with the assessed person. The nurse in John's case gave you the opportunity to identify closely with the situation and your professional response should have considered the impact that overidentification could have had on your decision-making.

Reflective supervision for BIAs is often only available in a group environment rather than on a one-to-one basis. Group reflective supervision may be compromised by the control wielded by whoever runs the group – often the local authority supervisory body – as it can be difficult to admit when things go wrong or when practitioners feel unsure. Janis's (1982) idea from social psychology of 'groupthink' can help us to understand how decisions made in groups can reach unanimous decisions rather than the best one for the circumstances. This model can be a useful tool for reflecting on group decision-making, such as best interests meetings as well as group supervision forums, and needs conscious reflection in order to avoid. BIAs may not want to admit to others their mistakes or feelings of inadequacy. It is your responsibility, however, to ensure that you receive the reflective supervision you need, so it may be more appropriate to approach your supervisory body for individual support, or experienced peers, if you are an independent BIA.

Hemmington et al (2021) noted that the COVID-19 pandemic has increased the isolation of BIAs at the same time as increasing caseloads, while opportunities for supervision, especially highly valued peer supervision, were reduced (p 112) in a context where it was reported that 'a significant number of … BIAs said they did not receive dedicated supervision' (p 116). Making sure that you have access to BIA-specific supervision in whatever format works for you is a priority for positive and ethical practice and something you should raise with your supervisory body if this is not routinely available.

REFLECTIVE ACTIVITY

Supervision

What can I expect in the way of supervision as a BIA?

- How often do you engage in reflective, BIA-specific supervision?
- In group supervision, if the group disagrees with your reasoning on a particular matter, how would you respond?
- Would this make you change your mind?
- If you don't change your mind, how do you feel about standing alone on a decision?
- How do you maintain an open mind?

> – What beliefs and values do you hold, and how could these impact (positively or negatively) on the person you are assessing?

Discrimination in decision-making

Anti-oppressive and anti-discriminatory practice (Nzira and Williams, 2009) have a significant role to play in BIA decision-making. The best interests checklist (MCA Code of Practice, DCA, 2007, pp 65–6) guides all those making best interests decisions to avoid making assumptions about what the person needs or would have wanted on the basis of their age, appearance, condition or behaviour. As a BIA, you have great power to decide whether a deprivation of liberty is in the person's best interests as a result of your training and professional background. Discrimination and oppression can take many forms, and BIAs need to be alert, not just to the potential for overt oppressions such as sexism, racism and homophobia, but also to the way that the interplay between people, professionals and organisations may inflict harm.

The relationship between the powerful (the BIA, the Mental Health Assessor, the supervisory body, the managing authority, the Lasting Power of Attorney or deputy and the person's family) and the powerless (the person being assessed) is being scrutinised by you as the BIA when you carry out your assessment. It is important to recognise the impact this power may have on the person's ability to be involved, to participate in the process and to interact with others involved. Acting in an oppressive manner is not likely to be the intention of most professionals, but this often occurs when they do not appreciate and reflect on the power they hold.

Gilbert and Powell (2010) use concepts from Michel Foucault regarding power to unpick the dual and often contradictory ways that social workers can both wield power 'as an instrument of governmentality, an agent that reproduces dominant state discourses' (p 4) and resist power in their use of discretion to act with autonomy in the interests of individuals rather than state authority (p 15) in a way that is equally applicable to BIAs. The priority that social work places on anti-oppressive practice and the empowerment of those they work with is an expression of this resistance to acting purely as agents of state power. It is telling that those who have embraced the role of the BIA as a social justice role, as noted by Hemmington et al (2021, p 111), are most likely to be conscious of the nature of the power they wield and the potential to subvert its application.

The conscious exercise of power involves awareness of your personal values and beliefs and how they may have a negative impact on the person you are working with (Thompson, 2012). For example, is your view of how and where a person is cared for likely to be influenced by their age? Should an older person with dementia be cared for in a care home or should they be at home with their family? Would your view of whether that person should be cared for at home change depending on whether the main family carer was male or female? Would your view change if the person needing care and support was an adult of working age with a learning disability?

It is essential to be self-aware when considering what levels of restriction may be in the person's best interests, to ensure that your decisions do not discriminate. Since people aged 60 and older have consistently made up the largest group subject to DoLS applications, according to the DoLS data gathered annually by the Health and Social Care Information Centre and NHS Digital from 2008 to 2021, the risk of ageism affecting such applications is particularly high. Tanner and Harris (2008, cited in Constable, 2010) suggest that 'older people are seen as taking up health and social care resources, as a burden, because of ageing populations in the Western world' (p 44). The relatively lower levels of funding available from local authorities to fund residential placements for older people rather than those with learning disabilities, which is something you may encounter as a BIA, could be seen as evidence for this view.

On a legal basis, it is your professional responsibility to act in accordance with the requirements and spirit of the Equality Act 2010.

 ESSENTIAL INFORMATION: LAW

Equality Act 2010

This law consolidates the main laws on equality (gender, race and disability) that have been enshrined in British law since the 1970s. The Equality Act also includes various other categories of discrimination and defines the following nine protected characteristics under the law:

1. Age
2. Disability
3. Gender reassignment
4. Marriage and civil partnership
5. Pregnancy and maternity
6. Race
7. Religion or belief
8. Sex
9. Sexual orientation

This legal framework allows those affected by the protected characteristics to address discrimination where they have been affected adversely whether directly or indirectly. The areas of life the law covers include work, education and access to goods and services as well as harassment and victimisation as a result of many of the protected characteristics.

Considering John's case at the start of this chapter, is there discrimination taking place? Would you consider that the Equality Act 2010 has been breached? Are assumptions being made about his acquired brain injury and its impact on his ability to live independently? Would you feel confident to challenge any of the views being expressed about what he has the capacity to decide about?

REFLECTIVE ACTIVITY

Asher, 48, Black British

Asher lives in a care home, funded under Section 117 of the Mental Health Act (MHA) 1983 (2007). He was admitted there following treatment for psychosis in a psychiatric hospital under Section 3 MHA for more than a year. Asher does not like living in the care home as he does not like the other residents and does not see the point of being there as he can look after himself. He wants to return to his flat and does not think the DoLS should be used to keep him in the care home. He is often asked to stay when he asks to leave the home and staff will often go to his flat to ask him to return to the home if he is out for a long time.

During your DoLS assessment, you speak to Asher's social worker, who says they are planning to encourage Asher to release the tenancy on his flat. The social worker does not want Asher to return to his flat, as there have been complaints from other residents in the building that Asher has been hostile towards them and that he has started fires there.

Questions
- Would you consider that the placement at the care home meets the four requirements of the DoLS best interests assessment?
- What rights does Asher have?
- Can you identify an oppressive or discriminatory factor that might be affecting decisions about Asher?
- How might the risks identified by the social worker influence your decision?

We would consider the following in these circumstances:

- We would want to explore his mental capacity to consent to the placement and the reasoning for why he is placed there, if he is able to care for himself. There do appear to be restrictions amounting to a deprivation of his liberty, as staff either try to prevent him leaving or try to get him to return if he does leave. It is not clear if these measures are necessary, proportionate or in his best interests.

- Asher often asks to leave the home and would rather not live there, which indicates he is objecting to his residence for care. If a DoLS is authorised, he will need a Relevant Person's Representative who is willing to support a Section 21A appeal to the Court of Protection.
- The reasoning about his flat being unsuitable seems to be based on his risk to others more than himself, which needs exploring. More suitable alternative accommodation may need to be explored if both his flat and the care home are unsuitable for him; for example, supported living where the fire risk can be managed by onsite staff but he has his own front door.
- There is a need to reflect on whether unconscious bias in terms of the risk he poses is a factor in the decision-making regarding the risks identified at his flat.

Other considerations for reflection

- What do you mean by 'risk'? Is risk always negative or positive?
- How can you separate the likelihood or probability of an event occurring from the actual outcome?
- What do you think about when deciding whether a decision is sound or unsound? Do you weigh up the likelihood or probability of an event occurring, or only consider the actual outcome?
- Think of a life-changing decision you have made in your own life in the past. How does it feel to think about this now? Do you think you reached the right decision? Has the outcome of the decision affected how you might make this kind of decision in future?
- What are the challenges of making independent decisions as a BIA?
- How do you know they are independent from the influence of others?

Bias in decision-making

When making decisions, BIAs may be influenced by conscious or unconscious bias as a result of previous experience or their working context. Rutter and Brown (2015, p 7) have summarised five common categories of bias that can affect BIA decisions:

- *Anchoring effect:* BIAs tend to rely or anchor themselves to one particular type, trait or category of information over other considerations, for example when a professional opinion is taken to be superior to another or when the BIA feels subordinate to another professional's status.

- *Bandwagon effect:* Particular ways of working in a supervisory body or with a particular individual may influence your work as a BIA. It may mean you are influenced by others to go along with their way of thinking rather than critiquing or questioning the practice of others.
- *Confirmation bias:* This may lead you to look for familiar events or features in assessments that lead you to making similar decisions. If you look for confirmation of your pre-existing ideas, you are not entering into the assessment with an open mind and you may only consider what fits with your prejudices. This is one of the challenges of reading DoLS application paperwork, case files and records before talking to the person, as it may mean that during your assessment of the person you fail to notice information that does not fit with your pre-existing view.
- *Pseudo-certainty effect:* This may lead you to assume that you know what will happen as a result of your decisions when, in reality, the outcome is often uncertain. For example, when considering whether restrictions are necessary to prevent harm, you may be certain that the person's cognitive impairment as a result of dementia may make it dangerous for them to walk unaccompanied by a busy road, and as a result you would support a restriction that prevents them from leaving a care home unaccompanied. This assumption may never have been tested, however, so your certainty may be based on bias rather than evidence.
- *Outcome bias:* This is the tendency to judge a situation by its outcome, rather than the quality of the decision-making at the time the decision was made. This tendency to judge risk in hindsight may lead to risk-averse practice when we assume we know what the outcome is likely to be.

This list is by no means exhaustive, but it is important for the BIA to be aware of the potential range of biases that may affect what appears to be a sound decision. Thinking again about John's case study, what emotions or thoughts did you have when you read that a motorbike instructor had incurred a brain injury in an accident while speeding and wearing a poorly fitted helmet? What impact did the consultant's views have on your decisions considering their professional status? Did the ward sister's view that John should not be on the ward influence you? Did you identify with the wife's pleas that John not come home?

The possibility that bias affects all our decisions must be acknowledged so that you can honestly consider what is actually driving the decisions you make and what evidence you are using to come to these conclusions. Reframing the situation, and reflective discussion with a supervisor or a peer supervision group, could allow you to become aware of biases that are operating in your decision-making and provide you with the opportunity to rigorously question your views.

Evidence-based decisions

Although it is essential when making decisions under DoLS not to make assumptions about what the person would want based on the medical condition they have been diagnosed with, it is important to acknowledge the different experiences people will have had as a result of those conditions and what varying needs and responses may be required to ensure that each person has an equal chance of the greatest level of freedom possible.

People with dementia

Most of the people you are likely to assess as a BIA will be older people with dementia. Since dementia was highlighted as a subsection of mental illness (HSCIC, 2012, p 17), subsequent annual DoLS data reports (from HSCIC and NHS Digital until 2017 when this data stopped being reported) have shown that DoLS applications for people with dementia have continued to make up more than half of the total number of applications, even after the *Cheshire West* [2014] judgment.

O'Connor and Purves (2009) note that the assumptions made about those with dementia focus on the condition's impact on the person's ability to make meaningful choices about their lives and the resulting assumption that 'over time, the person with dementia will become progressively more dependent upon others for all aspects of his or her care' (p 11). The risk for the person with dementia is that this results in the lack of 'retention of personal social identities beyond that of dementia patient' (O'Connor and Purves, 2009, p 14) and the presumption that a dementia patient needs caring for with little personal autonomy.

Tom Kitwood has written persuasively on the subject that people with dementia can maintain their 'personhood' if five areas of needs are attended to: comfort, attachment, inclusion, occupation and identity (Kitwood, 1997, cited in Kaufman and Engel, 2016, p 776). To ensure that people with dementia who are assessed by BIAs achieve some measure of wellbeing, these areas of need must be considered and addressed in assessments, and, where consideration is not found in care planning, conditions can be created to address these failings. If this does not happen, BIAs need to be prepared to 'challenge poor decisions or discriminatory practice that affects a person with dementia negatively' (DH, 2015c, p 27).

People with learning disabilities

The policy change in caring for people with learning disabilities from institutional settings to community-based homes is now, in most respects, a matter of social history. However, it is our experience that for many people you assess as a BIA, it is also a matter of personal experience. Many older adults with learning disabilities have lived in long-stay hospitals and moved to smaller group homes in the 1980s and 1990s, where they may now be subject to DoLS assessment.

When considering whether restrictions are necessary to prevent harm in such cases, it is important to consider the life history perspective of those whose lives have been significantly restricted in the past and the relative freedom offered by their current circumstances, as evidenced in research by the Open University (2022). This should not lead you to assume that there is no potential to continue to increase the amount of choice and control in the lives of those you assess.

It is also important to recognise that plans to reduce the number of assessment and treatment units in the UK following the care scandal at Winterbourne View Hospital (Flynn, 2012) have not yet meant that people with complex and challenging needs are no longer cared for in restrictive, institutional environments. These kinds of care settings still exist – often far away from residents' family and communities and with concerning levels of restrictions in place that repeated policy objectives have yet to significantly change, as evidenced in the Care Quality Commission's *Out of Sight – Who Cares?* report (CQC, 2020) and annual updates (CQC, 2022b). Where there remains the potential for increased freedom and autonomy in the lives of people with learning disabilities, BIAs have a responsibility to identify such potential and promote the rights of people to be in control of their futures.

People with mental disorders

The MHA does not apply in all situations where the person's Article 5 (ECHR) rights need to be protected, so there may be times when BIAs are asked to assess those with mental disorders other than dementia. For example, people with mood disorders or psychosis living in care homes may need assessment under DoLS where their mental disorder is affecting their ability to make decisions about their care and residence. The fact that the person has a mental disorder does not always mean the person will lack capacity to make such decisions or that residence in a care home or hospital will be in their best interests, so as with assessments of people with dementia, learning disabilities or brain injuries, the BIA must gather clear information on the person's wishes and beliefs to inform their decision.

In the *Wye Valley NHS Trust v B* [2015] case, Jackson J gives the view that the fact that a person lacks capacity to make a decision does not act as an 'off-switch' for the person's rights and freedoms, and their views should not carry lesser weight just because they lack capacity to decide as a result of a mental disorder. The case concerns Mr B, who clearly stated his view that he did not want his leg amputated above the knee. The health trust involved suggested that his views should be given less weight as he lacked capacity to make this decision, characterising his belief system as 'religious delusions' (Series, 2016, p 1106). The judge took exception to this description, suggesting that despite Mr B's diagnosis of paranoid schizophrenia, his belief in angels and the Virgin Mary that guided him was part of his faith and his idiosyncratic identity, rather than a symptom of his psychiatric condition. Series (2016, p 1106) suggests that this judgement is 'a stark example of how wishes and feelings can outweigh clinical conceptions of best interests under the MCA' that BIAs must consider when making decisions about people eligible for DoLS whatever their mental disorder.

People with acquired brain injury

The Acquired Brain Injury and Mental Capacity Act Interest Group (2014), in a report following the House of Lords Select Committee post-legislative review into the MCA (House of Lords, 2014), noted that action was required to ensure that the specific needs of adults with acquired brain injury (ABI) were recognised in mental capacity practice. The group noted that the 'consequences of acquired brain injury are ... often invisible and can be subtle but devastating for the sufferer and their family and community' (p 4). These consequences, it continued, may include issues with 'memory, planning, organising, initiating activity, problem solving, with rigidity of thinking, disinhibited behaviour, predicting and understanding the consequences of one's actions, impulsivity and aggression. The sufferer rarely has complete insight into their condition' (Acquired Brain Injury and Mental Capacity Act Interest Group, 2014, p 4).

This makes assessing capacity complex, especially where assessors are not aware of the features of brain injury, causing potentially increased levels of risk where the person may be assessed to have capacity even though the person's brain injury prevents them from acting consistently with their expressed views. The report sets out the challenges facing those assessing the mental capacity of people with brain injuries, using case studies and guidance to help practitioners take a more evidence-informed approach in these circumstances.

Holloway (2020) suggests BIAs need to consider the following when assessing those with ABI:

- Understand the nature and impact of brain injuries (pp 130–1, 133).
- Not take the person's statements about how they manage risk in relation to decisions at face value – triangulate with the views of others involved in their care about whether what they say they do is what they actually do (pp 139–40).
- The structure of a mental capacity assessment can create the conditions for the person to demonstrate their mental capacity (p 132) – that is, the person may be able to show they have mental capacity because you have structured the assessment for them but this may not accurately reflect their everyday decision-making processes.
- Mental capacity is about what people do, not just what they say they will do, and intellectual awareness is not the same as mental capacity (p 134–5).

ESSENTIAL INFORMATION: PRACTICE GUIDANCE

Executive capacity

The structure of mental capacity assessments within the MCA, involving the two-stage test of capacity (the *diagnostic* and *functional* tests), have been criticised for not including their *executive* functioning. Ruck Keene et al (2022 p 15) describe this as where a person 'gives superficially coherent answers to questions, but it is clear from their actions that they are unable to carry into effect the intentions expressed in those answers'. This suggests that the person's ability to actually apply the risk management measures they may identify in the mental capacity assessment may be in question. Those with ABI are noted to often experience cognitive impairment to an extent that means they may be able to evidence they can understand, retain, use, weigh and communicate their decision during a capacity assessment, but their ability to apply these measures in everyday life may be impaired. A loss of insight or self-awareness of their functioning in reality may not be reflected in their conversation with the assessor and their abstract reasoning may be impaired in a way that makes a realistic self-assessment of their own decision-making abilities difficult.

Norman et al (2018) surveyed case managers working with people with ABI and found that 63 per cent had disagreed with other people or agencies regarding their service user's mental capacity regarding welfare, risk taking and their living arrangements. These case workers suggested that the part of the functional test of mental capacity where their service users would have most difficulty was in using and weighing information in relation to a decision and would be least likely to have difficulty communicating their decision (p 8). These specialist ABI case managers often found that those they worked with where they assessed them to lack capacity to make certain decisions were often assessed by others to have capacity to decide, including in situations relating to deprivation of liberty (p 13).

This makes consultation with others to check out whether the person's actual problem-solving and risk-managing behaviour matches their own estimation of this an essential element of the DoLS mental capacity assessment, as well as linking with specialist ABI practitioners as part of assessments to ensure that inexperience of working with impaired executive capacity does not adversely affect decision-making.

Neurological conditions, such as Parkinson's disease, multiple sclerosis, Huntington's disease and motor neurone disease, are not mental disorders as defined by the MCA or MHA, but they can, in some cases, be related to mental disorders, such as depression or cognitive impairments, that may come within the scope of DoLS assessments.

Conclusion

The most crucial time in your BIA assessment is the time you spend once all the information has been gathered to think about each decision you need to make and what the evidence tells you. Think about who gave you the information during consultation, what documentation you have seen and what it demonstrates, what weight each view should be given and whether you have concerns about bias. Consider how independent you are as a decision-maker from the most powerful voices you have heard during your assessment, and ensure that the voice of the person is heard as clearly as possible. Be explicit about what influences have acted on you the most and what you have done to balance them, especially if they are similar to the emotional responses that John's case may have brought up for you. Each time you carry out an assessment, a different set of circumstances will influence and drive your decision-making. As long as you are able to explicitly set out the decision-making process you have been through, the evidence base for your decisions and the reasoning that led to your conclusions, your assessment and decisions are likely to be defensible to the scrutiny of others.

 KEY MESSAGES

- AS a BIA, you must be aware of the potential for bias to affect the decisions you make.

- REFLECTIVE supervision is vital to acknowledging these biases and identifying ways to address them. You have a professional responsibility to ensure that you access and make best use of this essential tool for ethical practice.

- BIAs are professionals who wield considerable power over vulnerable people's lives. Reflecting on your values and beliefs is essential to ensure that you do not discriminate against or oppress the person you are assessing.

- THEORETICAL understandings of decision-making can help you to understand how BIA decisions can be made and ensure that they are made in the most effective and well-considered manner possible.

KNOWLEDGE REVIEW

- **WHAT** is the role of theory and research in BIA decision-making?

- **HOW** can your decisions be influenced and what can you do to be aware of and address these influences?

- **WHAT** function does reflective supervision have on your role as a BIA?

- **WHAT** role does anti-oppressive and anti-discriminatory practice have in your practice as a BIA?

- **IN** what ways will you maintain up-to-date knowledge of medical conditions and symptoms that affect a person's ability to make their own decisions?

 FURTHER READING

- Acquired Brain Injury and Mental Capacity Act Interest Group (2014) *Recommendations for Action following the House of Lords Select Committee Post-Legislative Scrutiny Report into the Mental Capacity Act: Making the Abstract Real*

- Brammer, A. (2020) 'Discrimination', in A. Brammer, *Social Work Law*, 5th edn, Harlow, Pearson Education, Ch 6

- Maclean, S. (2010) *The Social Work Pocket Guide to Reflective Practice*, Lichfield, Kirwin Maclean Associates

- Rutter, L. and Brown, K. (2015) *Critical Thinking and Professional Judgement in Social Work*, 4th edn, London, Sage Publications

7

Ethical dilemmas in BIA practice

This chapter explores some of the ethical dilemmas you may encounter in practice as a Best Interests Assessor (BIA) and explores frameworks to help you make considered decisions in these situations. The chapter covers the following:

- Ethical dilemmas in BIA practice.
- Theories of ethical decision-making, including professional ethics.
- Ethical BIA decision-making in action, including carrying out assessments that comply with the Mental Capacity Act (MCA) 2005 within Deprivation of Liberty Safeguards (DoLS) timescales, and safeguarding best interests.
- Key messages, knowledge review and further reading.

Ethical practice is at the core of BIA practice. Without the core ethics and values of BIAs driving their assessment and decision-making, those they work with may be subject to unnecessary and unlawful restrictions, and wider opportunities for freedom in often highly restrictive settings may be missed.

Lucy Series (2022, p 28) identifies BIAs as 'reformers, "empowerment entrepreneurs" ... working to effect changes within the system using the new tools and legal technologies of social care detention to prod, interrogate and sometimes loosen the grip of carceral practices in the community'. This highlights how BIAs fundamentally have access to use the ethical structures of law, professional ethics and personal values regarding rights-driven practice to improve people's care experiences overall.

PERSPECTIVES: ACADEMIC

Interview with Lucy Series

What do you see as the key contribution/s and value of the BIA role in DoLS?

> There's a certain kind of BIA that I call an 'empowerment entrepreneur'. These are people who are passionate about using the law – including the Mental Capacity Act 2005, the Human Rights Act 1998, perhaps the Care Act and

other progressive bits of law – to leverage improvements in people's living situations. Empowerment entrepreneurs may not know this themselves, but they are the descendants of a rich tradition of social care practitioners who fought to get people out of large institutions and into the community, who are steeped in concepts like 'person-centred' support, 'supported decision-making', 'independent living' (in the disability rights sense), 'choice and control' and – if they're really up to date with things – the UN Convention on the Rights of Persons with Disabilities. Empowerment entrepreneurs use their professional role and status to find ways to push back restrictions in people's care, to try to secure better living arrangements if possible, to ensure that the person's voice is front and centre of the discussions, to challenge others if necessary and use the law to back up that advocacy. If you can finish the following sentence, you are probably an empowerment entrepreneur, and bonus points if you know who said it: 'What good is it making someone safer if it merely makes them ...?

What particular challenges do you see BIAs facing to maintain a rights-driven perspective in practice?

Empowerment entrepreneurs operate within bureaucratic and political environments that are hostile both to disabled people and other social care users, and – increasingly – the very concept of social care itself. Social care has the potential to be a truly radical project, in the words of Social Care Future, of supporting and enabling everyone 'to live in the place we call home with the people and things that we love, in communities where we look out for one another, doing the things that matter to us'. Yet social care is underfunded, bureaucratised, stigmatised. There is no space or time to sit with the messy complexity of people's lives, to get to know them and build and sustain trusting relationships. People who draw on care and support are increasingly reduced to a bundle of tasks to be performed, the minimum necessary to keep them alive and avoid major scandal (and sometimes not even that). Empowerment entrepreneurs hold a set of values and ideals that cannot be realised within the landscape of care as it currently exists. Sometimes, they will find themselves reduced to (as one put it to me the other day) 'just making things a bit less shit'.

What are your hopes and fears for the BIA role in the future?

I hope they carry on carrying the light for social care's radical potential and connecting this with the law. I hope they carry on supporting each other, and supporting a new generation, to carry forward and develop these radical ideals. To work with disabled and older people as allies in their politics, while doing the best they can with what they have in their everyday practice. Because for a lot of people they are their last hope.

Dr Lucy Series, Senior Research Fellow and Lecturer in Law, Wellcome Society and Ethics Research Fellowship holder, Cardiff School of Law and Politics, Cardiff University

Ethical dilemmas in BIA practice

BIAs are asked to make decisions in a wide range of circumstances. Although the questions they must consider – about best interests and deprivation of liberty – are the same each time, the context for the person being assessed and the consideration needed to come to conclusions that respect the person's right to autonomy and safety vary greatly. Many of these situations involve ethical dilemmas, without clear answers, that require BIAs to draw on a range of perspectives to come to a conclusion. Arriving at the 'right' thing to do in a range of situations takes skill. You need to identify an appropriate action, but also consider differing contexts that may make the same decision less ethical. Johns (2016, p 15) identifies the key question of ethics as follows: 'Is something wrong because the action itself is simply wrong, or does the degree to which it is right or wrong depend on who carried out the action, in what circumstances, with what intent and for what purpose?'

Cave (2015, p 192) explains that:

> In courts of law … judges hear the evidence, bring together past cases, precedents and what the law says. They then 'weigh' matters, compare cases with cases, maybe concluding that the defendants were negligent or acted unreasonably; other expert judges may judge differently. Hence, majority votes often determine legal outcomes.

It may be possible to see BIA practice in this light, as akin to a judge considering evidence and writing judgments. However, the individual nature of the BIA's assessment and the sometimes complex nature of the assessed person's situation brings a greater level of subjectivity to the role.

Cave (2015, p 192) notes that with individual ethical dilemmas, 'majority votes have no foothold' and often no single, fixed solution. Ethics and values may guide decision-making, but do not give certain answers in all circumstances: 'No science, no accountancy, is available to resolve ethical dilemmas – to measure the value of family life against a career; or freedom of speech against the nation's security' (p 191). In the same way, a BIA must gather evidence and reach a conclusion in situations when the 'right' or 'wrong' thing to do are not easily defined.

Let us give you an example of an ethical dilemma, loosely based on an experience of a BIA we know. The BIA was asked to assess Jack, a middle-aged, White British man who had a long history of mental illness, including psychosis. Jack lived in a care home and had been prevented from leaving at night as staff were concerned that he was putting himself at risk by asking passers-by on a busy main road for money or cigarettes. When the BIA visited to assess Jack, he refused to talk to them. They were concerned that without speaking to them, he would not understand that the BIA had the power to choose whether or not the restriction remained in place and that they would be unable to hear his voice when making their decision.

Question: What should the BIA have done?

The BIA responded to the situation in the following way – think about whether you would have done the same things or not:

- Tried to talk to Jack again in different circumstances.
  - He refused to speak to them again.
- Asked care staff who worked with Jack about their understanding of his views.
  - They told the BIA that his reaction to them was common, as he distrusted all professionals and refused to speak to any of them, especially about where he lives as he had been moved without his agreement in the past. They also gave the BIA a capacity assessment they had recently completed about him deciding where to live. This showed that he did not acknowledge that he put himself at any risk by leaving the home at night and did not engage in any discussion of the risks and benefits of living in the home. In the view of the care staff, Jack's desire for cigarettes clouded his judgement about his safety. He had no family or friends to consult and so an Independent Mental Capacity Advocate (IMCA) had been appointed for the DoLS assessment.
- Asked the IMCA about what they had learned about Jack's views.
  - Jack had refused to speak to the IMCA on the two occasions they visited.
- Talked to the Mental Health Assessor.
  - Jack had also refused to see the Mental Health Assessor. They were concerned that he was paranoid at the time they tried to assess him.

Dilemma

Without hearing Jack's views of the risks of him leaving the home, how he kept himself safe or how he experienced being prevented from leaving at night, all the BIA could consider were the anxieties of the staff about his safety. The BIA was also unable to hear in Jack's own words whether he could understand, retain, use and weigh or communicate his decision. Jack was clearly able to communicate his refusal to engage with them, but the BIA was concerned that if they were to return to try to speak to him again, they would become more of an irritation and possibly increase his paranoia.

Decision

The BIA considered that the symptoms of Jack's mental disorder (paranoia), observed by both the Mental Health Assessor and the BIA, were affecting his ability to decide about the restrictions to the extent that he refused to engage with the assessment. The BIA was not absolutely certain that Jack lacked capacity to agree to the restrictions he was subject to, but decided on the balance of probabilities that the evidence from those who knew him well and from the Mental Health Assessor strongly suggested that this was the case.

The BIA considered that the benefits of increased scrutiny on decisions about his care outweighed the fact that he would be subject to a legal process that supported this deprivation of his liberty. The BIA ensured that he had a paid representative and placed conditions on the DoLS authorisation that the home should continue to explore less restrictive alternatives to prevent him from leaving the home when he chose to at night (for example by suggesting he use electronic cigarettes), as well as continuing to talk to him about the risks the restriction was designed to prevent to gather more information on his views.

The BIA chose a short authorisation period of a few months to ensure that his situation would be reviewed as soon as possible with the desired outcome that the restrictions could be reduced and the authorisation removed.

Commentary

The BIA considered this decision to be a pragmatic one. Ideally, they would have assessed Jack's capacity thoroughly and come to a decision based on what he said during the assessment with the aim of meeting the principles of the MCA as fully as possible. In this situation, their ability to do this was compromised by Jack's unwillingness to engage with any professionals or advocates involved in the DoLS assessment. The BIA decided on an outcome that promoted Jack's rights and aimed to reduce or remove the restrictions in place.

The following questions remain:

- Was this a 'good-enough' decision?
- Should the BIA have done more to engage Jack in the assessment, for example returned to the care home or asked others to help them to assess?
- What would you have done if you had assessed Jack?
- At what point could you take a capacity assessment, where the person refuses to be assessed, to the Court of Protection for a ruling?

A key point from case law is to identify the difference between a person needing to be assessed who is *unwilling* or *unable* to engage in the DoLS assessment process (Ruck Keene et al, 2022, p 17). For example, in *QJ v A Local Authority* [2020], the judge noted that 'QJ's behaviour included his reluctance to answer certain questions. It should not be construed from this that he is unable to. There is a good deal of evidence which suggests that this is a choice.' In the case of Jack, it may have been possible that in other areas of his life he was able to exercise choice, which could have been established through discussions with those responsible for his care.

The following frameworks show the various ways in which BIAs can explore the ethical dilemmas they encounter in BIA practice, such as that described in this section, how they link to the legal frameworks that BIAs operate within and how to consider responses based on these perspectives.

Theories of ethical decision-making

Over centuries, philosophers have developed a range of theories on how to decide what to do in complex situations. Here, we summarise some of the key ethical theories that may be of value to BIAs:

- deontological ethics
- utilitarianism
- virtue ethics
- social justice, egalitarian and care ethics.

Deontological ethics: following the rules

Deontological ethics aims to work to a set of moral principles that should guide all the decisions we make. Whether derived from religion, the law, professional codes or value systems, this approach assumes that universal principles are available to us all to guide our behaviour. Immanuel Kant (1724–1804), a key figure in this view of ethics, maintained the need to obey what reason shows is the 'right thing to do' and gives us the 'categorical imperative' (Cave, 2015, p 43) to always do the right thing. Johns (2016) suggests that this approach leads us to modern ideas of equality, as it encourages us to consider all people as equals, irrespective of their age, sex, gender identity or expression, race, religion, disability, sexual orientation and so on, and links closely with ideas of social justice.

As a BIA, you have a duty to abide by various sets of rules including your profession's standards and the principles set down in the legal frameworks you work within. These are summarised in the following panel. Abiding by these standards as a priority when making decisions can be seen as applying deontological principles.

ESSENTIAL INFORMATION: PROFESSIONAL STANDARDS

Professional standards and ethics

All four of the eligible BIA professions have regulatory ethical standards that must be demonstrated in practice. Some professions have frameworks applicable across the UK and others have separate frameworks for the four countries of the UK.

Social workers
British Association of Social Workers (BASW)
The BASW Code of Ethics for Social Work (BASW, 2021)
This is aimed at social workers who are BASW members across the four nations of the UK, and states that:

> The Code is not designed to provide a detailed set of rules about how social workers should act in specific situations. Instead it comprises statements of values and ethical principles relating to human rights, social justice and professional integrity, together with guidance on practising ethically as a social worker. (p 4)

BASW also produced a *Code of Ethics Addendum* (BASW, 2014), which sets out how independent social workers can maintain ethical practice. This is relevant to social workers who work independently as BIAs.

Social Work in England – Social Work England (SWE)
Social Work England Professional Standards (SWE, 2019b)
These professional standards are designed to be a baseline for ethical and safe practice for registered English social workers and come with guidance on how they should be applied to practice. The *Professional Standards Guidance* (SWE, 2020a) describes the ethical practice expected as:

> Ethics in the context of social work is about the professional responsibilities and values social workers have and how they conduct themselves inside and outside the workplace. Social workers respect the distinct beliefs and lifestyles of people, their families, communities and networks. They consider their own personal values, views and preferences and take measures to prevent them from impacting on their work with people.

Social Work in Wales – Social Care Wales (SCW)
Code of Professional Practice for Social Care (2017)
Code of Practice and Guidance (SCW, 2021)
Welsh social care workers, including registered social workers, must abide by SCW's 2021 Code to

> ensure that their conduct and practice do not fall below these standards, and that no action or omission on their part harms the well-being of individuals. Workers are encouraged to use the Code to examine their own conduct and practice and to look for areas in which they can improve.

Occupational therapists and psychologists
Health and Care Professions Council (HCPC)
Standards of Conduct, Performance and Ethics (HCPC, 2018a)
The overall standards for all HCPC qualifying professions, which affirms these as 'the values that guide a person's behaviour or judgement'.

Nurses
Nursing and Midwifery Council (NMC)
The Code (NMC, 2018)

> The Code sets out common standards of conduct and behaviour for those on our register. This provides a clear, consistent and positive message to patients, service users and colleagues about what they can expect of those who provide nursing or midwifery care. (p 4)

These codes and standards are designed to give a framework for professional practice and ethical decision-making and provide a measure by which practice that causes concern can be judged.

For health and social care professionals working within the MCA, the deontological, principle-driven approach resonates with the five principles that govern all MCA practice. These are intended to be universal in their nature and inform all decision-making with those who potentially lack capacity about their lives. Deontological theory makes it clear that it is our duty (in Latin, *deon* means duty) to abide by these laws and apply them to all that we do. It does not ask that we consider the outcome, however. As Cave (2015, p 42) explains, 'deontological morality demands that we do the right thing even if good does not result'. This poses a dilemma. How should we act if the rules say this is how we should act but we know that it will not have a positive outcome for a service user?

To explore this further, we need to look at another principle that BIAs apply – Article 5 of the European Convention on Human Rights (ECHR). Johns (2016, p 150) points out that the right to liberty 'is not an absolute', as it is lawful to interfere with this right with those who have broken the criminal law, those who are of unsound mind or for the purpose of limiting the spread of infectious diseases (as relevant to COVID-19 quarantine).

The legal frameworks for restricting people's access to their right to liberty, such as the Mental Health Act (MHA) 1983 (2007), Deprivation of Liberty Safeguards (DoLS), domestic deprivation of liberty process via the Court of Protection and related case law, support a universal view of access to the right to liberty. This has not always been the case if you consider the Court of Appeal's judgment in *Cheshire West and Chester Council v P* [2011]. In this case, Munby LJ judged that 'what may be a deprivation of liberty for one person may not be for another' (p 16) when deciding whether a man with a learning disability was deprived of his liberty. He suggested that rather than comparing what level of restriction might be a deprivation of liberty with 'the able-bodied man or woman on the Clapham omnibus' (p 33), it was more appropriate to make a comparison with 'the kind of lives that people like X would normally expect to lead' (p 33). This suggested that the law considered that a person with a disability had no right to expect more than was available to them and that they were, by their disability, restricted in their access to appealing their rights.

Baroness Hale overruled this view in her judgment on the same case in the Supreme Court [2014], with reference to the UN Convention on the Rights of Persons with Disabilities (CRPD, 2006). She highlighted 'the universal character of human rights, founded on the inherent dignity of all human beings' (pp 18–19) and explained that 'what it means to be deprived of liberty must be the same for everyone, whether or not they have physical or mental disabilities' (p 19). Johns (2016) confirms that, on first examination, the Supreme Court has taken a universal, principles-based approach to deciding what a deprivation of liberty looks like for a person with a disability. He also notes that since the right to liberty may be interfered with by decision of the court, there may be a hierarchy at work where 'an exception to the right to liberty is allowable because there is a higher duty or obligation in relation to protection of the vulnerable' (p 154).

Considering the assessment of Jack, the BIA's practice did not match the principles and standards set out in the MCA because they did not fully include the person in the capacity assessment, and could therefore be considered unethical, if not unlawful, although they did serve the higher purpose of protecting a vulnerable person. Other ethical viewpoints may view this decision differently, but in deontological terms, the practice was not fully ethical.

Utilitarianism: the greatest good for the greatest number

The utilitarian approach, by contrast, aims to 'direct the attention towards the intentions or consequences of individual actions' and to 'look for good consequences, and as many as possible' (Johns, 2016, p 18). The result of BIA practice is what matters, not whether the rules were followed in reaching a decision. This suggests that where BIAs assess the capacity of people who have never objected to the restrictions in their care and who have been settled in a stable placement that meets their needs with the support of those around them, their work may have little ethical value as it does not increase their 'pleasure or happiness', as the philosopher Jeremy Bentham would put it (Johns, 2016, p 18).

Johns (2016) suggests that Munby LJ may have been taking a utilitarian approach to the decision he made in *Cheshire West and Chester Council v P* [2011], when suggesting that there was little point in bringing such cases through the expensive process of a court appeal. As P lived where the DoLS did not apply (that is, in supported living), there was a risk, if Munby LJ had agreed that P's care was a deprivation of his liberty, that many more similar cases would need to come to court for authorisation. Considering that no one questioned that the restrictions in place for P were unnecessary, disproportionate or not in his best interests and that the care planning had been supported by all those involved, what was to be gained by taking the case to court for the deprivation of liberty to be legally agreed? Taking a utilitarian view, access to the court did not change the care that was available to P and therefore was of no value.

To develop this argument, the decision in the Supreme Court can be seen to have damaged the 'pleasure' of others as public funds for care are being diverted from the provision of care services to meet the increased demand for DoLS assessments. Johns (2016) suggests that rule utilitarians, who look beyond individual good to see ethical behaviour as establishing rules for others to live by, would see value in the *Cheshire West* decision, as it has created a simpler and more accessible definition of deprivation of liberty, which has allowed a greater number of people to have their circumstances scrutinised and improved where necessary.

In utilitarian terms, the BIA's capacity assessment decision did not make Jack's life more 'happy or pleasurable', as it did not alter the restrictions he lived under, although it may have given the home the time and inclination to find alternatives that would do so.

Virtue ethics: doing the right thing

An alternative view of ethics places the focus not on the rules to follow or effect of the actions taken, but on the person making the choice. A virtuous person (characterised by Aristotle) has the qualities and intentions that mean they will make ethical decisions in all given situations. Johns (2016) suggests the following as qualities that make a virtuous person: being 'courageous, honest, kind, loyal or conscientious' (p 19). In addition, a virtuous social worker would have the following qualities: 'temperance, magnanimity, gentleness, truthfulness, wittiness, friendliness, modesty, justice, professional wisdom, care, respectfulness and courage' (p 19). Cave (2015, p 66) suggests that 'courageous individuals require sufficient perceptiveness and sensitivity to tell when "brave" actions are appropriate – when whistleblowing would help matters, when it would be wiser to adopt other tactics', so an element of personal judgement is essential.

This view suggests that 'virtuous' people know implicitly what is the 'right' thing to do, as their personal qualities ensure that they always know what this is and are never motivated by greed or self-interest. Johns (2016) suggests that social worker training should encourage the development of 'reflection, empathetic understanding and sensitivity' (p 19) so that such virtue is available to social workers for their practice. If this were the case, you could be led to wonder why there is any need to think about ethical decision-making when all these virtuous social workers (and BIAs) have been trained to always do the right thing.

In Jack's case, if the BIA is virtuous, you can trust that the decision they have made is ethical, as they have shown professional wisdom, person-centred values and respectfulness in how they reached their decision. Without an external measure to judge by, however, how could you disagree that they may have acted unethically?

Social justice, egalitarian and care ethics: fairness for all

Social justice is concerned with the application of what is just to a social context. This may include the law, how society works and how people relate to each other on an individual level. It may include rights, responsibilities, the distribution (or redistribution) of wealth and resources, and the way in which social policy affects how decisions are made and services are provided. Social justice is concerned about the individual's relationship with the state. The frameworks of human rights law within which BIAs operate are a manifestation of that state power and control. Johns (2016, pp 35–40) sets out the views of a range of thinkers on social justice, including those of John Stuart Mill (1806–73) and John Rawls (1921–2002), and shows how the practice of social workers using the law can be informed by their views. Considering that not all BIAs are social workers, it is valuable to consider that social work – a key profession to BIA practice – highly values the social justice approach.

 ESSENTIAL INFORMATION: PROFESSIONAL STANDARDS

The BASW Code of Ethics for Social Work

The BASW Code of Ethics (2021, p 7) sets out five principles of social justice that members should adhere to:

1. Challenging oppression
2. Respecting diversity
3. Distributing resources
4. Challenging unjust policies and practices
5. Working in solidarity

As evidenced in the BASW Code of Ethics, social work as a profession explicitly asks its members not only to recognise and work to address inequality as it affects individuals but also to question and challenge structural inequity and support others to protest injustice.

As BIAs assessing, questioning and, at times, challenging care decisions, the social justice approach is a valid means of framing our judgements.

In the case of Jack's capacity assessment, on the one hand, the BIA can be seen not to have supported him sufficiently to exercise his right to challenge and remove an overprotective restriction (that is, to take a risk to go out at night unaccompanied) by not trying harder to gain his views of the risks and the deprivation of liberty. On the other hand, the BIA's actions in providing the protections, rights and advocacy available through the DoLS legal framework can be seen to have given the means for Jack to exercise greater power over the decisions made about his life, if he chooses to use them.

This egalitarian view, supported by the theories of John Rawls, suggests that there is value in state involvement (such as a DoLS authorisation) if it maximises the person's opportunities, that is, gives access to advocacy to enable the person's views to be heard, thereby reducing disadvantage. Johns (2016) notes the irony in the observation that by 'controlling one aspect of people's lives someone is enabled to participate in society, so that ... a deprivation of liberty is empowering' (p 159). As BIAs, we could be seen to be acting out an egalitarian process that aims to give the chance to improve the rights and self-determination of people with a disability and expand their capabilities. It is not always clear that this is the case, particularly when assessments and authorisations do not actually make any change to how the person is cared for or the levels of freedom or autonomy they experience.

Ethical assessment and BIA decision-making in action

Ethical theories are a helpful aid in reflecting on practice dilemmas. This section explores two common BIA practice dilemmas in the context of these approaches: completing MCA–compliant assessments with DoLS timescales, and safeguarding best interests. They do not provide definitive solutions, but offer BIAs the opportunity to explore different approaches.

How can BIAs carry out MCA-compliant assessments within DoLS assessment timescales?

Issue

The DoLS Code of Practice (Ministry of Justice, 2008) sets out a timescale for assessment under an urgent authorisation of seven calendar days, with an option to increase for a further seven days, although this requirement has been routinely breached since the increase in applications following the *Cheshire West* judgment.

There remains a pressure to complete DoLS assessments as quickly as possible, as supervisory bodies and managing authorities must protect the person's rights to ensure that the care they provide complies with human rights law, which is not the case if applicants remain on a waiting list for assessment.

BIAs and Mental Health Assessors often note that waiting times contravene Principle 2 MCA Code of Practice, which requires that those assessing capacity take 'all practicable steps to help' the person to make decisions for themselves (DCA, 2007, p 22). These practicable steps are likely to take time and the requirement for BIAs to have had no prior involvement in the person's care means that they have no prior knowledge of the person's preferred methods of communication or time to build a relationship. The DoLS timescales for assessment also affect the time needed to explore the decisions that have brought the person to their current care arrangements, and explore any less restrictive options, as well as the time needed to discuss the past, present and future of the person with their friends, family and advocates. The time limitation means there is a significant risk that existing arrangements will be 'rubber-stamped' rather than challenged. Are we then to say that the rules themselves are at least contradictory or at worst unethical?

Relevant ethical models

The *deontological* view may not offer any easy answers to the ethical assessor. The assessor completing the capacity assessment may try to assess in detail according to the MCA's five principles while aiming to complete the assessment within 7 or 14 calendar days according to the DoLS legal framework, or the even shorter timescales required by supervisory body rotas; for example, one assessment in one day a month, or three assessments in five days.

The tension this creates between two different, contradictory sets of rules puts the assessor in a compromised position where neither set of demands may be satisfied. The MCA's principles are designed to be 'universal' and apply to all people who lack capacity, regardless of age (over the age of 16), disability or gender, and yet the DoLS appears to ask the assessor to apply these principles in a more limited manner. How can this be considered acceptable? Johns (2016) cites Ross, 'who argues that there is a hierarchy of duties and obligations' (p 154) that allows for some principles to be set aside when more important rights are at stake. In this situation, it could be considered that the wider goal of scrutinising care and capacity decisions and promoting less restrictive care under DoLS is a higher purpose than a capacity assessment that is fully compliant with Principle 2 MCA.

Johns (2016) points out that when assessing a person who may be subject to DoLS, their Article 5 right to liberty is already potentially compromised and may be compromised further if they have not been fully assessed. There is, however, a risk that the 'natural' desire of people working with adults who are perceived to be vulnerable to avoid risky situations as 'protecting people who are unable, for clearly identifiable reasons, to protect themselves always seems the right thing to do' (Johns, 2016, p 154). If the MCA's principles are ignored in favour of the speedier DoLS timescales, the risk of protective, rather than person-centred decisions, becomes greater.

The *utilitarian* view may guide the assessor towards making a pragmatic decision to offer a more limited assessment to a greater number of people, thereby ensuring that the benefit of the 'direct independent legally based professional assessment' (Richards, 2016, p 5) provided by a BIA is more widely available. It offers the enticing prospect to supervisory bodies that more of those on waiting lists for assessments will be seen and the potential for fewer people to be unlawfully deprived of their liberty while assessors are working diligently on other assessments, but raises the possibility of perfunctory, uncritical assessment becoming the norm. Guidance to undertake proportionate assessments supports this view – to provide equity of access to your professional services for as many people as possible – but this should not take precedence over the purpose of the assessment – to ensure that care planning does not infringe individual human rights without justification.

A *virtue ethics* approach places greater emphasis on the assessor's 'integrity, honesty and probity' (Johns, 2016, p 156) in making decisions, and values the respect that the assessor shows the person during the assessment as well as the 'virtuousness' of the decisions they reach. This offers support to the well-intentioned assessor that 'ethical decisions are those that result in the well-being of the individual in a holistic sense' (p 156) – decisions that can be validated in a court of law or be informed by existing case law. By conforming to the prevailing view of well-informed, legally supported practice, the assessor remains ethical. Cases such as *London Borough of Hillingdon v Steven Neary and others* [2011] and *CC v KK and STCC* [2012] show what can happen when the principles of the MCA are ignored. The resulting suffering of people subject to the unnecessary restrictions of the DoLS can be avoided by adopting the key elements of case law into ethical assessment practice.

Summary

There are compromises inherent in the DoLS assessment process, especially concerning the quality of mental capacity assessments when time pressures apply. As a BIA, you are treading the line between each of these approaches, making decisions based on the principles you must uphold, in the context of pressure to offer your professional expertise to as many people as possible while maintaining the quality and virtue of your assessment practice in the knowledge that it may be judged in court. How skilfully you weigh and balance the decision-making process is at the heart of your ethical practice.

What should a BIA do if the person's current care is not in their best interests?

Issue

It can be very clear when a BIA assesses a person that their current care is not in their best interests; for example, the care is of a poor quality or is not appropriate for the person's cultural or emotional needs or wellbeing and is causing them harm. There may be no possibility of changing the person's care arrangements immediately, as there may be no appropriate alternative available and it may cause more harm to stop the care. While BIAs have the option to state that a deprivation of liberty is occurring that is not in the person's best interests, and that the deprivation of liberty must cease immediately, and have the power to raise a safeguarding concern (see the panel below on Section 42 of the Care Act 2014), this rarely happens in practice as it may mean leaving the person without care and support entirely.

In this situation, BIAs tend to recommend the authorisation be in place for a short period of time before it is reassessed, stipulate conditions to address the areas of concern with the care provider, ensure that there is effective monitoring in place via a Relevant Person's Representative (RPR), an IMCA appointed under Section 39D MCA 2005 or paid representative, and make recommendations to the funding authority on ways they can address the issues and raise the safeguarding concern. This does not always feel satisfactory to BIAs, as it leaves the person with the care that has already been assessed as inadequate and asks them to trust the managing authority and care manager to address the issues promptly and effectively.

We are aware of a case where a BIA did not want to recommend authorising a deprivation of liberty for a person in a care home where overly restrictive care techniques were being used and alternative options were not being tried by the nursing home out of concern about the risk involved to the person and other residents. In the BIA's view, the care was unnecessarily restrictive, a view supported by other health professionals involved. The BIA did not want their assessment to give legitimacy to the restrictions by stating in their decision that they were in the person's best interests even for a brief period of time.

 ESSENTIAL INFORMATION: LAW

Care Act 2014, Section 42: Enquiry by local authority

1) This section applies where a local authority has reasonable cause to suspect that an adult in its area (whether or not ordinarily resident there) –

> a) has needs for care and support (whether or not the authority is meeting any of those needs);
>
> b) is experiencing, or is at risk of, abuse or neglect; and
>
> c) as a result of those needs is unable to protect himself or herself against the abuse or neglect or the risk of it.
>
> 2) The local authority must make (or cause to be made) whatever enquiries it thinks necessary to enable it to decide whether any action should be taken in the adult's case (whether under this Part or otherwise) and, if so, what and by whom.

The BIA in this case liaised with the local authority's safeguarding team responsible for organisational abuse to investigate whether there were any safeguarding concerns raised about the care provided by the home and found that there were. The BIA provided the local authority with information relating to their own concerns to contribute to its enquiry under Section 42 of the Care Act 2014 and recorded their reluctant recommendation for a short DoLS authorisation.

As a general guide, where a regulated care setting has been given an inadequate rating by the CQC (or Welsh equivalent), this should trigger:

- a high priority DoLS assessment for those residents on a waiting list;
- Part 8 review of those with existing DoLS authorisations as there needs to be scrutiny of the best interests assessment and weighing of whether the risk of remaining somewhere unsuitable outweighs the risk of moving the person.

Relevant ethical models

A *deontological* perspective on this situation would suggest the necessity to apply the rules set down in the DoLS and refuse to authorise the deprivation of liberty because the care was not in the person's best interests. The BIA's professional, legal and ethical obligation to report the safeguarding concern would be met, so enquiries could be made and an action plan drawn up to address the concerns. However, the short-term impact on the person would very likely be a rushed move to another care home with no guarantee of an improvement in their circumstances. As Munby J has noted in *Local Authority X v MM and another* [2007] and elsewhere: 'What good is it making someone safer if it merely makes them miserable?' The principles set out in law do not consider that the impact of keeping the person safe may at times increase the risk to their emotional wellbeing – or was their emotional wellbeing already at significant risk and there is a chance that the harm might be reduced by moving them from their current home? It is difficult to answer this question without being able to see into the future.

A *utilitarian* view might suggest that recommending the DoLS authorisation for a short time with conditions in place to address the concerns about the person's care is a pragmatic solution that could increase the person's physical and emotional wellbeing without causing any further disruption. The BIA's actions do not increase the level of harm occurring and will ensure that, as the person is subject to a DoLS authorisation, they have the right to appeal, the right to further professional scrutiny of their care soon and the right to an advocate to ask for a review and check that the conditions are being addressed. This view is also supported by the Court of Appeal's judgment in *North Yorkshire County Council and A Clinical Commissioning Group v MAG and GC* [2016], which stated that the care provided in those circumstances would only have been an unlawful breach of the person's rights if the care had been 'seriously inappropriate' (para 43). The fact that care continues to be provided, albeit not in an ideal form, is better for the person than living on the streets.

Summary

The two potential options considered here suggest that harm would be caused to the person whatever was decided. It is concerning that the first ethical approach would not consider the potential negative outcome for the person in the short term (such as a hastily planned alternative placement or withdrawal of care), which may make the second, less palatable but more pragmatic solution more acceptable. It is also important to be clear that DoLS cannot be used as a means to 'safeguard' a person (that is, remove them from their home and family without other legal authority) as DoLS does not give the power to breach the person's Article 8 (ECHR) right to private and family life in this way. The two cases below show that DoLS has been misused in this way and it is not lawful.

ESSENTIAL INFORMATION: LAW

Somerset County Council v MK and others [2014]

MK was 19 and lived with her family. She became distressed during a school trip in May 2013 and returned home where her mother noticed bruising to her chest. She reported the bruising to the GP and to staff at the respite placement where P was due to stay during a family holiday. Staff at the respite placement noticed further bruising and safeguarding procedures started. The investigation failed to note that MK had been seen to hit herself heavily on the chest during the school trip. Instead, the decision was made for MK to remain permanently at the placement, although her family sought her return home. She was prescribed aripiprazole, an antipsychotic medication with a sedating effect. In November 2013, she was moved to a second placement and in December 2013 a standard

DoLS authorisation was granted and the local authority applied to the Court of Protection. The judge found that not only was she removed unlawfully from her family with no grounds to do so, but that the detention was unlawful until the DoLS application was made in November, that Somerset County Council had not investigated the safeguarding concern and it had also breached her Article 8 (ECHR) right to private and family life.

Milton Keynes Council v RR and others [2014]

RR was an elderly woman with dementia who was removed from her home by Milton Keynes Council in October 2012 following safeguarding concerns about her welfare, which included bruising to her face. RR was taken from her home and placed in a care home. Her son, SS, was away at the time and was not told for another 19 days where his mother was. There had been no safeguarding investigation into the concerns that had been raised. The council did not seek the court's authorisation for RR's removal and placement in the care home. A standard DoLS authorisation was sought but not put in place for two weeks after she was taken to the care home. She remained at the home for 16 months until the Court of Protection heard her case, by which time the council decided not to pursue the safeguarding allegations against SS. The judge found that RR was deprived of her liberty unlawfully until the DoLS authorisation was in place and that her (and her son's) Article 8 rights had been breached. The council apologised to them both.

 KEY MESSAGES

- **BIA** practice often asks BIAs to make decisions where there is no clear right or wrong answer.

- **THERE** is a range of different ethical models that support the BIA's critical thinking by proffering rules and principles to guide your decision, including the benefits for the individual or wider society, the actions you take and how you take them, and the value of the outcome to the person.

- **CRITICALLY** reflective ethical practice asks BIAs to think carefully about what motivates the decisions they make, to be explicit about their values and ensure that they are ultimately of benefit to the person whose rights they are maintaining or promoting.

- **A** confident understanding of the legal rights of those detained, including advocacy and appeal and the roles of those who support these processes, is essential for ethical BIA practice.

KNOWLEDGE REVIEW

- **THERE** are some decisions required of BIAs that have no right answers. How can you ensure that the decisions you reach are ethical?

- **WHICH** ethical approaches fit closest with the ways you usually make difficult decisions? Are there others that you have read about that you want to explore further?

- **WHAT** value do ethical models add to making complex BIA decisions?

- **WHAT** rights and roles are available to those detained under DoLS and what is your role in ensuring that these are available without conflict of interest?

 FURTHER READING

- Cave, P. (2015) *Ethics: A Beginner's Guide,* London, Oneworld Publications

- Johns, R. (2016) *Ethics and Law for Social Workers*, London, Sage Publications, Chs 1, 2 and 8

8

BIA recording

This chapter focuses on the central task of recording your Best Interests Assessor (BIA) assessment. It acknowledges how fundamental it is to all BIA practice to evidence the decisions you have made and how you made them. It will help you to explore the key elements you need to record BIA assessments effectively and support defensible decision–making, and covers the following areas:

- Completing Form 3 in a professional and legally compliant manner.
- Keeping records of your consultation process.
- Writing enough (but not too much) to cover all the requirements.
- Considering previous and other assessments and relevant viewpoints.
- Writing recommendations and conditions.
- Getting the details right.
- Recording objection.
- Writing for your audience.
- Recording your decision not to recommend authorisation of the deprivation of liberty.
- Key messages, knowledge review and further reading.

Introduction

The huge increase in Deprivation of Liberty Safeguards (DoLS) assessments following the *Cheshire West* judgment (see Chapter 1) has led to efforts to streamline the DoLS assessment and recording processes. Efforts were made in the immediate aftermath of *Cheshire West* to streamline the standard DoLS forms. Separate, similar but not identical versions were devised for England and Wales (Welsh Government, 2015; DHSC, 2018). This highlights the crucial role recording has in BIA practice. BIAs handle a significant number of assessments and it is essential that person-centred assessment practice does not deteriorate under pressure to complete more assessments. To maintain standards in BIA recording, it is essential to keep records of decision–making that are proportional to the risks and complexities for the person involved.

A time study of BIA practice for Cornwall Council (Goodall and Wilkins, 2015) showed that recording is a 'primary component' of BIA work. In this study, BIAs were asked approximately how long they spent writing up all of the documents, and responses ranged from 30 minutes to 10 or more hours (p 46).

The study notes factors that BIAs identified to explain this variation, including 'the "complexity" of the work and the bureaucracy of the scheme' (p 48). In reality, most assessments take between three and four hours to write up depending on the nature of the assessment.

Hemmington et al (2021, p 88) highlighted that 'a significant number of respondents highlighted difficulties in getting enough information to make a reasoned recommendation'. This was exacerbated further if the BIA was independent and not employed by the local authority as access to care records was more challenging, adding to the bureaucracy felt by BIAs accessing hospitals and care homes, and speaking with key professionals.

Completing Form 3 in a professional and legally compliant manner

Professionalism

All professionals eligible to qualify and practise as BIAs are required by their respective professional bodies to maintain good practice in record keeping.

ESSENTIAL INFORMATION: PRACTICE GUIDANCE

All BIA professions must follow professional standards for recording as part of their registration. These are:

Social workers
- Social Work England (SWE): standards 3.11, 4.3, 4.7, 5.3 and 6.3 regarding recordkeeping (SWE, 2019b)
- Social Care Wales (SCW): standard 6.2 on recordkeeping (SCW, 2017).

Occupational therapists and psychologists
- Health and Care Professions Council (HCPC): standard 10 relating to recordkeeping (HCPC, 2018a):
  - occupational therapists (HCPC, 2018b)
  - practitioner psychologists (HCPC, 2018c).

Nurses
- Nursing and Midwifery Council (NMC): standard 10 on recordkeeping (NMC, 2018).

Every professional is bound to standards that prize accurate, comprehensible and secure records. Prideaux (2013, p 1450) found evidence that 'good standards of record keeping … [can be] linked with improving the quality of patient care'. McCaw and Grant (2009, p 203) note that occupational therapists 'should document the clinical reasoning behind their care planning and service provision … a task, it has been argued, they are not always good at'. Recording has been described as a 'necessary evil' in social work, 'resented as a distraction from the real work' on the one hand, and noted as 'absolutely essential' on the other (O'Rourke, 2009).

Sadly, the quality of recording mental capacity and best interests decisions is inconsistent and may be implicated in significant harm caused to individual wellbeing. Preston-Shoot et al's review of Safeguarding Adults Reviews (SARs) from April 2017 to March 2019 highlights poor practice in the application of the MCA 2005 generally in cases where significant harm or death occurred (2020, pp 118–21), and notes in respect of recording that 'in some cases [recording] of capacity assessments was noted to be poor: one ambulance service record did not state what decision the individual lacked capacity to make, another made no capacity record about a hospital admission refusal. A psychiatrist's assessment was not formally recorded' (p 120).

BIAs may find recording the decisions they make challenging. It is vital to remember as a BIA that the record of the assessment and the decision you have made is your evidence of the necessity that a person's human right to liberty should be taken away from them for a period of time. The power the BIA holds to recommend that a person is deprived of their liberty should never be used without well-evidenced documentation that clearly sets out the grounds for that decision. Form 3 allows BIAs to show their reasoning, but the BIA should never see this as a routine or casual piece of work. Your evidence should answer the question 'on what authority [are] we acting to impose … our views and decisions upon others?' (Graham and Cowley, 2015, p 155). The quality of recording should be a priority for all BIAs as documentary evidence of the way that essential choices are made on behalf of often voiceless people.

Completing Form 3

The English and Welsh Form 3s (Welsh Government, 2015; DHSC, 2018) combine the assessments that BIAs complete (age, no refusals, best interests and, where requested by your supervisory body, mental capacity assessments, although this is completed on Form 3a in Wales). This aimed to prevent the duplication of information formerly contained in separate assessment forms. Form 3 includes sections to record background information about the person and their deprivation of liberty, the views of the person and others involved in their care, and the BIA's recommendation for the length of the authorisation and an appropriate Relevant Person's Representative (RPR). Practice guidance is available for completion of both the English and Welsh DoLS forms (Welsh Government, 2015; DHSC, 2018) to aid practitioners to use the forms to evidence the decision-making process in all the essential requirements of the DoLS assessments.

REFLECTIVE ACTIVITY

Download a copy of Form 3 (Welsh Government, 2015; DHSC, 2018) and Form 3a, for Wales. Look out for the following kinds of information that must be recorded in the different sections:

– factual information such as dates, names, addresses, phone numbers, titles of documents and so on;
– boxes to tick, for example to summarise your decision, to show whether a decision in a particular area needs to be made or to indicate that you have completed that assessment;
– text boxes for recording views and opinions, listing the evidence you used to come to your decision, and explaining why you made your decision.

Highlight the different types of information in different colours.

– What different kinds of information do you need to prepare to gather in order to complete all of these sections?

ADASS (2016) gave advice to supervisory bodies on how to streamline their DoLS assessment processes as an 'emergency interim measure' post-*Cheshire West*, which included proposals for a 'desktop assessment' and short assessment (Form 3b) to be used in certain situations where, for example, the person's care is settled and there are no objections to care or safeguarding concerns (pp 5–6), although this has rarely been used. DoLS-specific software packages (such as DoLSPro) were also made available to help BIAs spend less time on writing up their assessment.

As with all approaches to streamlining processes that are concerned with maintaining person–centred practice and meeting legal obligations, as a BIA you should take a considered view as to whether your chosen method fulfils the following requirements:

• meets the expectations of the supervisory body you work for;
• meets the ethical practice standards of your professional body;
• does not expose the person you are assessing to a lower quality assessment.

Keeping records of your consultation process

Completing Form 3 is not the only writing required for making your assessment. As with all health and social care practice, in order to write assessments accurately you will need to make notes while you gather information. This is particularly important when noting the person's exact response (for example verbal responses or behaviour) to questions asked during the capacity assessment or gathering their views to inform your best interests decision.

As BIAs ourselves, we have often made pages of notes during assessments, including records of documents we have seen, dates of incidents, summaries of what we have been told by those we have consulted and lists of medication the person has been taking, and how much and how often. We note exact phrases from conversations with the person, their family and friends and other people involved in their care so that we can quote directly from what they have told us. From the information about the person that we have gathered, we decide what we consider the 'salient points' for the capacity assessment to be, so that during the assessment:

- we know what we need to inform the person of;
- we know in what form to present this information, so that we can support the person as far as is practicable;
- we can assess how the person understands, retains, uses, weighs and communicates these points;
- we can subsequently record this information clearly in the capacity assessment.

REFLECTIVE ACTIVITY

Think about the following questions.

Contemporaneous notes

- What notes do you keep and where do you keep them?
- What do you do with them after you have completed your assessment?
- How would you evidence what you did during your assessment if you were asked to justify your decision-making afterwards?

Running records

- How do you record what the people you consult have said?
- How do you know who said what when?
- How do you evidence how you made your decisions as a BIA?
- Where do you keep these records and what do you do with them when your assessment has been completed?
- What impact does your employment role (rota, full-time or independent BIA) have on what and how you record your assessment?

As the legal principle for evidence is 'if you didn't write it down, it didn't happen', would you feel confident you have written evidence available

> that shows the efforts you have made to assess and consult thoroughly? Is there more you need to do or are you confident you keep detailed enough records?

Writing enough (but not too much) to cover all the requirements

The most important thing to remember when writing BIA assessments is that they should be proportionate to the person's circumstances. Ruck Keene et al (2022, p 20) summarise this as follows: 'What is reasonable to expect by way of documentation will depend upon the circumstances under which the assessment is conducted.' A complex situation, for example, where capacity has been challenging to assess, the person is objecting or there are disagreements over less restrictive options, will require a more detailed explanation than a situation where the person is happy with their care and there are few, if any, alternative options.

Common pitfalls when completing BIA assessments include the following:

- making statements or offering opinions about the situation without evidence to support your view;
- repeating information recorded elsewhere in your assessment;
- quoting case law unnecessarily;
- including detailed information from care plans that is not relevant to the deprivation of liberty.

You can avoid these by checking back through your assessment and taking the following actions:

- Each time you make a statement or give an opinion, add an example such as: 'I have not made assumptions based on Mrs X's age, condition and appearance as I have considered a range of alternative best interests such as returning home, supported living and extra care housing as well as her current care home placement, and not assumed that an older person with dementia is best cared for in an institutional setting.'
- If you need to refer to certain information more than once, include a complete explanation in the first instance, and then refer back to it on subsequent occasions using the relevant page number or section of the form. For example, refer to your capacity assessment when considering the subjective element of deprivation of liberty rather than repeating your judgement.
- Use key elements of case law as headings to structure your explanation. For example, explain the features of the care plan that make you think the person is under 'continuous supervision and control', rather than listing the case law that defines deprivation of liberty.
- Reread your assessment to ensure that the evidence you have considered is relevant. For example, ask yourself whether you have focused on the

restrictions the person is subject to or have written general comments about their care provision.

Considering previous and other assessments and relevant viewpoints

The touchstone case for why it is important to consider all potential viewpoints and maintain your independence when writing BIA assessments is *London Borough of Hillingdon v Steven Neary and others* [2011].

 ESSENTIAL INFORMATION: LAW

London Borough of Hillingdon v Steven Neary and others [2011]

The Court of Protection found in June 2011 that Steven Neary had been illegally deprived of his liberty between 5 January 2010 and 23 December 2010, despite one urgent and three standard DoLS authorisations having been in place since April 2010. The judge ruled that as well as Steven's Article 5 right to liberty under the European Convention of Human Rights (ECHR) having been breached, his Article 8 (ECHR) right to a private and family life had also been unlawfully breached as he had been kept away from his home and father.

Steven Neary was 21 at the time the borough arranged a respite placement for him at a Hillingdon-run support unit in December 2009. Steven has diagnoses of severe learning disability and autism and he had been cared for at home by his parents, and then by his father Mark, when his parents separated, with support from the London Borough of Hillingdon. The borough continued the respite placement for a year without Mark's explicit consent and in the face of both Steven's and Mark's objections. Steven's case was taken to court eventually once an Independent Mental Capacity Advocate (IMCA) had been appointed under Section 39D MCA 2005 in October 2010.

The judge criticised the actions of the supervisory body on the following grounds:

- The decision-making about the DoLS authorisation was too close to the management of both the support unit and the decision-making about Steven's care. Mark Neary criticised this as the supervisory body 'rubberstamping' the care plan made by the same organisation's social workers (para 147).
- The supervisory body lacked robust scrutiny. The judge commented: 'Where, as here, a supervisory body grants authorisations on the basis of perfunctory

scrutiny of superficial best interests assessments, it cannot expect the authorisations to be legally valid' (para 33(3)).

The assessments completed by the three BIAs were identified as being inadequate. Criticisms included the following:

- A 'cursory' assessment by the second BIA, who spoke to Mark Neary only briefly and copied and pasted sections from the first BIA assessment into their own, which suggested that their assessment was not an independent view of the circumstances (para 96).
- 'A best interests assessment which makes no reference to the person's wishes and feelings or those of their family, to alternative care options or to the need for an IMCA, is crucially deficient' (para 137).

For further information, read the Honourable Justice Peter Jackson's judgment in this case. There is also a summary and commentary on the case in Johns (2014, pp 117–18).

Each time you write a BIA assessment, whether it is the first one ever to be written about the person or whether it follows many previous assessments, your writing must show an independent and critical view of the current situation. You need to record any varying points of view and consider new information available since the previous assessment, rather than merely repeating what has happened or been decided before.

There are circumstances in which quoting explicitly from other assessments may be appropriate, for example when referring to factual information from previous BIA assessments that will not change from one assessment to the next when reviewing or reassessing an authorisation. This should be done with caution, as the information may not be accurate and is likely to be subject to change.

You should refer only to verifiable facts such as:

- the conditions set for the managing authority as part of a previous DoLS authorisation that will enable you to review progress in the current case;
- factual information that has not changed, such as the person's background history, leading up to the DoLS authorisation made by a previous BIA assessment.

You may also find it useful to quote verbatim from other assessments completed as part of the overall DoLS assessment process, such as the Mental Health Assessor's, IMCA's or paid representative's reports. Information given that is quoted word for word from another source should be presented in quote marks and should refer to the name and role of the person who wrote the document quoted as well as the date of that document. You must also ensure that you list the other assessments and reports you are considering as part of coming to your own independent conclusion.

Carter (2020) reported on the suspension of a social worker from the Social Work England register for 12 months because they had been found guilty of copying and pasting information between a number of BIA DoLS assessments. Evidence heard at a SWE tribunal (SWE, 2020b) included that the social worker admitted that they were under additional pressure in their work because of being on a BIA rota and that they copied and pasted information from one Form 3 to another that was incorrect. The social worker was acting in the belief that their practice was acceptable but admitted at the hearing that their actions were 'unprofessional, stupid, naïve and potentially put service users at risk of being unlawfully deprived of their liberty' (SWE, 2020b, para 22). In particular, it was noted that the text the social worker had copied and pasted was not general information about the DoLS process but details of the assessment that the BIA had conducted and descriptions of the person's responses to questions. This case emphasises the professional duty to maintain high standards of practice in recordkeeping as a BIA and the risks to the person of poor recording practice that might remove their personal experiences, views and wishes from records of their assessments and decision-making. This issue was identified by a practitioner who was scrutinising BIA recording and therefore also emphasises the importance of careful and considered examination of DoLS recording before authorisation by supervisory bodies.

Writing recommendations and conditions

As well as completing the relevant assessments, the BIA is asked to make recommendations on Form 3 relating to any authorisation for a deprivation of liberty. Such recommendations include the following:

- any conditions relating to the authorisation that the relevant managing authority should fulfil before the authorisation expires;
- any recommendations for the social worker or health professionals involved;
- the duration of authorisation;
- the most appropriate individual to act as the RPR, including whether this should be a paid representative.

We have often heard it said by experienced DoLS coordinators that BIAs are confused about what they are being asked to recommend and how to record their recommendations. If you identify issues in the person's care that directly relate to reducing the level of restrictions to which they are subject, you should make recommendations and related conditions that assign responsibility for addressing those issues and a realistic timeframe for these issues to be addressed.

When checking your BIA assessment, it is useful to ensure that there is a logical thread through the following elements:

- *Proportionate restrictions* that are in the person's best interests while less restrictive alternatives are being considered; for example, an identified need to explore less sedating medication.
- *Conditions that specifically set out the issues to be addressed*, the person responsible for addressing these issues and a realistic timescale in which to achieve this; for example, a referral from the care home to the person's doctor for a medication review to look into options for reducing levels of sedation within eight weeks.
- *Length of authorisation that is tailored to the issues to be addressed*; for example, a six-month authorisation to allow the doctor to review medication and try a new regime.
- *Recommendation for a representative* who can monitor whether the conditions are being addressed and will challenge the managing authority, if necessary.

When writing conditions, it is helpful to keep in mind the acronym SMART – specific, measurable, achievable, relevant, time-specific. In the context of DoLS conditions, this helps the BIA to write conditions that are:

- *Specific* to reducing the deprivation of liberty: that is, the conditions are in the control of the managing authority to address, the responsibility of a particular person or team and it is clear what the managing authority needs to do to address them.
- *Measurable:* it is clear to those who read and monitor the conditions that they know when they have been met.
- *Achievable:* the care home or hospital responsible for implementing the conditions has access to the necessary resources; for example, for a review or a referral for a service rather than a specific level of service.
- *Relevant:* the conditions are directly related to reducing the level of restriction and therefore reducing the deprivation of liberty.
- *Time-specific:* there is a realistic timescale for implementation.

REFLECTIVE ACTIVITY

SMART conditions

Consider the following two examples relating to DoLS conditions:

1. The managing authority will refer to the local authority for a care review within two weeks of receiving the DoLS paperwork to consider support to access the community.

2. A care review is needed as the person has not been seen by a social worker for more than a year.

Reflection

Decide which of these examples you think is SMART and which is not. How have you come to your decision?

- Think of a condition you might attach to a DoLS authorisation. Write it as a SMART condition.

Question

What is the difference between conditions and recommendations?

- *Conditions* are about issues the managing authority can address. They directly relate to reducing the need to deprive the person of their liberty and should be addressed during the time for which the DoLS is authorised.
- *Recommendations* are issues that social workers or health professionals should consider when planning the person's future care, such as looking at alternative placements or care packages via care reviews.

Getting the details right

Accuracy

DoLS coordinators for busy supervisory bodies check the quality of BIA assessments every day, and we have already noted concerns about details that are recorded inaccurately. In our experience of practice, we have often come across minor errors in details such as names and dates of birth, addresses and phone numbers of family members, local authorities, dates of key events in the person's history (such as the date of a loved one's death) and so on. With so much work to do, there is little wonder that mistakes happen. We understandably tell ourselves that 'Busy professionals make mistakes' and 'We are all human'. Mughal and Richards (2022, p 200) suggest that the '*de minimis* principle' applies to DoLS assessments. This means that a minor error, such as an incorrect name or address, should not invalidate the assessment as a whole. However, while such mistakes appear to be minor, relatives may find them distressing and indicative of a wider lack of concern or care. The brief additional time required to check through an assessment after it is completed for typing or factual errors is invaluable to eliminate unnecessary mistakes and avoid potential distress.

BIAs often have difficulty getting the details right in their assessment because of a lack of accuracy in the information provided to them by others. Sometimes, the information held by the managing authority (for example the care home) differs from the information held by the organisation involved in making decisions about the person's care (the local authority or NHS body), which may not have been checked with family or friends. It is the BIA's responsibility to make sure that the information they put in the assessment is correct, so checking factual information is essential. This can be quite a challenge if you are an independent BIA with no idea of who is responsible for the decisions made about the person's care up to the point you assess them or what alternative options have already been tried. This is where the supervisory body should be available to assist you, so do not be afraid to contact them for information and advice.

Measuring degree and intensity of restrictions, risk and proportionality

The purpose of the DoLS is to restrict people's human right to liberty only in circumstances where a risk of harm has been identified and the restrictions in place are the least restrictive way to manage that risk of harm. As a BIA, you provide evidence relating to your decision-making on issues such as the degree and intensity of restrictions, and whether these restrictions are necessary to prevent harm and proportionate to the risk of harm. It is difficult to measure the degree and intensity of restrictions – that is, how the person subject to the restrictions experiences them – without identifying exactly what those restrictions are.

When making decisions on restrictions, you may want to consider the following:

- Environmental restrictions in the home and the person's room that affect their ability to move around or leave, such as locks, sensors, alarms and barriers.
- The size of the home; for example, how many people live there and what relationships they have with people in the home.
- How often the person receives care and of what kind; for example, whether a care worker assists them with washing, dressing, going to the toilet, transferring or mobilising safely, eating, drinking, taking medication, taking part in activities and maintaining their health in terms of checking dressings, taking blood tests and so on.
- How many people assist or check on the person, whether during the day or night, and how often.
- Type, dosage and timing of medication, especially that which affects their behaviour, including whether it is taken regularly or 'as required' and how often it has actually been taken.
- Autonomy; for example, how much control the person has over their life, including whether they have chosen where they live and who they live with, what they do each day, where they go and so on, or whether these choices were made by others in their best interests.
- How often the person has the opportunity to engage in activities that interest them or to leave the care home or hospital for outings of their own choosing.

- The person's expressed views on where they live or behaviour in response to their environment and restrictions in place, and how often these views or behaviours are expressed and in what situations.
- How often the person tries to leave or says they want to leave, where they want to go to and why.
- The person's responses to staff and the care and support they provide; for example, whether the person accepts or rejects help with intimate care, how often and in what circumstances they do this, and what approach staff take to providing help in the least restrictive manner possible.
- Other details relevant to the person's situation.

Much of this information can be gathered from a detailed examination of the person's care records and discussing the person's care regime with key care staff. If this level of detail is not available, you may want to add a condition in your assessment asking the managing authority to record this information.

It is essential that BIAs clearly explain the link between the risk of harm, and justify the restriction in place and whether or not it is proportionate. Taylor (2013, p 95) states that 'the capacity of any person to predict a particular harmful event through either experience (clinical) or statistical (actuarial) methods is limited', as people do not always act in accordance with their past behaviour or with data available about their particular social group. People are unpredictable, and yet BIAs are asked to give evidence for a judgement about whether harm would occur to a person if their life were not restricted in some way. This requires a detailed analysis of past harmful events, whether measures taken to prevent them from reoccurring have been successful or unsuccessful and what impact restrictions have had on the person deprived of liberty.

We have come across cases where BIAs have included a general list of concerns about vulnerability and risk in the section relating to necessity to prevent harm, with little sense of whether the identified harm has actually occurred to the person, and if so, when and how often it has occurred, or whether it is a generalised risk of harm that has not yet taken place that is presumed the person might be at risk of.

REFLECTIVE ACTIVITY

Mr Jones does not leave the care home in which he lives without a member of staff or a family member:

Example 1
Mr Jones would be at risk if he left the home as he is vulnerable. He is not safe near roads and would get lost.

Example 2

Mr Jones has a hearing impairment and does not like to wear his hearing aid. On two reported occasions when care staff have accompanied Mr Jones to the local shops, he has stepped into traffic without being aware that a car was approaching. He no longer goes to the shops unaccompanied, as last month he did not return from a regular unaccompanied shopping trip and was brought back to the home by an off-duty member of staff who spotted him two miles away from where he was meant to be.

Questions

- Which example gives you detailed enough evidence on which to base your judgement? Why?
- Is there anything else you would like to know about Mr Jones' trips out of the home?

Recording objection

The right of the person to object to their care and/or treatment that amounts to a deprivation of their Article 5 (ECHR) right to liberty is an essential safeguard. As the person recording the majority of the DoLS assessment in relation to the person and their views and wishes, the BIA has the responsibility to ensure that it is clear when the person is objecting and an application for a Section 21A appeal to the Court of Protection should be pursued. This should be recorded in the following locations on Form 3:

- *Mental capacity assessment:* if the person stated their objection to their care and/or residence during the mental capacity assessment, this should be recorded with the assessment of their ability to communicate their decision during the functional assessment.
- *Person's views and wishes:* the evidence suggesting or stating that the person is objecting to their care and residence should be included, how this was communicated, how often this has been communicated if the managing authority have kept records of this and, if available, a verbatim account of the person's objection. A note that you consider this an objection requiring support to access a Section 21A appeal to the Court of Protection would be appropriate to include here.
- *IMCA's views:* if an IMCA (for example, Section 39A) or existing RPR have been involved in your assessment, include their views on the person's objection, if relevant.
- *Conditions:* the managing authority should be guided to keep a record of when and how the person objects to their care and/or residence, if they are not doing so already.

- *Best interests:* the person's objection to their current care and/or residence must be included in the circumstances of the person's care and considered as a burden of the current care option on the balance sheet.
- *Appointment of the RPR:* consideration of whether a family member or friend recommended to be the person's RPR must include that they have been notified that they will need to support the person's likely objection and they are willing to do so. If not, you will need to record the necessity for a paid rep to be appointed so their objection can be pursued to appeal.
- *Timescale:* the recommended authorisation period should be shorter than the maximum 12 months to reflect that the person is objecting to their care and/or residence and this should be noted as one of the reasons why this period of time is being recommended.

Writing for your audience

The benchmark often given by practitioners for written assessments is whether they will stand up in the Court of Protection if necessary. However, it is important to recognise that the court is not usually the audience for your BIA assessment, and is never the only reader. When your form has been checked and authorised by the supervisory body, it is sent to the person affected by the DoLS authorisation, the managing authority where they currently reside (the hospital or care home) and to those consulted during the assessment (professionals, family and friends involved in the person's care), as noted by Valois (2016). This means that your assessment needs to be clearly written in plain language, with no unexplained jargon and with accurate details that focus on the person and the circumstances directly related to their deprivation of liberty.

It is not advisable to directly quote the DoLS statute, Codes of Practice or case law in your assessment, as a layperson may find this intimidating and impersonal. You can show you are acting within legal principles by clearly applying these to your assessment. Some supervisory bodies do ask BIAs to quote case law in their assessments where relevant, in which case you should comply with the request, although it is worth checking to ensure that you are clear about the policy of the supervisory body you work for.

Form 3 is laid out in a way that encourages you to apply the relevant legal frameworks and principles without having to explain why. For example, the section on the person deprived of their liberty asks the assessor to consider whether they think the requirements for lawful deprivation of liberty under Article 5 (ECHR) have been met, that is, the objective (including the 'acid test'), subjective and imputable to the state elements. As Mughal and Richards (2022, pp 204–5) identify, this may require you to break down the restrictions in place and note how they fit into the Guzzardi framework (type, duration, effect, manner, degree and intensity) without any need to quote the case law to show why you have broken them down in this way (see Figure 5.1 for more information on the Guzzardi framework). Using these elements of the Guzzardi framework as headings in this section will help you to organise your list of restrictions and how they affect the person, and will show that you have explored each element in your description of the restrictions. Other things to remember when writing for your audience include the following:

- Avoid using acronyms such as DoLS, RPR or IMCA where possible. If you do need to use them, include the phrase in full in the first instance with the abbreviation in brackets, and use the abbreviation subsequently.
- Try not to use social care or health jargon. We have seen assessments that talk about 'personal care' or that use abbreviations for medical treatment without explaining what they mean. If you need to describe the kind of care a person receives, use everyday terms such as 'washing', 'dressing' or 'help to use the toilet'.

Recording your decision not to recommend authorisation of the deprivation of liberty

BIAs may decide not to recommend the authorisation of a deprivation of liberty. Often this happens because the person's circumstances have changed, for example their care needs or accommodation have changed or they died before the assessment was complete. A decision not to apply for a DoLS authorisation is recorded on Form 3a in England (DHSC, 2018) and Form 6 in Wales (Welsh Government, 2015).

The BIA must record the evidence they have gathered towards their assessment up to the point that they decided the person was not eligible for the DoLS. For example, if you decide the person has the mental capacity to consent or not to their care and residence, then you should complete all sections of the capacity assessment on Form 3 with the evidence from the assessment that informed your decision. These include the sections relating to the practicable steps taken to ensure that the person was involved in the assessment, the diagnostic test and the functional test, including why you believe the person demonstrated their capacity in this area.

In the concluding statement, you must explain why you think the person's mental disorder does not affect their ability to make decisions relating to their care. If you have had difficulty making decisions in any particular area, it is worth recording how you thought this through and came to your conclusion. In cases where you have identified suitable future courses of action in your assessment, you may also find it useful to add recommendations for other decision–makers involved in the person's care.

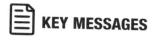 **KEY MESSAGES**

- **EVIDENCE-INFORMED**, critical recordkeeping underpins professional and ethical BIA practice.

- **ACCURACY** is important, not just for the decisions you make, but for the person you are writing about.

- **EVERY** decision you make or opinion you state should be supported by evidence from your assessment.

- **EVERY** assessment you write is a separate, independent piece of work, so be cautious of copying from one assessment to another.

- **THERE** is no need to quote the legal framework or case law that has guided how you have made your decision; show you know it by using it to structure your writing.

 KNOWLEDGE REVIEW

- **WHICH** forms do BIAs use in your region to record their assessment and decisions?

- **WHICH** DoLS assessments and recommendations can you complete on these forms?

- **WHO** is responsible for the accuracy of the information recorded?

- **WHAT** other records might a BIA need to keep and why?

 FURTHER READING

- Links to the English and Welsh DoLS forms are in the References; see DHSC (2018) and Welsh Government (2015) respectively

- For detailed guidance on completing the English Form 3 (also relevant for those completing the Welsh DoLS forms), see Mughal, A. and Richards, S. (2022) *Deprivation of Liberty Safeguards Handbook*, 2nd edn, Hounslow, BooksWise, pp 201–9

Part 3
Developing good practice

9

BIA continuing
professional development

This chapter explores the learning required to become a Best Interests Assessor (BIA), the ongoing learning required for practice in the role and how it links with your existing continuing professional development (CPD) requirements.

The chapter covers the following:

- Qualifying as a BIA in England: requirements, issues and resources.
- Qualifying as a BIA in Wales.
- Post-qualifying BIA CPD requirements.
- Maintaining your knowledge, skills and practice as a BIA: critical reflection and self-directed learning.
- The future.
- Key messages, knowledge review and further reading.

Introduction

The BIA role is a challenging one that takes place in the context of ongoing legal, professional and organisational change. Thus, qualifying as a BIA takes time, commitment and professionalism. BIA practice requires you to maintain and develop your knowledge and skills to a high level and be prepared to revise and adapt your practice quickly and flexibly. As has been acknowledged in other chapters in this book, BIAs often practise in the role alongside other work and demands on their time, so it is essential to develop robust ways to access information, learning and support, and remain up to date with developments in the field. This chapter will help you to develop good habits for learning and help you embed the BIA role into your continuing professional development (CPD).

ESSENTIAL INFORMATION: PRACTICE GUIDANCE

CPD requirements for professionals eligible to train as BIAs

Social workers in England

Social work BIAs in England must register with Social Work England (SWE). To maintain their registration, they must meet the requirements for CPD set out in the CPD guidance (SWE, 2022a), which linked to standard 4.7 to 'Record my learning and reflection on a regular basis and in accordance with Social Work England's guidance on continuing professional development' (SWE, 2019b). Those social workers who are qualified as BIAs and are annotated as BIAs on the SWE register must provide annual evidence of the completion of BIA-specific CPD.

Social workers in Wales

Those BIAs registered with the Social Care Wales (SCW) must meet the requirements of its Code of Professional Practice (SCW, 2017) and Practice Guidance (SCW, 2019), to be accountable for the quality of your work and take responsibility for maintaining and developing knowledge and skills, in particular 'undertaking relevant learning and development to maintain and improve your knowledge and skills to ensure you are fit to practise, and contributing to the learning and development of others' (Section 6.9, p 16).

Occupational therapists and psychologists

Those registered with the Health and Care Professions Council (HCPC) must meet the requirements set out in its standards (HCPC, 2018d) to 'maintain a continuous, up-to-date and accurate record of their CPD activities'. This means:

- Carrying out regular CPD activities.
- Keeping a record of what you do in whatever way is most convenient for you.
- Adding to your record on an ongoing basis. If you are audited, the HCPC will be interested in what you have done over the previous two years (the length of each registration cycle).
- Your record needs to be a true reflection of the activities that you have carried out.

This is to ensure that 'you continue to develop new skills throughout your career, meaning you can practise safely' (HCPC, 2018d).

Nurses

Those registered with the Nursing and Midwifery Council (NMC) must meet its CPD requirements (NMC, 2021), which states that nurses must maintain accurate records of the CPD they have undertaken including: what kind of CPD was undertaken, what they learned about and how it relates to their practice, the dates and number of hours involved, linking their learning to the relevant part of the Code and evidence that they completed the CPD activity.

BIA qualifying training and practice represents specialist professional development that provides valuable evidence that you have continued to learn and develop new skills.

Your experience of learning to become a BIA and learning from practice can be used as evidence of CPD towards renewal or revalidation of your professional registration, as well as helping you meet the CPD requirements for the BIA role itself. Rutter (2013) notes, in relation to social work, that CPD asks practitioners to 'go beyond a requirement to passively update skills and knowledge; it becomes an individual responsibility to actively make sense of ongoing learning and build expertise in its widest sense' (p xi). Since you must be a qualified and experienced professional before becoming a BIA, the role represents a specialist level of practice over and above your day-to-day work. Moreover, the complexity of the Deprivation of Liberty Safeguards (DoLS) means that you cannot merely be passive in your learning; rather, you must be active in order to apply your understanding of the DoLS framework ethically to the role.

Qualifying as a BIA in England: requirements, issues and resources

When the DoLS were first being implemented, universities registered with the Department of Health (DH) were given the opportunity to deliver BIA qualifying training in England by providing post-qualifying social work programmes, as set out in the Mental Capacity (Deprivation of Liberty: Standard Authorisations, Assessments and Ordinary Residence) Regulations 2008. After implementation, The College of Social Work (TCSW) was commissioned by the DH to develop an endorsement programme for universities offering BIA qualifying training. When TCSW was closed by the government in 2015, responsibility for endorsing BIA qualifying training went back to the DH and, in 2016, a revised list of providers of BIA training was published (DH, 2016). SWE has now taken on responsibility for regulating BIA training (SWE, 2020c). These arrangements apply regardless of the profession of those studying on BIA qualifying programmes.

BIA qualifying programmes are academic modules that are taken either at the final year of undergraduate degree study or at Master's level. The number of academic credits they attract, the length of the course and the cost of the modules depends on the university running the course. The methods of assessing students also vary across courses, with some requiring students to complete a portfolio, and some assessing through written assignments and interviews or law exams. Some universities have embedded BIA qualifying courses within training programmes for Approved Mental Health Professionals

(AMHPs) or professional award frameworks, while others offer the qualification as a stand–alone module.

Potential BIA students should be aware of the following key points:

- BIA qualifying programmes are academic courses for those of you who have already completed professional qualifications and are designed to ensure that you have the legal, professional and practice knowledge and skills to practise as a BIA.
- The qualifying programmes are short courses, designed to cover a range of complex content, such as statutes, case law, professional perspectives and research. They demand high levels of critical learning, so it is important that you have the time, energy and commitment required to undertake the training.
- You will be expected to have a working knowledge of using the Mental Capacity Act (MCA) 2005 in your professional practice before you begin the course. If you are not confident of your understanding of the MCA, you are advised to become familiar with it before the course begins to ensure that you are not out of your depth.

Increasingly, BIA qualifying courses require students to shadow qualified BIAs carrying out assessments as part of the programme, so students get a real flavour of current practice. This experience is central to developing a sense of the BIA role, its challenges and boundaries. It should enable you to step beyond the information you acquire during taught sessions at university – 'something certain and absolute, usually in the hands of experts' (Rutter, 2013, p 18) – so that you can develop the means to 'interpret, adapt and evaluate knowledge in use, and produce ideas of your own as a result' (Rutter, 2013, p 19).

In practical terms, it is important to note that it is the responsibility of the student, not the university running the programme, to arrange shadowing opportunities before applying for a BIA qualifying course. This means that if you want to train as a BIA, and do not already have the support of a local authority, you should contact supervisory bodies in the area where you intend to work to see if they are willing to offer you this experience. Depending on their workload and the number of existing students they are supporting, supervisory bodies may or may not be able to offer shadowing opportunities. They may attach conditions to providing shadowing opportunities, such as requiring BIA students to carry out a number of free assessments for the supervisory body after qualification.

Of fundamental importance is the need for professionals training to become BIAs to recognise that training as a BIA is about developing a specialist professional role and identity, developed from, but not identical to, your existing profession and role.

Qualifying as a BIA in Wales

When planning for the implementation of DoLS, the Welsh Government decided to train BIAs locally and did not require academic qualifications as a prerequisite to BIA practice. As a result, Welsh BIAs are often trained by lawyers commissioned by local authorities and health boards that were not academically accredited. This means that BIAs trained in Wales are unable to practise in England, although English BIAs may practise in Wales (DH, 2015d, p 10). In recent years, especially since the *Cheshire West* judgment (see Chapter 1), more Welsh BIAs are coming to English universities to gain accredited BIA qualifications. The Care and Social Services Inspectorate Wales (CSSIW) and Healthcare Inspectorate Wales (HIW) recommended in a report following the Supreme Court's judgment in 2014 that BIA training in Wales should be accredited and that 'capacity will need to be increased to ensure that Wales sustains access to the appropriate quantity and range of professionals to carry out this function' (CSSIW/HIW, 2014, p 10).

Post-qualifying BIA CPD requirements

The Mental Capacity (Deprivation of Liberty: Standard Authorisations, Assessments and Ordinary Residence) Regulations 2008 set out the expectation that BIAs, once qualified, must undertake 'further training relevant to the role' every 12 months (p 3). What form this takes has been left for the supervisory bodies to decide, since they are responsible for appointing suitable BIAs to assess under DoLS. Many supervisory bodies require BIAs to attend annual refresher training days, often run by lawyers; some also offer peer supervision to BIAs who work for them or other tailored training relevant to the role, such as access to AMHP legal updates to maintain knowledge on the interface between the MCA and the Mental Health Act 1983 (amended 2007). Since the start of COVID-19 pandemic in March 2020, many providers of BIA refresher training moved online, which may be a more accessible way of getting your annual BIA refresher training, especially if you work independently.

The now-traditional, one-day BIA refresher training course offers some valuable benefits to BIAs. It should provide the following:

- updates on current relevant case law;
- updates on national issues and challenges around DoLS implementation and planned legislative changes;
- the chance to refresh your knowledge of the main assessment and decision-making requirements for BIA work;
- the chance to explore key issues for current practice with peers and knowledgeable trainers;
- a forum to explore decision-making dilemmas using case studies.

However, if this is all you do, there may be individual areas of practice you find challenging that are not addressed. BIAs need to understand the practice and ongoing learning that moves beyond 'basic ideas and methods' towards 'wider and more critical debates ... or with deeper and more theoretical ideas and research ... [to] provide you with alternative ideas to critically consider' (Rutter, 2013, p 19).

Many BIAs find that writing assessments, dealing with complex situations, including family dynamics, and assessing capacity where people have complex communication needs are as significant as maintaining case law knowledge in terms of learning needs, so a range of ways to access support and learning is needed. Without clear guidance on the learning BIAs are expected to complete beyond qualifying, the responsibility rests with individual BIAs to come to their own conclusions about what they need to do to maintain their knowledge and skills for effective practice. This means that tools for self-reflection to identify knowledge gaps and ways to meet learning needs are essential if BIAs are to maintain their knowledge.

The BIA key capabilities (The College of Social Work, 2013) offer a structured way to think about the skills and knowledge you have and where you may need to develop more confidence, as 'directionless reflection is not very useful for CPD' (Rutter, 2013, p 32). You could check your confidence against the capability statements once you have qualified as a BIA to identify which areas you want to develop. It is also an excellent way to plan areas of learning when returning to the BIA role after a break.

Maintaining your knowledge, skills and practice as a BIA: critical reflection and self-directed learning

Case law

An essential skill for practising as a BIA after qualifying is the ability not just to keep up to date with new case law but also to be able to interpret it for use in practice. Decisions made in the Court of Protection, Court of Appeal and Supreme Court in the UK, as well as in the European Court of Human Rights, have a direct impact on the work you do as a BIA, including the decisions you need to make and how to make them. This means that at times you will need to be able to read and understand judgments written about case law.

Issues when working with case law include the following:

- Sometimes, you will find written summaries and interpretations of case law online, and it is tempting to just read these rather than the original judgments, as they are often shorter, more clearly written and give clear interpretations. However, you must bear in mind that legal summaries are the interpretations of one lawyer – they are not the only or 'correct' interpretation. If your actions as a BIA are to be informed by case law you have read, check your interpretation with the supervisory body first to ensure that they will support your conclusions.

- Some judges write in more coherent ways than others, so it is important to read key judgments to gain an understanding of how judges explain their decisions, how they refer to and acknowledge cases that have come before and the authority that their judgment has over your practice. If you refer to legal judgments, whether in writing academic assignments for BIA qualifying training or because your supervisory body asks you to quote case law in your assessments, make sure you quote from the judgment itself rather than from a summary or interpretation of the judgment.
- Case law (or 'common law') works by precedent. This means that if a court makes a judgment on a case, its interpretation becomes the one you must work by. If another, higher court then makes another judgment in the same case, that ruling should be the one that guides your practice.
- Supervisory bodies have access to legal advice, so if you are unsure what effect a judgment will have on your work as a BIA, ask your supervisory body what legal advice they have received about how to interpret it.

There are websites that will send you regular updates and monthly newsletters to help you keep up to date with case law as it becomes available in England and Wales (see the Further Reading section at the end of this chapter).

Sources of support and learning

Supervisory bodies should be your first point of contact for ongoing learning as a BIA. It is in their interests that you become a skilled and capable BIA, so the onus is on them to support your development as much as they can. You should keep in contact with the supervisory body you work for to ensure that you do not miss out on opportunities for training or development activities for assessors.

Some supervisory bodies offer individual support to newly qualified BIAs from experienced BIAs who can shadow and advise you on your early assessments or offer feedback on draft assessments. Some supervisory bodies commission additional training for their BIAs because of feedback from assessors. For example, one of us, as a DoLS coordinator and training officer, has experience in organising CPD training courses for BIAs:

- on medication, particularly for non-medically qualified BIAs;
- on the Mental Health Act for non-AMHP BIAs;
- on pictorial communication tools for capacity assessments on behalf of a supervisory body to develop the skills of their BIAs.

Your BIA learning should be ongoing and regular to ensure that you do not lose the skills and knowledge you have worked hard to acquire. Ongoing BIA practice is essential in this respect, as it is easy to forget what you have learned if you do not apply your knowledge in practice.

Developing critical reflection and self-directed learning

It should be clear from all that you have read so far that the BIA role is one that demands detailed knowledge, a range of sophisticated interpersonal skills, practice wisdom and ongoing critical professional judgement. Confidence to work in this way takes time to develop, as BIAs grow skills in 'accountable professional decision-making as well as risk assessment and management, and therefore with the ability to predict the future and manage risk of harm … based on realistic conceptions of human strengths and weaknesses' (Rutter and Brown, 2015, p 18). Higham (2013, p 143) states that 'critical reflection is essential for developing practice capability' and points out that theory considers this kind of reflection a '"self-researching" experience' (p 143), which firmly places it as the individual professional's responsibility.

As a professional who has qualified as a BIA, you will develop expertise from critical reflection on your practice and the constructive opinions of others. This is why peer supervision is another important tool in BIA CPD, as it offers an opportunity to share decision-making processes with other experienced practitioners. It can also be valuable once you have gained some experience as a BIA to have others observe and offer critical analysis on your practice. The observation of others is valuable for maintaining a conscious awareness of your own skills and knowledge, as it provides an external perspective and may highlight strengths and areas for development that you are unaware of.

REFLECTIVE ACTIVITY

Consider the following questions, and think about whether you take these actions regularly and what you can do to enhance the critical reflection of your BIA CPD.

- Do you take the initiative in identifying your learning needs?
- How did you identify what you need to learn? From feedback, supervision, assessment experiences, gut feeling?
- Who was involved in helping you identify this learning? The assessed person, families and friends, other BIAs, advocates, the Mental Health Assessor, the supervisory body?
- How honest are you with yourself about your strengths and areas for development?
- What enables you to learn or stops you from learning?

- Do you recognise and capture the learning potential of everyday practice?
- How do you note what you have learned from the assessments you carry out or from your discussions with colleagues?
- If you reflect on what did not work this time, how do you make sure you address it next time?
- Do you critically reflect on your practice and its outcomes?
- Who critically questions you?
- Have you recently asked for an experienced BIA to shadow you and give feedback?
- Do you regularly record reflections on your practice and keep it as evidence of your BIA CPD?
- Did you ensure that your reflection focused on your strengths as well as areas for development?
- Do you create your own learning objectives for your CPD?
- From your reflections, did you plan particular things you were going to learn?
- Did you discuss this with anyone? It could be your usual supervisor, a peer forum for BIAs, another experienced BIA or the supervisory body. If you are a social worker in England, SWE now ask for one annual piece of reflection on your CPD with a peer.
- Do you identify, locate and evaluate the resources you need?
- If you couldn't find anything, who did you ask to assist you?
- Do you choose and use appropriate learning strategies?
- Do you use a range of resources as well as those you prefer?
- How do you ensure that you use your new knowledge and skills in practice and not just leave them as notes or handouts?
- If your organisation does not embrace new learning or ideas, how can you overcome this?
- Do you evaluate what you learned?
- Have you revisited your learning objectives?
- Did you test whether your practice has changed and how?
- Did you seek and reflect on more critical feedback from other BIAs?
- No one can be expected to know everything or practise perfectly – how can you judge whether your aims and expectations are set too high?
- Do you explore how you can apply what you have learned?
- Do you explicitly use your learning when supporting other BIAs?
- Do you connect what you have learned to other reading?
- Have you used your knowledge to develop new resources or to undertake research?

Adapted from Williams and Rutter (2015, pp 174–5)

Bogg and Challis (2016) suggest that maintaining a CPD portfolio is the most effective way to 'support professional development and to evidence learning outcomes' (p 30). Keeping a robust and regularly updated portfolio allows BIAs to evidence their professional development to their professional body and their employing supervisory body to show they are suitable to be appointed to assessors. Some supervisory bodies will only appoint BIAs who can provide a copy of a completed assessment, so it is worth keeping an anonymised assessment in your portfolio.

All the work you do to develop greater depth to your practice, and how you continue to grow and learn as a BIA, generates evidence of your increasing specialist capability and ability to fulfil professional and BIA CPD requirements. It will also enhance your ability to meet the challenges of BIA practice now and in whatever future role the BIA becomes.

The future

As you will see in Chapter 10, the plans for the implementation of the Liberty Protection Safeguards (LPS) will involve new learning for all those currently practising within DoLS as well as in wider health and social care. You will have a number of options for your future practice as a BIA in the LPS and all of them will require refreshed and new learning whether you choose to:

- use your deprivation of liberty assessment skills in frontline practice;
- become a pre-authorisation checker of necessary and proportionate assessments for a responsible body;
- convert to the new Approved Mental Capacity Professional (AMCP) role.

Whatever role you choose to take on, your learning in relation to DoLS, and LPS in the future, never stops. There is always new case law, new practice challenges, new people with new and complex needs and circumstances for you to meet and, as a BIA, you need to be prepared to meet these challenges with an appetite for learning, curiosity and enthusiasm.

 KEY MESSAGES

- **BIAs** should complete a rigorous qualifying programme to equip them for the challenges of this specialist professional role.

- **DEVELOPING** good practice in applying the MCA is essential to success in both training and practising as a BIA.

- **SETTING** up good habits for post-qualifying CPD is essential for your ongoing skills and knowledge as a BIA.

- **CRITICAL** reflection and the ability to develop your own programme of learning for practice are key skills for ongoing BIA practice. BIAs should develop these skills during training and continue to apply them afterwards.

 ## KNOWLEDGE REVIEW

- **WHAT** are the requirements for qualifying as a BIA?

- **WHAT** ongoing learning must you undertake once qualified as a BIA?

- **HOW** does this connect with the CPD requirements of your profession?

- **WHICH** area of knowledge is most important for you to maintain?

- **HOW** can you access support and advice about CPD?

- **HOW** can you identify what further learning you may need for the BIA role?

 ## FURTHER READING

Email alerts from online resources are an excellent way to keep up to date with practice developments:

Case law
- Mental Health Law Online for regular updates on mental health case law: www.mentalhealthlaw.co.uk/Main_Page

- 39 Essex Chambers for monthly newsletters including case law summaries and guidance relevant to the MCA and DoLS: www.39essex.com/tag/mental-capacity-newsletter

- Court of Protection Hub for notifications of judgments from the Court of Protection linked to the Court of Protection User's Guide: www.courtofprotectionhub.uk

News
- *Community Care* reports on mental capacity and deprivation of liberty issues alongside social work and social care: www.communitycare.co.uk/adults

Learning resources
- Social Care Institute for Excellence MCA Directory: www.scie.org.uk/mca/directory

Social media

- For ongoing peer supervision and up-to-date information and resources, join the Facebook group for student and practising BIAs (ask the group admin if you can join): www.facebook.com/groups/816590018376985

For guidance on continuing professional development and exploring critical reflection, see:

- Bogg, D. and Challis, M. (2016) *Evidencing CPD: A Guide to Building Your Social Work Portfolio*, 2nd edn, Northwich, Critical Publishing

- Rutter, L. (2013) *Continuing Professional Development in Social Work*, London, Sage Publications

- Rutter, L. and Brown, K. (2015) *Critical Thinking and Professional Judgement for Social Work*, 4th edn, London, Sage Publications

10

BIA futures

This chapter focuses on what will happen to the Best Interests Assessor (BIA) role when the Deprivation of Liberty Safeguards (DoLS) are repealed and replaced with the Liberty Protection Safeguards (LPS). It includes the main features of the LPS framework as it is understood at the time of writing (May 2022), including the processes set out in the draft revised Mental Capacity Act (MCA) Code of Practice (which was under consultation at the time of writing). It includes the roles that BIAs are likely to be able to carry out in the new structure, including the role of the Approved Mental Capacity Professional (AMCP). This is a summary rather than a detailed exploration of the legal measures, *so you will need to ensure that you directly consult the statute and final Code before practice*. See 'Further reading' at the end of this chapter for links to the draft MCA Code and LPS consultations.

This chapter includes the following:

- The future of the BIA role and the law on deprivation of liberty.
- The Liberty Protection Safeguards (LPS).
- Safeguards for the cared-for person in the LPS.
- Interface with the Mental Health Act (MHA) 1983.
- Deprivation of liberty and 16- and 17-year-olds.
- Training for LPS, including Approved Mental Capacity Professionals (AMCPs).
- Roles for BIAs in LPS.
- Implications of LPS.
- Key messages, knowledge review and further reading.

The future of the BIA role and the law on deprivation of liberty

When we were writing the first edition of this book in 2016–17, the initial Law Commission consultation on the replacement for the DoLS was being discussed and the final chapter reflected what was known then about what the replacement might look like. Now, more than five years later, much has changed. The Mental Capacity (Amendment) Act (MCAA) 2019 has received Royal Assent, which inserted Schedule AA1 into the MCA.

Two planned implementation dates for the Liberty Protection Safeguards (LPS) – October 2020 and April 2022 – have been heralded and then missed for reasons that include a global pandemic.

The long-awaited revision of the MCA Code of Practice, regulations and documents supporting the implementation of the LPS consultation for England (DHSC, Ministry of Justice, Department for Education and Welsh Government, 2022) and LPS consultation for Wales (Welsh Government, 2022a) were made available for consultation in March 2022, with the intention that these will close in July 2022. *This means that we know more about how a new MCA Code and LPS might look in practice but we do not yet know how exactly it will operate.*

ESSENTIAL INFORMATION

Revised MCA Code of Practice and LPS guidance

This is a *disclaimer*. Where we talk about the LPS and the role of BIAs in the future, beyond what is set out in the MCAA (Schedule AA1 MCA) itself, *there is a risk that there will be changes between the consultation and the final documents* as approved by Parliament for use in England and Wales that we will not be able to update before and after publication.

The wording, chapter and paragraph references to the draft revised MCA Code of Practice (HM Government, 2022) may be subject to change in the final version passed by Parliament, *so you are recommended to check the final version* before referencing the new MCA Code of Practice.

The date of implementation of the LPS has yet to be confirmed by the government, although current estimates suggest October 2023 or April 2024.

We recommend that you search for the Liberty Protection Safeguards on the relevant government websites to check for progress on the implementation of the LPS:

- England, Department of Health and Social Care: www.gov.uk/government/organisations/department-of-health-and-social-care
- Wales, Welsh Government: https://gov.wales

The Liberty Protection Safeguards

Schedule AA1 MCA only refers to 'the safeguards', but we now know that the new framework will be called the 'Liberty Protection Safeguards' (LPS) and this is what is referred to in the draft MCA Code, regulations and training plans. It is important to be aware that, although we will be working with a new framework, the purpose and underlying rights and case law will still apply. What is changing is procedural. There will no longer be DoLS assessments or Section 16 MCA applications to the Court of Protection for community deprivation of liberty, as both of these systems will be combined within the LPS. The systems of how people who might lack capacity to make decisions about restrictive care and treatment they need to protect them from harm are changing. Their underlying human rights and the principles of the MCA are not.

This can mean that language is different because of changing functions and responsibilities. For example, this terminology from the previous DoLS framework is to change in the LPS:

- 'Relevant person' becomes the *cared-for person*.
- 'Supervisory bodies' become *Responsible Bodies*.
- 'Managing authorities' have a different role as providers of care and treatment within care arrangements.
- The role of the Best Interest Assessor will be abolished and replaced by the *Approved Mental Capacity Professional (AMCP)*.
- 'Relevant Person's Representative' will become the *Appropriate Person*.
- Sections 39A, 39C and 39D Independent Mental Capacity Advocate (IMCA) roles will be replaced with *one LPS IMCA role*.
- Eligibility assessment regarding the MHA/MCA interface is now called *excluded arrangements*.

Overall, the LPS introduce new legal provisions in England and Wales for those aged 16 years and above who are deprived of their liberty by their care arrangements, as in their care plans, rather than their residence, as previously. Deprivation of liberty is defined by case law (HM Government, 2022, paras 12.1–12.54). The settings in which LPS can be authorised include the person's own home, residential schools, supported living schemes, extra care provision, shared lives, as well as hospitals and care homes. The LPS focus is on the care arrangements that have been put in place or are planned and whether the restrictions in place are necessary and proportionate to prevent harm to the cared–for person.

The conditions required for the LPS to be authorised are:

- The person lacks capacity to consent to the care arrangements.
- The person has a mental disorder, as defined by the MHA 1983.
- The arrangements are necessary to prevent harm to the person and proportionate to the likelihood and seriousness of the risk of harm to the person.

Three assessments will need to be completed in order to show that the LPS authorisation conditions are met:

- a mental capacity assessment regarding the care arrangements;
- a medical assessment to determine mental disorder;
- a 'necessary and proportionate' assessment.

The LPS work on the presumption that assessments will form part of the usual care planning processes for the cared-for person. These could be aligned to the Care Act 2014, using existing assessments where they remain valid, reasonable and appropriate, hospital or community health assessments, including those for NHS Continuing Healthcare (CHC). The responsible body is the ultimate decision-maker as to whether an authorisation for a deprivation of liberty is given, following checks and specialist scrutiny of the assessment where considered appropriate within the framework, although in some circumstances this may be authorised by an AMCP.

Who the cared-for person's *responsible body* is depends on who is mostly responsible for their care arrangements at the time. The draft Code (HM Government, 2022, para 14.3) gives the following guidance:

1. Are the arrangements being carried out mainly in an NHS hospital? If so, in England the Responsible Body is the NHS Trust or NHS Foundation Trust. In Wales, it is the Local Health Board.
2. Are the arrangements being carried out mainly in an independent hospital in England? If so, the Responsible Body is either the local authority who is meeting the person's needs or the local authority within whose area the hospital is situated.
3. Are the arrangements being carried out mainly in an independent hospital in Wales? If so, the Responsible Body is the Local Health Board for the area in which the independent hospital is situated.
4. Are the arrangements being mainly carried out through the provision of NHS Continuing Healthcare in England or Continuing NHS Healthcare in Wales? If so, the Responsible Body is the Clinical Commissioning Group (CCG) in England or the Local Health Board in Wales.
5. In all other cases the Responsible Body is a local authority.

The draft Code includes a range of guidance regarding which responsible body will be responsible for the cared-for person's LPS application in terms of geographical location (HM Government, 2022, Ch 15).

Anyone can make a *referral* believing that a cared-for person is deprived of their liberty by their care arrangements to a responsible body and, if they are not the correct responsible body, they will pass this referral on to the correct one under the government's 'no wrong door' principle (HM Government, 2022, pp 299–300).

The responsible body then has a responsibility to identify whether there is an *Appropriate Person* to support the cared-for person during the LPS process. They should be appointed as soon as the LPS process is triggered, so they can be involved in as much of the assessment process as possible. The Appropriate Person can be a family member, friend or someone holding a Lasting Power of Attorney (LPA) or a court-appointed deputy. There are criteria for who the Appropriate Person can be and the appointed person must consent to being nominated for this role. Their role is to represent and support the cared-for person, provide them with information and support their appeal, if required. If there is no one suitable to appoint as an Appropriate Person, an IMCA should be appointed by the responsible body (HM Government, 2022, Ch 15).

The *assessment* of whether these arrangements are necessary and proportionate to the risk of harm will be conducted by frontline professionals. The assessment must include all relevant consultations where these are reasonable and practicable, including with the cared-for person, those they nominate for consultation, those involved in planning their care, any LPA, deputy, appropriate person or IMCA involved (HM Government, 2022, Ch 17). The draft MCA Code states that: 'Where possible, the LPS assessments, determinations, reviews and renewals should be embedded in the assessments and review processes carried out under these other legislative frameworks' (HM Government, 2022, para 16.3), such as health reviews and reviews of the Care Act 2014, Section 27. It is also possible to use equivalent assessments that have been made that meet the standard of evidence needed for the LPS assessments.

The draft MCA Code states that: 'To ensure that decisions taken regarding deprivations of liberty are not arbitrary, there should be no fewer than two professionals involved in carrying out the three assessments and determinations required under the LPS' (HM Government, 2022, para 16.8). The draft MCA Code states that the professionals carrying out the assessments and determinations should have *a degree of independence* from each other (HM Government, 2022, para 16.9). The draft Code also notes that they need 'the skills and experience appropriate to carry out the assessment, including an applied knowledge of the MCA and the related Code of Practice, and the ability to keep appropriate records and to provide clear and reasoned reports in accordance with legal requirements and good practice' (para 16.10), among other requirements.

The draft Mental Capacity (Deprivation of Liberty: Assessments, Determinations and Pre-Authorisation Reviews (England) Regulations 202X set out the following professions that are able to carry out the three LPS assessments, among other criteria, where the professional is registered with the appropriate professional body:

- *Capacity assessment*: medical practitioner, nurse, occupational therapist, social worker, psychologist or speech and language therapist.
- *Medical assessment* (of the cared-for person's mental health): medical practitioner or psychologist.
- *Necessary and proportionate assessment*: medical practitioner, nurse, occupational therapist, social worker, psychologist or speech and language therapist.

Once the assessments are complete, the *pre-authorisation review* must be arranged by the responsible body. This must be completed by a person who is not involved in the cared-for person's day-to-day care or providing treatment to them (HM Government, 2022, paras 13.44–13.48), in order to preserve their independence from the cared-for person's care decision-making. This review should scrutinise the assessments that have been undertaken to ensure that there is sufficient evidence established as to whether the LPS criteria have been met and an authorisation is required. These assessments will be checked before they are authorised by responsible bodies.

In certain circumstances, these assessments will be passed to the *Approved Mental Capacity Professional* (AMCP) for further scrutiny and may be authorised by the AMCP. AMCPs will be involved where it is reasonable to believe that the cared-for person is objecting to their care arrangements or residence for care, when they are admitted to an independent hospital and where the responsible body refers a case to the AMCP and they accept the case. This means that the AMCP has some discretion to accept cases for scrutiny outside those two main criteria (HM Government, 2022, Ch 18).

Once the LPS assessments have been reviewed and all decisions (or 'determinations' as the LPS refers to them) have been made that the cared-for person's circumstances require the protection of the LPS, the responsible body may authorise the arrangements.

The LPS draft *authorisation record* should set out the arrangements that have been authorised, including:

- When the authorisation is due to come into effect.
- The length of time for the authorisation. A person's first and second authorisations can be up to 12 months, and thereafter authorisations can last for up to 36 months.
- The conditions for the authorisation. For example, contact arrangements, issues relevant to the person's culture or any other issues related to the deprivation of liberty which – if not dealt with – would mean that the deprivation of liberty would not be justified.
- A programme for reviews. This may for example specify that a planned review takes place on fixed dates or that reviews will take place at certain intervals. (HM Government, 2022, para 13.37)

The LPS authorisation can include either planned reviews as above, or in response to a reasonable request by someone with an interest in the arrangements, the person is detained under the MHA, or becomes subject to mental health requirements, such as a condition of their community treatment order under the MHA. A review can also be called if the responsible body becomes aware that the person does not wish to reside or receive care or treatment in that place and an AMCP has not reviewed this case previously, or if the responsible body becomes aware of a significant change in the person's conditions or circumstances (HM Government, 2022, para 13.88). The review could result in a variation of the LPS authorisation, changes to the person's care or termination of the authorisation.

When the authorised period is coming to an end, a decision about whether to *renew* or not can be made. The responsible body must be satisfied that the conditions for authorisation are still met. This may or may not necessitate a full reassessment, as the cared-for person's mental health and, possibly, mental capacity may not have changed. The person's wishes and feelings and the nature of the restrictions in place may have changed, so it will need to be decided whether a further necessary and proportionate assessment and determination need to be made.

ESSENTIAL INFORMATION: LAW

Safeguards for the cared-for person in the Liberty Protection Safeguards

The cared-for person has a number of safeguards within the LPS to ensure that their right to liberty is protected according to law. The main safeguards are similar to DoLS:

- vital acts;
- right of appeal to the Court of Protection;
- right to representation and support;
- right to specialist scrutiny of LPS assessments in certain circumstances;
- right to a review of the authorisation.

Vital acts
Under Section 4B MCA, there are occasions when deprivation of liberty is urgently needed for life-sustaining treatment or carrying out a vital act and there is no time to wait for an LPS authorisation. Four conditions must be met to be able to use Section 4B (HM Government, 2022, para 19.1):

Condition 1: the steps must wholly or partly be for the purpose of giving the life-sustaining treatment or any vital act. For example, restraining a person to enable a medical treatment to be administered which would help sustain the person's life, such as dialysis, or consist of giving the life-sustaining treatment or the vital act. For example, using antipsychotic medication with a sedative effect to prevent a serious deterioration in the patient's dementia and stop them from leaving the hospital and disengaging with the treatment.

Condition 2: the steps must be necessary in order to give the life-sustaining treatment or carry out the vital act.

Condition 3: the decision-maker must reasonably believe that the person lacks capacity to consent to the steps.

Condition 4: one of the following applies:

- a relevant decision is being sought from the court (eg, a decision relevant to whether a decision-maker is authorised to deprive the person of liberty),
- a Responsible Body is determining whether to authorise arrangements under the LPS, or
- there is an emergency.

If these four conditions apply, then a decision-maker can take steps that deprive the person of their liberty. Acts under Section 4A are only available until other legal measures are in place, such as an order of the Court of Protection, detention under the MHA or LPS authorisation, or there is no longer a need for care or treatment.

Right of appeal

Under Section 21ZA of Schedule AA1 MCA, the cared-for person, the Appropriate Person or an IMCA can make an appeal to the Court of Protection that can be funded via non-means-tested legal aid. This appeal can consider any of the decisions or determinations relating to the LPS authorisation, whether the authorisation conditions are met, what period the authorisation has effect for and what the authorisation relates to. The court can make an order to vary or terminate the authorisation or direct the responsible body to vary the authorisation.

Right to representation and support

- *Appropriate Person:* During the LPS process of assessment, determination, authorisation and review, the cared-for person has the right to have an Appropriate Person appointed to represent and support the cared-for person either by the cared-for person themselves or by the responsible body in the cared-for person's best interests.
- *Independent Mental Capacity Advocate (IMCA):* Where the cared-for person does not have an Appropriate Person to support them or the Appropriate Person needs support with the role, the responsible body must take all reasonable steps to appoint an IMCA.

Right to specialist scrutiny of LPS assessments in certain circumstances

- *Approved Mental Capacity Professional (AMCP):* AMCPs are involved in LPS where the cared-for person is reasonably suspected to be refusing either their care arrangements or their residence for care, or both, or they are being cared for in an independent hospital, or where the AMCP agrees to accept a case from the responsible body. The AMCP should be appointed to scrutinise the LPS assessments, speak to the cared-for person, their Appropriate Person or IMCA and others involved in their care and consider whether the requirements are met for LPS authorisation. The authorisation can then either be made by the responsible body or the AMCP themselves. AMCPs are expected to be managed outside usual health and social care management structures to ensure independent and accountable decision-making. The draft MCA Code (HM Government, 2022, para 18.11) suggests a model where in a local area all responsible bodies contribute AMCPs to a 'central AMCP team', which could be run by the local authority for the area as well as having measures in place for duty and out of hours referrals – a similar model to that of Approved Mental Health Professional (AMHP) provision.

Right to a review of the authorisation

Grounds for a review of the LPS authorisation can include if the responsible body becomes aware that the person does not wish to reside or receive care or treatment in that place and an AMCP has not reviewed this case previously, or if the responsible body becomes aware of a significant change in the person's conditions or circumstances (HM Government, 2022, para 13.88) and could result in the cessation of the authorisation.

Interface with the Mental Health Act 1983

As with DoLS, there are times when the Mental Health Act interacts with the Mental Capacity Act and the Liberty Protection Safeguards. This is covered in significantly more detail in Chapter 22 of the draft MCA Code (HM Government, 2022) than in this section. The framework of the MHA has not changed as yet, so in many respects the principles for deciding on whether the MHA or LPS should be used to make lawful detention for mental health treatment is not greatly different. Some of the nuances of the interaction have been revised in the draft MCA Code (HM Government, 2022, Ch 22), *so this is worth reading in more detail and updating your knowledge when the final MCA Code becomes available.*

It is clear that there will always be interaction between the MCA and MHA as: 'People who lack relevant mental capacity suffer mental health problems like everyone else and may need to be treated under the MHA. The MCA applies to people subject to the MHA in the same way as it applies to anyone else with four exceptions' (HM Government, 2022, p 416).

These four exceptions are:

- if someone is detained under the MHA, decision–makers cannot normally rely on the MCA to give treatment for mental disorder or make decisions about that treatment on that person's behalf
- if somebody can be treated for their mental disorder without their consent because they are detained under the MHA, healthcare staff can, with some exceptions relating to more invasive treatments, administer treatment to them even if it goes against an advance decision to refuse that treatment

- if a person is subject to guardianship under the MHA, the guardian has the exclusive right to take certain decisions, including where the person is to live
- IMCAs do not have to be involved in decisions about serious medical treatment or long-term accommodation, if those decisions are made under the MHA. (HM Government, 2022, p 417)

The draft MCA Code (HM Government, 2022, p 416) explains the following about the MHA in relation to LPS:

> Where the LPS and the MHA meet, there is an interface. Decision-makers may need to decide which is the most appropriate regime to deprive a person of their liberty under, or if the person is subject to certain sections of the MHA, whether an LPS authorisation is also required. The interface between these two regimes only occurs in a very small number of specific cases.

When deciding whether the MHA or LPS is indicated, the first consideration is whether the person's care arrangements are mainly in hospital or the community for mental health treatment.

Hospital

The draft MCA Code (HM Government, 2022) states that for a hospital-based deprivation of liberty, professionals will need to choose between MHA and LPS. This depends on the following circumstances:

- If the criteria for detention in hospital under Section 2 or 3 of the MHA are met and the person *is* objecting, then LPS cannot be used and the MHA should be considered (paras 22.61–22.64). If the person is already detained in hospital under Section 2 or 3, then there is no need to use LPS.
- If the criteria for detention in hospital under Section 2 or 3 of the MHA are met and the person *is not* objecting, then a decision should be made regarding which regime should be used to make their deprivation of liberty lawful (para 22.70). Guidance in the draft MCA Code (HM Government, 2022, paras 22.70–22.74) on what to bear in mind in this situation includes:
  - 'Which is the least restrictive way of achieving the proposed assessment or treatment, by adopting a fact sensitive approach and having regard to all relevant circumstances.'
  - 'This decision should never be based on a general preference for one regime or the other, or because one regime is more familiar to the decision-maker than the other.'
  - 'Decision-makers should not proceed on the basis that one regime is generally less restrictive than the other. Both regimes are based on the

need to impose as few restrictions on the liberty and autonomy of patients as possible.'

- 'In the particular circumstances of an individual case, it may be apparent that one regime is likely to prove less restrictive. If so, this should be balanced against any potential benefits associated with the other regime.'
- 'Decision-makers should also consider whether an individual deprived of their liberty may regain the relevant capacity or may have fluctuating capacity. Such a situation is likely to indicate that use of the MHA to authorise a deprivation of liberty could be more appropriate than an LPS authorisation or Court of Protection order.'
- 'Hospitals should have policies in place to deal with circumstances where a disagreement results in an inability to take a decision as to whether the Liberty Protection Safeguards or MHA or [sic] should be used to authorise a deprivation of liberty. A clear decision-making process should be set out including how to access appropriate legal advice if required.'

Community

As with DoLS, where the person's care arrangements are in the community and community sections of the MHA are in place, LPS may still be needed to make restrictions amounting to a deprivation of liberty lawful. These community sections of the MHA are:

- Section 7 guardianship or a guardianship order
- Section 17 leave
- Section 17A community treatment order
- conditional discharge.

This is because, as with DoLS, these MHA powers alone cannot authorise a deprivation of liberty (see *Welsh Ministers v PJ* [2018]), and would need an LPS authorisation to run alongside them to do so, so long as there is no conflict with a mental health requirement, such as where the person resides.

People with learning disabilities

The draft MCA Code (HM Government, 2022) also makes it clear that, as with DoLS, the MHA exclusion criteria related to people with learning disabilities does not apply, so LPS will apply to those with diagnosed learning disabilities.

Children and young people and the MCA/MHA interface

Whereas the MHA has no lower age limit, the MCA and LPS can only be used for those who are 16 years old and above, meaning that for those under 16, the options for lawful deprivation of liberty are the MHA or other legal provisions for under-16s, such as within the Children Act 1989.

Deprivation of liberty and 16- and 17-year-olds

One significant change to the LPS from DoLS is the inclusion of 16- and 17-year-olds in the scheme, bringing the lower age limit down to match that of the MCA. Currently, DoLS applies only to those 18 and over, leaving matters of making deprivation of liberty lawful to other legal frameworks, such as Section 25 of the Children Act 1989, and the Family Division of the High Court or Court of Protection, depending on whether the young person is under or over 16 years of age.

The Court of Protection can currently authorise deprivation of liberty for those from the age of 16 (or under, if the young person is likely to continue to lack capacity regarding their care and treatment after 16). Other legal measures for deprivation of liberty under the age of 18 include Section 25 of the Children Act 1989 regarding placement in secure accommodation, or MHA 1983 (2007) regarding treatment for mental ill health, which has no lower age limit, as well as youth remand and custodial sentencing provisions, where relevant.

ESSENTIAL INFORMATION: CASE LAW

'Teen Bournewood' – the case of 'D'

Four judgments from 2015 to 2019 have clarified the status of parental responsibility and consent to deprivation of liberty in relation to one young person, 'D', who was diagnosed with ADHD, mild learning disability, Asperger's syndrome and Tourette's syndrome when he was 15. There was no disagreement that he lacked capacity to consent to his residence for care and treatment. Whether parental responsibility under Section 3(1) of the Children Act 1989 ('all the rights, duties, powers, responsibilities and authority which by law a parent of a child has in relation to the child and his property') could be used to authorise deprivation of liberty, and therefore not require court intervention to make lawful, was in question.

Trust A v X and A Local Authority [2015] EWHC 922 (Fam)

In *Trust A v X and a Local Authority* [2015], D was 15 and under continuous supervision and control and not free to leave a psychiatric unit. His parents were held to be able to consent on his behalf so he was not deprived of liberty for the purposes of Article 5 (ECHR), meaning that the subjective element of deprivation of liberty was not met. This was judged to be an appropriate exercise of parental responsibility.

Birmingham City Council v D [2016] EWCOP 8

In *Birmingham City Council v D* [2016], D had been discharged from hospital and, having turned 16, lived at a residential unit, funded by the local authority, with his parent's consent under Section 20 of the Children Act 1989. The main issues before the court were:

- whether his parents were still able to consent on his behalf;
- whether the arrangements were imputable to the state.

All agreed he was deprived of his liberty, that is, his care and treatment met the 'acid test'. Keehan J agreed that while he was under 16, D's parents could consent to his deprivation of liberty. However, once he reached 16, Keehan considered that his parents could no longer authorise a deprivation of liberty on his behalf as D now came under the MCA, which presumes 16-year-olds have the capacity to make their own decisions, and where assessed not to have capacity, a decision would need to be made in D's best interests by the Court of Protection (as he was not old enough for DoLS to be used).

D (A Child) [2017] EWCA Civ 1695

D's case was heard at the Court of Appeal and the judgment was that there is no 'bright line' at 16 in relation to the young person's capacity to consent to decisions such as deprivation of liberty, so parents can continue to consent to such confinement up to the age of 18 if that is an appropriate exercise of their parental responsibility.

As a result, although D satisfied the 'acid test' (the *objective* element that he was under continuous supervision and control and was not free to leave), he was not deprived of liberty because there was valid consent from his parents (the *subjective* element). The corresponding judicial safeguards (the need for the Court of Protection to give legal authorisation to impeding his Article 5 rights) were therefore not required until he became an adult.

This meant that for under-18s who were confined and unable to consent, parents were considered to be able to give valid consent as an appropriate exercise of parental responsibility and those under 18 who are able to make the relevant decision and object to their confinement will require Article 5 safeguards, that is, Court of Protection authorisation.

Re D [2019] UKSC 41

The Supreme Court held by a majority that where a 16- or 17-year-old child cannot (or does not) give their own consent to deprivation of liberty (defined by the *Cheshire West* 'acid test') and the state is aware (or should be aware) of the deprivation of liberty, then this meets the requirements for Article 5 (ECHR) and requires the protections offered there, whether or not those with parental responsibility are seeking or have given consent to those arrangements.

In other words, parental consent in this case does not take this situation outside human rights law and Lady Hale noted that she did not consider that making the decision to deprive D of his liberty was within the scope of parental responsibility as D was 16–17 years of age.

The judgment deliberately focused solely on deprivation of liberty decision-making and did not suggest that parents have no legal power to make other decisions on behalf of incapacitated 16- and 17-year-olds, leaving open the potential for other decisions, such as serious medical treatment, to remain within the scope of parental responsibility.

The Supreme Court's ruling in this case confirms that restrictions that amount to a deprivation of liberty for 16- and 17-year-olds are a matter that engages Article 5 (ECHR), as parental consent does not take this decision out of imputability to the state. When LPS is implemented, the legal framework for this decision-making will move from the Court of Protection to LPS in relevant cases.

This change to the LPS brings deprivation of liberty into residential schools and other settings where children's law usually applies and will mean that professionals in children's social care and health as well as education will need to be aware of the provisions and requirements of the LPS and be prepared to implement them.

Training for the Liberty Protection Safeguards, including Approved Mental Capacity Professionals (AMCPs)

Both the English (DHSC, Ministry of Justice, Department for Education and Welsh Government, 2022) and Welsh (Welsh Government, 2022a) consultations for implementing LPS include national workforce and training strategies (DHSC,

2022b; Welsh Government, 2022b), as well as draft regulations for the training and approval of AMCPs in England and Wales.

The Welsh training plan (Welsh Government, 2022b) does not have the detail of the English plan and notes that a more detailed plan is being developed with Social Care Wales that will be available for consultation in the future, although competency groups (A–F) are identified that align with those in the English training plan below.

These training plans all recognise that a considerably broader understanding of LPS will be required for implementation than was required for DoLS as LPS assessments will be part of everyday, rather than specialist, practice.

Those carrying out the following roles will require LPS training:

- *All those in health and social care* working with those from 16 years of age will need to know generally about the scope and application of the LPS, building on knowledge of the wider MCA.
- LPS necessary and proportionate assessments will be completed by frontline *health and social care professionals* rather than specially trained assessors, so social workers, nurses, occupational therapists, psychologists, speech and language therapists and medical practitioners will need training so they are ready to conduct these assessments.
- *Pre-authorisation reviews* will be conducted by responsible bodies before signing off by authorisers so those in these roles will need specific training.
- *IMCAs* will need update training as well as training for new LPS IMCAs.
- *Approved Mental Capacity Professionals (AMCPs)* will require a range of training:
  - Initial *AMCP qualifying training* will be approved by Social Work England (SWE) no matter which profession the student is qualified in or the professional body they are registered with. SWE is consulting on draft professional standards for the education of AMCPs, which the universities that will be offering AMCP qualifying courses will be expected to align to. The SWE consultation on these standards opened in May 2022 (SWE, 2022b) and at the time of writing (May 2022) was expected to close in August 2022. The draft LPS impact assessment (DHSC, 2022c, p 44) anticipates that AMCP qualifying courses will be 60 rather than 30 academic credits and will therefore take twice the study time to complete.
  - Existing qualified BIAs will need *conversion training* for the AMCP role. It is expected that local authorities will be responsible for the delivery of BIA to AMCP conversion training, with support of materials developed nationally, while qualifying training for AMCPs will remain the role of higher education. An annex to the LPS training plan for conversion of BIAs to the AMCP role is also included in the English consultation (DHSC, 2022d). It is anticipated in the draft LPS impact assessment (DHSC, 2022c, p 44) that 90 per cent of AMCPs will be recruited from existing BIAs via conversion and that conversion training will take 8 to 16 hours.

- The training plans and regulations include the need for a further 18 hours of annual *AMCP refresher training* once qualified that will also be delivered by universities (DHSC, 2022b, p 27).

These training plans set out common competency groups showing what level of knowledge and skills will be required of staff across health and social care according to their level of engagement with LPS.

The competency groups build on each other and are identified in the draft training framework (DHSC, 2022e, pp 5–6) as:

A   *Awareness raising:* an overview to all staff who need to know about LPS.
B   *Identification and referral:* for clinical staff and supervisors or managers of staff or volunteers, who may need to identify when a person may be deprived of their liberty, and when authorisation may be required to protect their rights under the LPS.
C   *Assessment, determination and consultation:* for all roles that under the regulations might undertake assessments, determinations and consultation on behalf of a responsible body, within the LPS process.
D   *Pre-authorisation review and authorisation:* for designated staff in responsible bodies who might undertake pre-authorisation reviews or make the decision whether or not to authorise a deprivation of liberty under the LPS on behalf of the responsible body.
E   *IMCA:* for existing and new IMCAs.
F   *AMCP:* for people who meet the requirements set out in regulations to undertake full AMCP training, or BIA to AMCP conversion training.

The draft LPS training framework for England (DHSC, 2022e) also sets out the learning outcomes for each competency group across five subject areas (p 7):

1. Human rights as a basis for LPS
2. Concepts of the MCA
3. The LPS process
4. Understanding of deprivation of liberty
5. Young people.

The SWE (2022b) draft education and training standards for AMCPs cover the following five areas:

- Admissions
- Course governance, management and quality
- Learning environment
- Curriculum and assessment
- Supporting students.

These standards suggest that SWE expects that AMCP qualifying education will ensure that applicants have prior knowledge, skills and experience in applying mental health, mental capacity and human rights law to practice. The draft standards also suggest that core to AMCP qualifying education will be academic teaching alongside practice learning experiences supported by qualified and experienced practitioners. It is a matter for discussion between local authorities, as AMCP employers, and universities as to how the education standards when they are finalised actually translate into qualifying courses. In our view, the draft standards read similarly to the AMHP education standards, which require placements to allow students to spend time building confidence in developing the knowledge and skills to apply the law to practise in this complex area. This seems likely to mean that the one-off, part-time modules, which BIA qualifying study has been up to this point, may be replaced by longer postgraduate, full-time programmes. This will not be clarified until the final SWE education and training standards are agreed.

Roles for BIAs in Liberty Protection Safeguards

There are a number of ways in which the knowledge, skills and expertise of BIAs will be valuable in the LPS. Your experience in assessing and making decisions in relation to mental capacity and best interests in situations relating to restriction and deprivation of liberty, your understanding of applied human rights law and principles for practice and decision-making from case law, as well as communicating with people subject to restrictive care regimes, their families and friends and other professionals, advocates and care staff will be essential to whichever role you take on in the future.

There are three main areas where your BIA knowledge, skills and experience will be particularly useful:

1. *Frontline professional care practice*, where you may complete LPS assessments alongside your usual work; for example, in adult social work when completing care and support assessments within the Care Act 2014 in the community, or as part of hospital discharge processes, as a CHC nurse assessor.
2. As a *pre-authorisation reviewer*, where you would be checking the assessments of frontline professionals and ensuring that the person's views, wishes and rights are recognised and that the assessments clearly evidence the need for an LPS authorisation. Your experience of acting independently from usual care and health decision-making will be invaluable for accountable scrutiny as will your understanding of good practice in deprivation of liberty assessment, decision-making and recording. Your BIA expertise may also be valuable for those who sign off LPS authorisations.
3. The role of the *Approved Mental Capacity Professional (AMCP)* is where the existing skills, knowledge, values and expertise of BIAs will be most valuable. The specialist focus and experience of acting as an independent and accountable

professional conducting thorough assessments, scrutinising restrictive care planning and questioning the decision-making of others will be an excellent grounding for the AMCP role, although the emphasis of the new role is rather different. As an AMCP, you will be scrutinising and authorising the assessments made by others rather than assessing yourself, although you will be able to consult those involved in the cared-for person's care. You will not be involved in all LPS assessments. You will be solely involved in cases where there is objection, where the person is being cared for in a setting that is otherwise considered to be too distant from other everyday scrutiny (such as independent hospitals) and you will have some discretion in other LPS authorisations you work on.

Whichever role you ultimately take on, your BIA skills, knowledge and values will not go to waste.

Who are Approved Mental Capacity Professionals (AMCPs)?

The professionals who will be able to practise as AMCPs, provided they are registered in the UK with a relevant professional body and have at least two years post-qualifying experience in their profession, are:

- Nurses
- Social workers
- Psychologists
- Speech and language therapists
- Occupational therapists.

All AMCPs will have to have completed either approved AMCP qualifying training or BIA to AMCP conversion training, if they were previously qualified as a BIA. All AMCPs will have to complete 18 hours of further training annually each year they are approved. Local authority responsible bodies will have the role of approving AMCPs annually and will need to be satisfied that the AMCP has completed this training and is practising to an acceptable standard.

The role of the AMCP

The draft MCA Code (HM Government, 2022, para 18.29) explains that the role of the AMCP is to carry out the pre-authorisation review of the person's case if:

- it is reasonable to believe that the person does not wish to reside in the place proposed in the arrangements,
- it is reasonable to believe that the person does not wish to receive care or treatment at the place proposed in the arrangements,

- the proposed arrangements are for the person to receive care or treatment mainly in an independent hospital,
- the Responsible Body refers the case to an AMCP and the AMCP accepts the referral.

The draft Code provides guidance on what might be considered as objection (HM Government, 2022, paras 18.30–18.37) and sets out a non-exhaustive set of circumstances in which an AMCP might be asked to carry out a pre-authorisation review by the responsible body. These circumstances include where the restrictions have a significant impact on the person, the assessments are borderline, where it is not clear if the case should be authorised within the MHA or MCA, or there is a significant level of complexity (HM Government, 2022, para 18.38).

The main task of the AMCP is to determine whether the LPS authorisation conditions are met. This involves reviewing the paperwork provided, which should evidence that an LPS authorisation is needed to make a deprivation of the person's liberty lawful. However, as with BIA practice, the safeguards offered by the AMCP are much wider than that. The AMCP has the opportunity to support the cared-for person to express their views about their care and treatment, identify and raise any safeguarding concerns with the appropriate bodies, identify and address unnecessary restrictions on their liberty and autonomy and ensure that their voice is heard regarding their objections to their care arrangements and residence. The AMCP will identify any differences of opinion between the cared-for person, their families and professionals, and will consider the essential questions of whether the restrictions in the person's care arrangements are necessary to prevent harm coming to the person and proportionate to the risk of that harm occurring.

It is expected that the AMCP will meet the cared-for person and will consult with others relevant to the person's care, as appropriate and practical. The AMCP has the power to make recommendations to the responsible body – the draft Code gives the following examples (HM Government, 2022, para 18.55):

- Suggesting a programme of support to enable the person to make their own decision.
- Exploring the suitability of a trial period with relevant, enhanced support at home.
- Suggesting new or different communication methods to enhance the person's participation.
- Challenging one or more of the assessments and advising the Responsible Body that new assessments and determinations are commissioned.
- Suggesting a second opinion for one or more of the assessments.
- Reviewing other information, including historic records about the person's care and treatment or safeguarding concerns.

- Visiting the location and seeing how the arrangements might work, and exploring whether they could be made less restrictive, and/or more acceptable to the person.
- If the AMCP isn't drafting the authorisation record, recommending conditions to be placed on the authorisation record.
- Suggesting less restrictive options.

The AMCP can ask the responsible body to apply conditions to authorisations and may be asked to become involved in an LPS review if the person is considered to be objecting and has not been reviewed by an AMCP previously. AMCPs, as BIAs before them, have a significant role in raising awareness of human rights-based practice as well as good practice in mental capacity, best interests and deprivation of liberty assessment and decision-making. This educative role will be even more valuable while LPS is being implemented as significant numbers of new health and social care staff become aware of the importance of this to their everyday practice.

Implications of Liberty Protection Safeguards

When the Law Commission first consulted on a replacement to DoLS in 2017, a number of issues with the changes were raised that remain relevant to the LPS as it exists on the statute books. In the first edition of this book, we noted that Walsh (2017) highlighted concern about the move from the necessity for a 'best interests' to a 'necessary and proportionate' assessment. Walsh (2017, p 15) suggested 'there is a need not to move too far away from the person-centred element that the concept of Best Interests has attempted to instil in assessors, albeit in limited ways at times'. From our experience, the 'necessary to prevent harm' and 'proportionate to the risk of harm' sections of the best interests assessment that BIAs complete are often the least understood and most superficially evidenced sections of their assessments. The best interests section tends to pull BIAs back to considering the person's views and wishes, their individual circumstances, the potential for discrimination to have affected their thinking and alternative ways for their care needs to be met. It is concerning to think that deprivation of liberty assessments will lose this essential rebalancing. Mark Neary (2017) calls this a 'rather big contradiction running through the narrative for the … scheme' and believes that 'when push comes to shove, it could be argued that something is necessary and proportionate, without being in the person's best interests at all'. Series (2022, p 192) states that the removal of best interests comes from the Law Commission concluding 'that the test "added nothing" to the more fundamental and human rights oriented question of whether the "arrangements" were necessary and proportionate to the risk of harm that might befall the person otherwise'. The Law Commission also suggested that the 'language of "best interests" implied a choice between different arrangements, when the reality was that public bodies were only willing to fund one option, which families or professionals might not consider "best" for the person' (p 192).

This suggests that the inadequacy of health and social care to offer options is going to drive how much weight the person's views, needs and wishes carry in decision-making. Series (2017) considered that the issues raised in *London Borough of Hillingdon v Steven Neary* [2011] regarding how close care decision-making is to deprivation of liberty decision-making are 'not addressed by the LPS, if anything it is exacerbated by the desire of the Commission to strengthen links between "the commissioning of the arrangements and responsibility for the authorisation"' (p 22). Mark Neary (2017) called this 'a huge challenge in maintaining independence'. The dual aim of reducing independent oversight through limited access to specialist scrutiny of assessments and decision-making, and putting responsibility for these assessments directly in the remit of commissioning organisations like adult social care and NHS CHC is worrying in this context.

These concerns have not diminished in the LPS as they will be enacted in the future. The identification of cases where deprivation of liberty might be an issue remains with busy health and social care workers, managers of care homes, hospitals and other care settings, although the local authority is ultimately responsible for ensuring LPS assessments take place. The assessment of those subject to deprivation of liberty in terms of their care arrangements will be passed to already overstretched frontline health and social care professionals, without a lot of time to devote to developing and maintaining their knowledge of complex legal and ethical matters.

Where these professionals have received BIA training or developed expertise in completing community deprivation of liberty applications to the Court of Protection, there is likely to be more confident practice but this will not be available to all. Current practice applying the MCA does not give confidence that there is a strong enough foundation to build this knowledge on, especially in children's services where the MCA principles are not well embedded in everyday practice with 16- and 17-year-olds. The safeguard offered by the pre-authorisation review and the independence of that role from care decision-making is valuable so far as it goes, considering it is a desktop review of secondary evidence reported by the assessor, rather than a direct examination of the actual care. However, the absence of any requirement for professional background or qualification for this role, or for LPS signatories, beyond the LPS learning outcomes (DHSC, 2022a), does not inspire a great deal of confidence. The absence of a direct assessment role for AMCPs is also of concern in this context.

One of the authors was a DoLS coordinator for a year in a busy city local authority DoLS team and spent their time examining hundreds of DoLS assessments to ensure they were of a sufficient standard for sign off by DoLS signatories. The similarity of this role to the pre-authorisation reviewer role in LPS has given cause for reflection and this experience suggests that these reviewers will need to be knowledgeable, detail-oriented practitioners with an appetite to question the practice of assessors where evidence is poorly presented or poor practice is evident. There will be little time to seek out those who need the safeguards of LPS that are not identified for assessment. A system that relies for its safeguards so much on the knowledge of human rights of health and social care practitioners and the quality of recording needs committed and knowledgeable practitioners to maintain standards.

Access to specialist scrutiny of care moving from universal to conditional status is a change that suggests a shift in ethical approach. We considered the deontological approach, in Chapter 7, where one rule applies to all, for example the universality of access to specialist assessment that applied in DoLS and links strongly to the universality of rights that Baroness Hale identified in the Supreme Court's judgment in *Cheshire West* (2014). The LPS represent a move to a more utilitarian approach, where detailed scrutiny by specialist practitioners is available only to those where there is objection, risk and complexity. And although this focusing of resources where need is greatest also echoes adult social care eligibility processes, there is also risk. Our experience is that the cared-for person's objection is not always identified or highlighted for action in BIA assessment recording, and we have concerns that not all those objecting to their care or residence will be identified for the additional scrutiny of an AMCP. Resistance to care or unhappiness are often not considered within the paradigm of objection. Series (2022, p 194) talks about how "'challenging behaviour" could be taken to indicate distress about a particular environment, treatment or restrictions, but could also be explained away as a symptom of "mental disorder"'. How behaviour and other communication are interpreted is a significant element in how likely a person is to be considered as objecting or not. The possibility that people who need the specialist and knowledgeable focus on their care arrangements and restrictions offered by the AMCP will miss out appears to be a weakness in the safeguards. The continuation of the Court of Protection as the route for appeal within LPS is also a missed opportunity to make the often slow and bureaucratic process of appeal more accessible.

The move to apply thresholds for access to the specialist review of rights within LPS also echoes the emphasis in the UK Government's consultation on a replacement to the Human Rights Act 1998 to focus only on those who have experienced 'significant disadvantage' as a result of interference in their human rights. This all contributes to an impression that the government thinks that access to rights is expensive and should only be available in limited circumstances. This fundamentally shifts the balance of power in human rights when the state, and agents of the state, like health and social care professionals, have the power to decide whose rights deserve scrutiny and whose don't.

This brings us back to the quote from Eleanor Roosevelt that we started this book with and the centrality of the person and their rights as they experience them:

Where, after all, do universal rights begin? In small places, close to home – so close and so small that they cannot be seen on any maps of the world. Yet they are the world of the individual person … Such are the places where every man, woman, and child seeks equal justice, equal opportunity, equal dignity without discrimination. Unless these rights have meaning there, they have little meaning anywhere. (Roosevelt, 1958)

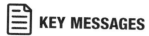

KEY MESSAGES

- **THE** LPS are coming soon and it is important to be aware of what impact these changes will have on your practice, not just as a BIA but across health and social care with those from the age of 16 upwards in England and Wales.

- **ALTHOUGH** a lot is changing, the fundamental rights and freedoms that DoLS was designed to protect remain very relevant to practice within LPS, and your role to ensure that these rights are available to all through person-centred practice also remains.

- **THE** shift from universal access to specialist assessment to frontline assessment with limited access to specialist review may impact those with least ability to make their voices heard.

KNOWLEDGE REVIEW

- **WHERE** and who will the LPS apply to that DoLS didn't, and what impact might this have on frontline and AMCP practice?

- **WHAT** are the new structures, roles and responsibilities within the LPS?

- **WHAT** safeguards are there for cared-for people within the LPS and how might you support the person to access them?

- **WHAT** new roles and responsibilities will you have as a frontline practitioner and as a BIA when the LPS are implemented?

FURTHER READING

As with all legislative change, we recommend starting with the statute itself – Schedule AA1 MCA: www.legislation.gov.uk/ukpga/2005/9/contents

Until the final MCA Code of Practice and regulations have been agreed by Parliament, it is important to make yourself familiar with the planned framework, as set out in:

- Department of Health and Social Care, Ministry of Justice, Department for Education and Welsh Government (2022) *Changes to the MCA Code of Practice and Implementation of the LPS*, www.gov.uk/government/consultations/changes-to-the-mca-code-of-practice-and-implementation-of-the-lps

- Welsh Government (2022b) *Liberty Protection Safeguards*, https://gov.wales/liberty-protection-safeguards

For insight into the expected nature of education for AMCPs, read:

- Social Work England (2022) *Consultation on New Education and Training Approval Standards for Approved Mental Capacity Professionals*, www.social workengland.org.uk/about/consultations/consultation-on-new-education-and-training-approval-standards-for-approved-mental-capacity-professionals

For more detail on the LPS, see:

- Mughal, A. and Richards, S. (2022) 'Liberty Protection Safeguards (LPS)', in *Deprivation of Liberty Safeguards Handbook*, 2nd edn, Hounslow, BooksWise, pp 213–34

- Series, L. (2022) 'Aftermath', in *Deprivation of Liberty In the Shadows of the Institution*, Bristol, Bristol University Press, pp 185–207

References

39 Essex Chambers (2017) 'R (Ferreira) v HM Senior Coroner for Inner South London and others', accessed 18/04/22 at: www.39essex.com/cop_cases/r-ferreira-v-hm-senior-coroner-inner-south-london-others

39 Essex Chambers (2020) 'London Borough of Tower Hamlets v A and KF', accessed 18/04/22 at: www.39essex.com/cop_cases/london-borough-of-tower-hamlets-v-a-kf

Acquired Brain Injury and Mental Capacity Act Interest Group (2014) *Recommendations for Action following the House of Lords Select Committee Post-Legislative Scrutiny Report into the Mental Capacity Act: Making the Abstract Real*, accessed 11/04/22 at: www.researchgate.net/publication/279535601_Making_the_Abstract_Real_Acquired_Brain_Injury_and_Mental_Capacity_A_report_making_recommendations_following_the_House_of_Lords_Select_Committee_review_of_the_Mental_Capacity_Act

ADASS (Association of Directors of Adult Social Services) (2014) *DoLS Prioritisation Tool*, accessed 11/04/22 at: www.adass.org.uk/adass-priority-tool-for-deprivation-of-liberty-requests

ADASS (2016) 'Advice note for managing and processing cases generated by the Supreme Court's decision in 2014 in relation to Deprivation of Liberty Safeguards: Additional emergency interim measures and safeguards', accessed 11/04/22 at: www.adass.org.uk/media/5297/additional-dols-safeguards-final.pdf

ADASS (2022) 'Deprivation of Liberty Safeguards Forms', accessed 02/06/22 at: www.adass.org.uk/mental-health-drugs-and-alcohol/public-content/new-dols-forms

Age UK (2022) *Factsheet 62: Deprivation of Liberty Safeguards*, accessed 20/04/22 at: www.ageuk.org.uk/globalassets/age-uk/documents/factsheets/fs62_deprivation_of_liberty_safeguards_fcs.pdf

Alzheimer's Society (2022) *Dementia Care Mapping*, accessed 20/04/22 at: www.alzheimers.org.uk/dementia-professionals/dementia-experience-toolkit/research-methods/dementia-care-mapping

Amnesty International (2020) *As If Expendable: The UK Government's Failure to Protect Older People in Care Homes during the COVID-19 Pandemic*, accessed 16/04/22 at: www.amnesty.org.uk/files/2020-10/Care%20Homes%20Report.pdf

BASW (British Association of Social Workers) (2014) *Code of Ethics Addendum: Additional Guidance for Independent Social Workers*, accessed 11/04/22 at: www.basw.co.uk/resources/basw-code-ethics-independent-social-workers

BASW (2021) *The BASW Code of Ethics for Social Work*, accessed 11/04/22 at: www.basw.co.uk/about-basw/code-ethics

BASW Wales (2020) 'BIA Workforce Survey', unpublished

Beddow, A., Cooper, M. and Morriss, L. (2015) *A CPD Curriculum Guide for Social Workers on the Application of the Mental Capacity Act 2005*, accessed 11/04/22 at: https://assets.publishing.service.gov.uk/government/uploads/system/uploads/attachment_data/file/467399/Pt2_Mental_Capacity_Learning_Accessible.pdf

Benn, T. (1993) 'The Independent Mind', lecture at Nottingham, 18 June, accessed 11/04/22 at: www.oxfordreference.com/view/10.1093/acref/9780191826719.001.0001/q-oro-ed4-00000892

BIHR (British Institute of Human Rights) (2021) *Explainer: The Report of the Independent Human Rights Act Review and the Government's Consultation on the Human Rights Act*, accessed 16/04/22 at: www.bihr.org.uk/explainer-the-report-of-the-ihrar-and-the-governments-consultation-on-the-human-rights-act

Bisson, J., Rosser, A. and Holm, S. (2009) 'Developing a care pathway for advance decisions and powers of attorney: qualitative study', *British Journal of Psychiatry*, 194(1): 55–61

Bogg, D. (2010) *Values and Ethics in Mental Health Practice*, Exeter, Learning Matters

Bogg, D. and Challis, M. (2016) *Evidencing CPD: A Guide to Building Your Social Work Portfolio*, 2nd edn, Northwich, Critical Publishing

Brammer, A. (2020) 'Discrimination', in A. Brammer (ed) *Social Work Law* (5th edn), Harlow, Pearson Education, Chapter 6

Bray, S. and Preston-Shoot, M. (2016) *Legal Literacy in Adult Social Care: Strategic Briefing*, Dartington, Research in Practice for Adults

Brooker, D. (2005) 'Dementia care mapping: a review of the research literature', *The Gerontologist*, 45(1): 11–18

Brown, R., Barber, P. and Martin, D. (2015) *The Mental Capacity Act 2005: A Guide for Practice*, 3rd edn, London, Sage/Learning Matters

Carter, C. (2020) 'Social worker suspended for copying and pasting information between DoLS forms', *Community Care*, accessed 19/04/22 at: www.communitycare.co.uk/2020/03/04/social-worker-suspended-copying-pasting-information-dols-forms/

Cave, P. (2015) *Ethics: A Beginner's Guide*, London, Oneworld Publications

Conan Doyle, A. (1902) *The Hound of the Baskervilles*, London, George Newnes

Constable, G. (2010) 'Older people', in C. Gaine (ed) *Equality and Diversity in Social Work Practice*, Exeter, Learning Matters, pp 42–54

CQC (Care Quality Commission) (2015) *Monitoring the Deprivation of Liberty Safeguards in 2014-15*, accessed 11/04/22 at: www.cqc.org.uk/publications/major-report/monitoring-deprivation-liberty-safeguards#old-reports

CQC (2020) *Out of Sight – Who Cares? Restraint, Segregation and Seclusion Review*, accessed 21/04/22 at: www.cqc.org.uk/publications/themed-work/rssreview

CQC (2022a) *State of Care: Deprivation of Liberty Safeguards*, accessed 11/04/22 at: www.cqc.org.uk/publications/major-reports/soc202021_03c_dols

CQC (2022b) *Restraint, Segregation and Seclusion Review: Progress Reports*, accessed 21/04/22 at: www.cqc.org.uk/publications/themed-work/restraint-segregation-seclusion-review-progress-reports

CRPD (2006) United Nations Convention on the Rights of Persons with Disabilities, accessed 19/04/22 at: www.un.org/development/desa/disabilities/convention-on-the-rights-of-persons-with-disabilities.html

CSSIW/HIW (Care and Social Services Inspectorate Wales/Healthcare Inspectorate Wales) (2014) *A National Review of the Use of Deprivation of Liberty Safeguards (DoLS) in Wales*, accessed 11/04/22 at: https://hiw.org.uk/national-review-use-deprivation-liberty-safeguards-dols-wales

CSSIW/HIW (2016) *Deprivation of Liberty Safeguards: Annual Monitoring Report for Health and Social Care 2014-15*, accessed 11/04/22 at: https://hiw.org.uk/deprivation-liberty-safeguards-annual-monitoring-report-health-and-social-care-2014-15

Dalrymple, J. and Burke, B. (2006) *Anti-Oppressive Practice: Social Care and the Law*, 2nd edn, Maidenhead, Open University Press

Davies, A. (1996) 'Risk work and mental health', in H. Kemshall and J. Pritchard (eds) *Good Practice in Risk Assessment and Risk Management*, vol. 1, London, Jessica Kingsley Publishing, pp 109–20

Day, J. (2013) *Interprofessional Working: An Essential Guide for Health and Social Care Professionals – Nursing and Health Care Practice*, 2nd edn, Hampshire, Cengage Learning EMEA

DCA (Department for Constitutional Affairs) (2007) *Mental Capacity Act 2005 Code of Practice*, accessed 30/6/16 at: www.gov.uk/government/publications/mental-capacity-act-code-of-practice

DH (Department of Health) (2014) *Carers Strategy: Second National Action Plan 2014–2016*, London, HMSO

DH (2015a) *Mental Health Act Code of Practice*, accessed 20/04/22 at: www.gov.uk/government/publications/code-of-practice-mental-health-act-1983

DH (2015b) *Local Authority DoLS Funding – Additional 2015/16 Grant*, accessed 20/04/22 at: www.scie.org.uk/files/mca/directory/la-dols-funding-returns-report-20-oct-15-final.pdf?res=true

DH (2015c) *A Manual for Good Social Work Practice: Supporting Adults Who Have Dementia*, accessed 20/04/22 at: www.basw.co.uk/resources/manual-good-social-work-practice-supporting-adults-who-have-dementia

DH (2015d) *Department of Health Guidance: Response to the Supreme Court Judgement Deprivation of Liberty Safeguards*, accessed 20/04/22 at: https://assets.publishing.service.gov.uk/government/uploads/system/uploads/attachment_data/file/485122/DH_Consolidated_Guidance.pdf

DH (2016) *Best Interests Assessor Training: Approved Providers*, accessed 11/04/22 at: www.gov.uk/government/publications/best-interests-assessor-list-of-organisations-providing-training

DH/OPG (Department of Health/Office of the Public Guardian) (2009) *Deprivation of Liberty Safeguards: A Guide for Relevant Person's Representatives*, accessed 20/04/22 at: www.manchester.gov.uk/download/downloads/id/14492/dols_guide_for_the_relevant_persons_representative.pdf

DHSC (Department for Health and Social Care) (2018) *Deprivation of Liberty Safeguards: Resources*, accessed 11/04/22 at: www.gov.uk/government/publications/deprivation-of-liberty-safeguards-forms-and-guidance

DHSC (2021) *The Mental Capacity Act (2005) (MCA) and Deprivation of Liberty Safeguards (DoLS) during the Coronavirus (COVID-19) Pandemic*, accessed 18/04/22 at: www.gov.uk/government/publications/coronavirus-covid-19-looking-after-people-who-lack-mental-capacity

DHSC (2022a) 'COVID-19 supplement to the infection prevention and control resource for adult social care', accessed 02/06/22 at: www.gov.uk/government/publications/infection-prevention-and-control-in-adult-social-care-covid-19-supplement/covid-19-supplement-to-the-infection-prevention-and-control-resource-for-adult-social-care

DHSC (2022b) *Liberty Protection Safeguards National Workforce and Training Strategy (England)*, accessed 22/04/22 at: https://assets.publishing.service.gov.uk/government/uploads/system/uploads/attachment_data/file/1061005/LPS-training-framework-england.pdf

DHSC (2022c) 'Mental Capacity (Amendment) Act 2019 Draft Impact Assessment', accessed 03/06/22 at: https://assets.publishing.service.gov.uk/government/uploads/system/uploads/attachment_data/file/1061618/LPS-impact-assessment.pdf

DHSC (2022d) *Transition from the Deprivation of Liberty Safeguards to the Liberty Protection Safeguards Annex to the LPS Training Framework (England)*, accessed 22/04/22 at: https://assets.publishing.service.gov.uk/government/uploads/system/uploads/attachment_data/file/1061001/annex-to-LPS-training-framework-england.pdf

DHSC (2022e) *Liberty Protection Safeguards Training Framework (England)*, accessed 22/04/22 at: https://assets.publishing.service.gov.uk/government/uploads/system/uploads/attachment_data/file/1060999/LPS-workforce-and-training-strategy-for-consultation.pdf

DHSC, Ministry of Justice, Department for Education and Welsh Government (2022) *Open Consultation: Changes to the MCA Code of Practice and Implementation of the LPS*, accessed 21/04/22 at: www.gov.uk/government/consultations/changes-to-the-mca-code-of-practice-and-implementation-of-the-lps

Dunning, D. (2011) 'The Dunning–Kruger effect: on being ignorant of one's own ignorance', in M. Zanna and J. Olson (eds) *Advances in Experimental Social Psychology*, vol. 44, pp 247–96

Fitzpatrick, R. (2018) 'Welsh Ministers v PJ [2018] UKSC 66', accessed 18/04/22 at: www.brownejacobson.com/health/training-and-resources/legal-updates/2019/01/welsh-ministers-v-pj-2018-uksc-66#:~:text=The%20Supreme%20Court%20unanimously%20allowed,the%20linked%20case%20of%20MM

Flynn, M. (2012) *Winterbourne View Hospital: A Serious Case Review*, accessed 21/04/22 at: http://sites.southglos.gov.uk/safeguarding/adults/i-am-a-carerrelative/winterbourne-view

Gast, L. and Bailey, M. (2014) *Mastering Communication in Social Work*, London, Jessica Kingsley Publishers

Gerrish, K. (2001) 'The nature and effect of communication difficulties arising from interactions between district nurses and South Asian patients and their carers', *Journal of Advanced Nursing*, 33(5): 566–74

Gilbert, T. and Powell, J. (2010) 'Power and social work in the United Kingdom: a Foucauldian excursion', *Journal of Social Work*, 10(1): 3–22

Goodall, E. and Wilkins, P. (2015) *The Deprivation of Liberty Safeguards: A Best Interest Assessor Time Study*, accessed 21/04/22 at: www.cornwall.gov.uk/media/tekiq0tv/bia-time-survey-cornwall-final-pdf-november-2015.pdf

Gordon Training International (2021) 'Learning a New Skill is Easier Said Than Done', accessed 16/04/22 at: www.gordontraining.com/free-workplace-articles/learning-a-new-skill-is-easier-said-than-done

Graham, M. and Cowley, J. (2015) *A Practical Guide to the Mental Capacity Act 2005: Putting the Principles of the Act into Practice*, London, Jessica Kingsley Publishers

Hargreaves, R. (2010) *Mental Health Alliance Briefing Paper 1 – Deprivation of Liberty Safeguards: An Initial Review of Implementation*, Mental Health Alliance, London

HCPC (Health and Care Professions Council) (2018a) *Standards of Conduct, Performance and Ethics*, accessed 19/04/22 at: www.hcpc-uk.org/standards/standards-of-conduct-performance-and-ethics

HCPC (2018b) *Standards of Proficiency for Occupational Therapists*, accessed 19/04/22 at: www.hcpc-uk.org/standards/standards-of-proficiency/occupational-therapists

HCPC (2018c) *Standards of Proficiency for Practitioner Psychologists*, accessed 19/04/22 at: www.hcpc-uk.org/standards/standards-of-proficiency/practitioner-psychologists

HCPC (2018d) *Our Standards for CPD*, accessed 20/04/22 at: www.hcpc-uk.org/cpd/your-cpd/our-standards-for-cpd

Hemmington, J., Graham, M., Marshall, A., Brammer, A., Stone, K. and Vicary, S. (2021) *Approved Mental Health Professionals, Best Interests Assessors and People with Lived Experience: An Exploration of Professional Identities and Practice*, accessed 15/04/22 at: www.socialworkengland.org.uk/media/4046/amhp-bia-research-report.pdf

Heron, C. (1998) *Working with Carers*, London, Jessica Kingsley Publishers

Higham, P. (2013) 'Understanding continuing professional development', in J. Parker and M. Doel (eds) *Professional Social Work*, London, Sage/Learning Matters, pp 132–51

HIW/CIW (Health Inspectorate Wales/Care Inspectorate Wales) (2022) *Deprivation of Liberty Safeguards (DoLS) Annual Monitoring Report 2020-21*, accessed 13/4/22 at: https://hiw.org.uk/deprivation-liberty-safeguards-dols-annual-monitoring-report-2020-21

HM Government (2022) *Mental Capacity Act 2005 Code of Practice Including the Liberty Protection Safeguards*, accessed 23/04/22 at: https://assets.publishing.service.gov.uk/government/uploads/system/uploads/attachment_data/file/1061499/draft-code-of-practice.pdf

Holloway, M. (2020) 'Hidden in plain sight: social work, acquired brain injury and missed opportunities for change', in S. Braye and M. Preston-Shoot (eds) *The Care Act 2014: Wellbeing in Practice*, London, Sage/Learning Matters, pp 129–43

House of Commons and House of Lords Joint Committee on Human Rights (2021) *The Government's Response to COVID-19: Human Rights Implications*, accessed 16/04/22 at: https://committees.parliament.uk/publications/2649/documents/26914/default

House of Lords (2014) *Select Committee on the Mental Capacity Act 2005: Report of Session 2013–14 Mental Capacity Act 2005: Post-legislative Scrutiny*, accessed 21/04/22 at: https://publications.parliament.uk/pa/ld201314/ldselect/ldmentalcap/139/139.pdf

HSCIC (Health and Social Care Information Centre) (2012) *Mental Capacity Act 2005, Deprivation of Liberty Safeguards Assessments – England, 2011–12, Third Report on Annual Data*, accessed 21/04/22 at: https://digital.nhs.uk/data-and-information/publications/statistical/mental-capacity-act-2005-deprivation-of-liberty-safeguards-assessments/mental-capacity-act-2005-deprivation-of-liberty-safeguards-england-2011-12-third-report-on-annual-data

HSCIC (2015) *Mental Capacity Act (2005) Deprivation of Liberty Safeguards (England) Annual Report, 2014–15*, accessed 21/04/22 at: https://digital.nhs.uk/data-and-information/publications/statistical/mental-capacity-act-2005-deprivation-of-liberty-safeguards-assessments/mental-capacity-act-2005-deprivation-of-liberty-safeguards-england-annual-report-2014-15

Hsieh, E. (2016) *Bilingual Health Communication: Working with Interpreters in Cross-Cultural Care*, New York, Routledge

Hubbard, R. (2012) 'Can you recognise us?', *Social Work Matters*, September

Hubbard, R. (2018) 'Best Interests Assessor role: An opportunity or a "dead end" for adult social workers?', *Practice: Social Work in Action*, 30(2): 83–98

IFSW (International Federation of Social Work) (2014) 'Global Definition of Social Work', accessed 16/04/22 at: www.ifsw.org/what-is-social-work/global-definition-of-social-work

Janis, I. (1982) *Groupthink: Psychological Studies of Policy Decisions and Fiascos*, 2nd edn, Boston, Houghton Mifflin

Johns, R. (2014) *Capacity and Autonomy*, Palgrave Macmillan, Basingstoke

Johns, R. (2016) *Ethics and Law for Social Workers*, London, Sage Publications

Jones, R. (2016) *Mental Capacity Act Manual*, 7th edn, London, Sweet & Maxwell

Jones, R. (2018) *Mental Capacity Act Manual*, 8th edn, London, Sweet & Maxwell

Kaufman, E. and Engel, S. (2016) 'Dementia and well-being: a conceptual framework based on Tom Kitwood's model of needs', in *Dementia*, 15(4): 774–88

Kitwood, T. (1997) *Dementia Reconsidered: The Person Comes First*, Buckingham, Open University Press

Kong, C., Coggon, J., Dunn, M. and Ruck Keene, A. (2020) 'An aide memoire for the balancing act? Critiquing the balance sheet approach to best interests decision-making', *Medical Law Review*, 28(4): 753–80

Kuylen, M., Wyllie, A., Bhatt, V., Fitton, E., Michelowski, S. and Martin, W. (2022) 'COVID-19 and the Mental Capacity Act in care homes: Perspectives from capacity professionals', in *Health and Social Care in the Community*, accessed 03/06/22 at: https://onlinelibrary.wiley.com/doi/full/10.1111/hsc.13747

Langan, J. and Lindow, V. (2004) *Living with Risk: Mental Health Service User Involvement in Risk Assessment and Management*, Bristol, Policy Press

Law Commission (2015) *Mental Capacity and Deprivation of Liberty: A Consultation Paper*, accessed 30/6/16 at: www.lawcom.gov.uk/app/uploads/2015/07/cp222_mental_capacity.pdf

Law Commission (2016) *Mental Capacity and Deprivation of Liberty: Interim Statement*, accessed 30/6/16 at: www.lawcom.gov.uk/project/mentalcapacity-and-deprivation-of-liberty

Law Society (2015) *Deprivation of Liberty: A Practical Guide*, accessed 21/04/22 at: www.lawsociety.org.uk/en/topics/private-client/deprivation-of-liberty-safeguards-a-practical-guide

Lennard, C. (2015) 'Deprivation of Liberty Safeguards (DOLS): Where do we go from here?', *Journal of Adult Protection*, 17(1): 41–50

LGA/ADASS (2015) 'Mental Capacity Act Including the Deprivation of Liberty Safeguards: An Improvement Tool', accessed 20/04/22 at: www.local.gov.uk/publications/mental-capacity-act-including-deprivation-liberty-safeguards

LGO (Local Government Ombudsman) (2019) 'Thousands of vulnerable Staffordshire people deprived of their liberty without proper assessment', accessed 3/6/22 at: www.lgo.org.uk/information-centre/news/2019/apr/thousands-of-vulnerable-staffordshire-people-deprived-of-their-liberty-without-proper-assessment

Liberty (2013) *Liberty's Submission to the House of Lords Select Committee on the Mental Capacity Act 2005*, accessed 10/1/17 at: www.liberty-human-rights.org.uk/policy/policy-reports-briefings

Local Government and Social Care Ombudsman (2019) 'Investigation into a complaint against Staffordshire County Council: reference number: 18 004 809', accessed 11/04/22 at: www.staffordshire.gov.uk/Contact-compliments-and-complaints/complimentscommentscomplaints/lgscodolsreport.aspx

McCaw, L. and Grant, J. (2009) 'Record and report writing', in E. Duncan (ed) *Skills for Practice in Occupational Therapy*, Edinburgh, Elsevier, pp 191–208

Maclean, S. (2010) *The Social Work Pocket Guide to Reflective Practice*, Lichfield, Kirwin Maclean Associates

McNicoll, A. (2015) 'Case backlog leaves "worryingly high" number of people deprived of liberty without authorisation, warns CQC', *Community Care*, accessed 21/04/22 at: www.communitycare.co.uk/2015/01/26/case-backlog-leaving-worryingly-high-number-people-deprived-liberty-without-authorisation-warns-cqc

McNicoll, A. (2016) 'Government to face legal challenge over deprivation of liberty safeguards funding', *Community Care*, accessed 21/04/22 at: www.communitycare.co.uk/2016/06/07/government-face-legal-challenge-deprivation-liberty-safeguards-funding

McNicoll, A. (2017) 'Councils lose court battle for more deprivation of liberty funding', *Community Care*, accessed 21/04/22 at: www.communitycare.co.uk/2017/05/03/councils-lose-court-battle-deprivation-liberty-funding

Manthorpe, J., Rappaport, J. and Stanley, N. (2009) 'Expertise and experience: people with experiences of using services and carers' views of the Mental Capacity Act 2005', *British Journal of Social Work*, 39(5): 844–900

Martin, W., Michalowski, S., Stavert, J., Ward, A., Ruck Keene, A., Caughey, C., Hempsey, A. and McGregor, R. (2016) *The Essex Autonomy Project Three Jurisdictions Report: Towards Compliance with CRPD Art. 12 in Capacity/Incapacity Legislation across the UK*, accessed 21/04/22 at: https://autonomy.essex.ac.uk/resources/eap-three-jurisdictions-report

Mental Health and Justice/Wellcome (2022) 'The person's capacity seems to fluctuate', accessed 18/04/22 at: https://capacityguide.org.uk/flashpoints/the-persons-capacity-seems-to-fluctuate

Ministry of Justice (2008) *Mental Capacity Act 2005: Deprivation of Liberty Safeguards: Code of Practice*, accessed 13/04/22 at: www.cqc.org.uk/files/deprivation-liberty-safeguards-code-practice

Ministry of Justice (2021) *Human Rights Act Reform: A Modern Bill of Rights*, accessed 17/04/22 at: www.gov.uk/government/consultations/human-rights-act-reform-a-modern-bill-of-rights

Mughal, A. and Richards, S. (2015) *Deprivation of Liberty Safeguards (DoLS) Handbook*, Hounslow, BooksWise

Mughal, A. and Richards, S. (2022) *Deprivation of Liberty Safeguards (DoLS) Handbook*, 2nd edn, Hounslow, BooksWise

Neary, M. (2017) 'The very protective safeguards', Love, Belief and Balls, accessed 21/04/22 at: https://markneary1dotcom1.wordpress.com/2017/03/14/the-very-protective-safeguards

NHS Digital (2016) *Mental Capacity Act (2005) Deprivation of Liberty Safeguards (England) 2015-16, National Statistics*, accessed 21/04/22 at: https://assets.publishing.service.gov.uk/government/uploads/system/uploads/attachment_data/file/556032/Deprivation_of_Liberty_Safeguards__England___Annual_Report_2015-16.pdf

NHS Digital (2017) *Mental Capacity Act (2005) Deprivation of Liberty Safeguards (England) 2017, Official Statistics*, accessed 21/04/22 at: https://digital.nhs.uk/data-and-information/publications/statistical/mental-capacity-act-2005-deprivation-of-liberty-safeguards-assessments/mental-capacity-act-2005-deprivation-of-liberty-safeguards-england-2016-17-official-statistics

NMC (Nursing and Midwifery Council) (2018) *The Code: Professional Standards of Practice and Behaviour for Nurses, Midwives and Nursing Associates*, accessed 19/04/22 at: www.nmc.org.uk/standards/code

NMC (2021) *Continuing Professional Development*, accessed 20/04/22 at: www.nmc.org.uk/revalidation/requirements/cpd

Norman, A., Moore, S., Wotus, R., Holloway, M. and Dean, J. (2018) *Supported Decision Making: Brain Injury Case Managers' Experience of Mental Capacity and the Mental Capacity Act*, accessed 20/04/22 at: www.babicm.org/wp-content/uploads/2019/07/SDM-Survey-Article-Feb-2018BABICM.pdf

Nzira, V. and Williams, P. (2009) *Anti-Oppressive Practice in Health and Social Care*, London, Sage Publications

O'Connor, D. and Purves, B. (2009) 'Decision-making, personhood and dementia: mapping the terrain', in D. O'Connor and B. Purves (eds) *Decision-Making, Personhood and Dementia: Exploring the Interface*, London, Jessica Kingsley Publishing, pp 11–21

OFH (2020) *Mental Capacity: Dealing with Fluctuating Capacity*, accessed 18/04/22 at: www.ofhcare.co.uk/mental-capacity-dealing-with-fluctuating-capacity

Open University (2022) *Timeline of Learning Disability History*, accessed 21/04/22 at: www.open.ac.uk/health-and-social-care/research/shld/timeline-learning-disability-history

OPG (Office of the Public Guardian) (2020) *Mental Capacity Act 2005 Code of Practice*, accessed 13/04/22 at: www.gov.uk/government/publications/mental-capacity-act-code-of-practice

OPG (2021) *Find out if Someone has a Registered Attorney or Deputy*, accessed 20/04/22 at: www.gov.uk/government/publications/search-public-guardian-registers

O'Rourke, L. (2009) 'Practitioners demand more guidance and training in record-keeping', *Community Care*, accessed 21/04/22 at: www.communitycare.co.uk/2009/04/09/practitioners-demand-more-guidance-and-training-in-record-keeping

O'Sullivan, T. (2011) *Decision Making in Social Work*, 2nd edn, Basingstoke, Palgrave Macmillan

Parker, J. and Doel, M. (eds) (2013) *Professional Social Work*, London, Learning Matters/Sage

Preston-Shoot, M., Braye, S., Preston, O., Allen, K. and Spreadbury, K. (2020) *Analysis of Safeguarding Adult Reviews April 2017–March 2019: Findings for Sector-led Improvement – Final Report*, accessed 19/04/22 at: www.local.gov.uk/sites/default/files/documents/National%20SAR%20Analysis%20Final%20Report%20WEB.pdf

Prideaux, A. (2013) 'Issues in nursing documentation and record-keeping practice', *British Journal of Nursing*, 20(22): 1450–4

Pulzer, M. (2008) 'Ninth annual regional conference: Buckfast Abbey', *Mental Health Nursing*, 28(5): 13

Pyramid Educational Consultants Ltd (2016) *What is PECS? Picture Exchange Communication System?*, accessed 21/04/22 at: https://pecs-unitedkingdom.com/pecs

RCN (Royal College of Nursing) (2022) *Principles of Nursing Practice*, accessed 21/04/22 at: www.rcn.org.uk/professional-development/principles-of-nursing-practice

RCSLT (Royal College of Speech and Language Therapy) (2022) *Supported Decision-making and Mental Capacity*, accessed 20/04/22 at: www.rcslt.org/speech-and-language-therapy/guidance-for-delivering-slt-services/supported-decision-making-and-mental-capacity

Richards, S. (2016) *Do BIA Assessments under DoLS have a Positive Impact for People? Results of a National Survey*, accessed 15/9/16 at: www.edgetraining.org.uk/DoLS%20survey%20of%20BIAs%20%E2%80%93%20final%20print%20pdf.pdf

Ripfa (Research in Practice for Adults) (2014) *Practice Tool: Supporting Good Assessment*, Dartington, Ripfa

Rogers, C. (1980) *A Way of Being*, New York, Houghton Mifflin

Roosevelt, E. (1958) 'Remarks at the United Nations, March 27, 1958', accessed 21/04/22 at: harpers.org/2007/12/roosevelt-on-human-rights-in-the-small-places

Ruck Keene, A. (ed) (2015) *Assessment of Mental Capacity: A Practical Guide for Doctors and Lawyers*, 4th edn, London, British Medical Association/Law Society

Ruck Keene, A., Butler-Cole, V., Allen, N., Lee, A., Bicarregui, A. and Edwards, S. (2016) 'Court of Protection: Health, Welfare and Deprivation of Liberty', Mental Capacity Law Newsletter December 2016: Issue 70, accessed 23/04/22 at: https://1f2ca7mxjow42e65q49871m1-wpengine.netdna-ssl.com/wp-content/uploads/2016/12/MC-Newsletter-December-2016-Compendium.pdf

Ruck Keene, A., Butler-Cole, V., Allen, N., Lee, A., Kohn, N., Scott, K. and Edwards, S. (eds) (2017) *Mental Capacity Law Guidance Note: A Brief Guide to Carrying Out Best Interests Assessments*, accessed 23/04/22 at: www.39essex.com/wp-content/uploads/2017/11/Mental-Capacity-Guidance-Note-Best-Interests.pdf

Ruck Keene, A., Butler-Cole, V., Allen, N., Lee, A., Kohn, N., Scott, K., Barnes, K., Edwards, S. and David, S. (eds) (2021a) *Determining and Recording Best Interests*, accessed 18/04/22 at: mental-capacity-guidance-best-interests-december-2021.pdf (proceduresonline.com)

Ruck Keene, A., Butler-Cole, V., Allen, N., Lee, A., Kohn, N., Scott, K., Barnes, K. and Edwards, S. (eds) (2021b) 'Guidance Note: Relevant Information for Different Categories of Decisions', accessed 18/04/22 at: https://1f2ca7mxjow42e65q49871m1-wpengine.netdna-ssl.com/wp-content/uploads/2021/05/Mental-Capacity-Guidance-Note-Relevant-Information-for-Different-Categories-of-Decision-1.pdf

Ruck Keene, A., Butler-Cole, V., Allen, N., Lee, A., Kohn, N., Scott, K. and Edwards, S. (eds) (2022) *Carrying Out and Recording Capacity Assessments*, accessed 18/04/22 at: https://1f2ca7mxjow42e65q49871m1-wpengine.netdna-ssl.com/wp-content/uploads/2021/11/Mental-Capacity-Guidance-Note-Capacity-Assessment-May-2022.pdf

Rutter, L. (2013) *Continuing Professional Development in Social Work*, London, Learning Matters/Sage

Rutter, L. and Brown, K. (2015) *Critical Thinking and Professional Judgement for Social Work*, 4th edn, London, Sage Publications

Schön, D. (1983) *The Reflective Practitioner: How Professionals Think in Action*, London, Maurice Temple Smith

SCIE (Social Care Institute for Excellence) (2017) *IMCA and Paid Relevant Person's Representative Roles in the Mental Capacity Act Deprivation of Liberty Safeguards: SCIE Guide 41*, accessed on: 20/04/22 at: www.scie.org.uk/mca/imca/roles

SCIE (2020) *MCA Directory*, accessed 20/04/22 at: www.scie.org.uk/mca/directory

Scott, K. and Ruck Keene, A. (2021) *Fluctuating Capacity in Context,* accessed 18/04/22 at: https://1f2ca7mxjow42e65q49871m1-wpengine.netdna-ssl.com/wp-content/uploads/2021/12/Mental-Capacity-Guidance-Note-Fluctuating-Capacity-in-Context-December-2021.pdf

SCW (Social Care Wales) (2017) *Code of Professional Practice for Social Care*, accessed 19/04/22 at: https://socialcare.wales/cms_assets/file-uploads/Code-of-Professional-Practice-for-Social-Care-web-version.pdf

SCW (2019) *The Social Worker: Practice Guidance for Social Workers Registered with Social Care Wales*, accessed 11/04/22 at: https://socialcare.wales/cms_assets/file-uploads/Practice-guidance-social-workers.pdf

SCW (2021) *Codes of Practice and Guidance*, accessed 11/04/22 at: https://socialcare.wales/dealing-with-concerns/codes-of-practice-and-guidance

Series, L. (2016) 'The place of wishes and feelings in best interests decisions: *Wye Valley NHS Trust v Mr B*', *Modern Law Review*, 79(6): 1090–115

Series, L. (2017) 'Liberty Protection Safeguards: a response', in A. Ruck Keene (ed) *Special Report: the Law Commission's Mental Capacity and Deprivation of Liberty Report (Law Com No 372)*, accessed 21/04/22 at: www.39essex.com/wp-content/uploads/2017/04/Law-Commission-MCD-Special-Report-April-2017-2.pdf

Series, L. (2022) *Deprivation of Liberty in the Shadows of the Institution*, Bristol, Bristol University Press

Series, L., Fennell, P., Doughty, J. and Mercer, A. (2017) *Welfare Cases in the Court of Protection: A Statistical Overview*, accessed 21/04/22 at: http://sites.cardiff.ac.uk/wccop/files/2017/09/Series-Fennell-Doughty-2017-Statistical-overview-of-CoP-Key-findings.pdf

SWE (Social Work England) (2019a) *Registration Annotations*, accessed 13/04/22 at: www.socialworkengland.org.uk/registration/registration-annotations

SWE (2019b) *Professional Standards*, accessed 19/04/22 at: www.socialworkengland.org.uk/standards/professional-standards

SWE (2020a) *Professional Standards Guidance*, accessed 19/04/22 at: www.socialworkengland.org.uk/standards/professional-standards-guidance

SWE (2020b) 'Social Worker: Wayne Lamming Reg number: SW30011 Fitness to Practise Committee: Final Hearing', accessed 19/04/22 at: www.socialworkengland.org.uk/media/2986/mr-lamming-template-final-2022020-1.pdf

SWE (2020c) *Best Interests Assessors Training*, accessed 13/04/22 at: www.socialworkengland.org.uk/education-training/best-interest-assessors

SWE (2022a) *CPD Guidance*, accessed 20/04/22 at: www.socialworkengland.org.uk/cpd/cpd-guidance

SWE (2022b) *Consultation on New Education and Training Approval Standards for Approved Mental Capacity Professionals*, accessed 10/05/22 at: www.socialworkengland.org.uk/about/consultations/consultation-on-new-education-and-training-approval-standards-for-approved-mental-capacity-professionals

Talking Mats (2022) *About Talking Mats*, accessed 20/04/22 at: www.talkingmats.com/about/our-resources

Taylor, B. (2013) *Professional Decision Making and Risk in Social Work*, 2nd edn, London, Learning Matters/Sage

The College of Social Work (2013) *Best Interests Assessor Capabilities*, accessed 19/04/22 at: www.skillsforcare.org.uk/Documents/Learning-and-development/social-work/psw/BIA-capabilities.pdf

Thomas, J., Pollard, K. and Sellman, D. (2014) *Interprofessional Working in Health and Social Care: Professional Perspectives*, 2nd edn, Basingstoke, Palgrave Macmillan

Thompson, N. (2012) *Anti-Discriminatory Practice*, 5th edn, Basingstoke, Palgrave Macmillan

Tribe, R. (2009) 'Working with interpreters in mental health', *International Journal of Culture and Mental Health*, 2(2): 92–101

Valois, N. (2016) 'Expert tips on how to improve your best interests assessor reports', *Community Care*, accessed 21/04/22 at: www.communitycare.co.uk/2016/03/04/expert-tips-improve-best-interests-assessor-reports

Walsh, C. (2017) 'Initial thoughts on the Law Commission's Liberty Protection Safeguards', in A. Ruck Keene (ed) *Special Report: the Law Commission's Mental Capacity and Deprivation of Liberty Report (Law Com No 372)*, pp 13–16, accessed 21/04/22 at: www.39essex.com/wp-content/uploads/2017/04/Law-Commission-MCD-Special-Report-April-2017-2.pdf

Welsh Assembly Government (2009a) *Guidance for Managing Authorities Working within the Mental Capacity Act Deprivation of Liberty Safeguards*, accessed 21/04/22 at: https://abuhb.nhs.wales/files/mental-health/deprivation-of-liberty-safeguards/dols-guidance-for-managing-authority-pdf

Welsh Assembly Government (2009b) *Guidance for Supervisory Bodies working within the Mental Capacity Act Deprivation of Liberty Safeguards*, accessed 21/04/22 at: www.wales.nhs.uk/sites3/Documents/744/Guidance%20for%20Supervisory%20Bodies.pdf

Welsh Government (2015) *Mental Capacity Act: Deprivation of Liberty Guidance and Forms*, accessed 12/04/22 at: https://gov.wales/mental-capacity-act-deprivation-liberty-guidance-and-forms

Welsh Government (2022a) *Open Consultation: Liberty Protection Safeguards*, accessed 21/04/22 at: https://gov.wales/liberty-protection-safeguards

Welsh Government (2022b) *The Liberty Protection Safeguards: Workforce Plan and Training Framework*, accessed 22/04/22 at: https://gov.wales/sites/default/files/consultations/2022-03/the-liberty-protection-safeguards-workforce-plan-and-training-framework.pdf

WFOT (World Federation of Occupational Therapists) (2012) 'Definition of occupational therapy', accessed 16/04/22 at: www.wfot.org/about/about-occupational-therapy

Whitaker, D. (2014) 'Social justice for safeguarded adults deprived of their liberty in the United Kingdom?', *Disability and Society*, 29(9): 1491–5

Williams, S. and Rutter, L. (2015) *The Practice Educator's Handbook*, 3rd edn, London, Sage/Learning Matters

Williams, S. and Tsui, W. (2008) 'The nature of practice wisdom in social work revisited', *International Social Work*, 51(1): 47–54

Wilson, E., Seymour, J. and Perkins, P. (2010) 'Working with the Mental Capacity Act: findings from specialist palliative and neurological care settings', *Palliative Medicine*, 24(4): 396–402

Y Weinyddiaeth Gyfiawnder (2008) 'Deddf Gallu Meddyliol 2005 Trefniadau diogelu rhag colli rhyddid', accessed 21/04/22 at: https://webarchive.nationalarchives.gov.uk/ukgwa/20130104224411/http://www.dh.gov.uk/en/Publicationsandstatistics/Publications/PublicationsPolicyAndGuidance/DH_085476

Statutes and case law

UK law operates by the principle of 'precedent', which means that when judges interpret statute in courts, they must consider the decisions made by other courts concerning the same situations, and where a binding decision has been made by a higher court, that judgement must be used to guide decisions in lower courts. Figure A1 shows the hierarchy of courts in which judgments relevant to mental health and mental capacity law practice are likely to be made.

Figure A1: Court structure relevant to Deprivation of Liberty Safeguards

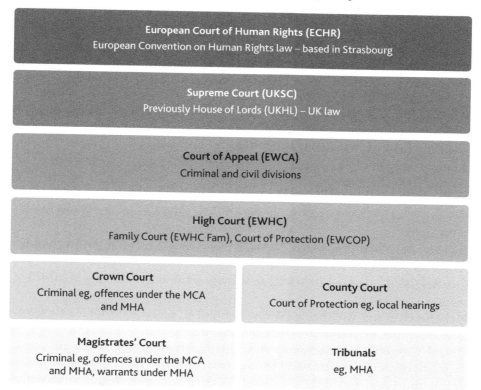

European Court of Human Rights (ECHR)
European Convention on Human Rights law – based in Strasbourg

Supreme Court (UKSC)
Previously House of Lords (UKHL) – UK law

Court of Appeal (EWCA)
Criminal and civil divisions

High Court (EWHC)
Family Court (EWHC Fam), Court of Protection (EWCOP)

Crown Court
Criminal eg, offences under the MCA and MHA

County Court
Court of Protection eg, local hearings

Magistrates' Court
Criminal eg, offences under the MCA and MHA, warrants under MHA

Tribunals
eg, MHA

Statutes, including statutory instruments and conventions

We have organised the statutes by date, from oldest to most recent.

Children Act (1989), accessed 22/04/22 at: www.legislation.gov.uk/ukpga/1989/41/contents

Human Rights Act (1998), accessed 20/04/22 at: www.legislation.gov.uk/ukpga/1998/42/contents

Mental Capacity Act (2005), accessed 20/04/22 at: www.legislation.gov.uk/ukpga/2005/9/contents

United Nations Convention on the Rights of Persons with Disabilities (2006), accessed 19/04/22 at: www.un.org/development/desa/disabilities/convention-on-the-rights-of-persons-with-disabilities.html

Mental Health Act (1983, as amended 2007), c 20, accessed 20/04/22 at: www.legislation.gov.uk/ukpga/1983/20

Mental Capacity (Deprivation of Liberty: Standard Authorisations, Assessments and Ordinary Residence) Regulations 2008 (SI 2008/1858), accessed 18/04/22 at: www.legislation.gov.uk/ukdsi/2008/9780110814773

Mental Health (Approved Mental Health Professionals) (Approval) (England) Regulations (2008) (SI 2008/1206), accessed 18/04/22 at: www.legislation.gov.uk/uksi/2008/1206/contents/made

Mental Health (Approval of Persons to be Approved Mental Health Professionals) (Wales) Regulations (2008) (SI 2008/2436), accessed 18/04/22 at: www.legislation.gov.uk/wsi/2008/2436/made

Coroners and Justice Act (2009), accessed 18/04/22 at: www.legislation.gov.uk/ukpga/2009/25/section/7

European Court of Human Rights (2010) European Convention on Human Rights, accessed 20/04/22 at: www.echr.coe.int/Documents/Convention_ENG.pdf

Equality Act (2010), accessed 20/04/22 at: www.legislation.gov.uk/ukpga/2010/15/contents

Care Act (2014), accessed 20/04/22 at: www.legislation.gov.uk/ukpga/2014/23/contents/enacted

Social Services and Well-being (Wales) Act (2014), accessed 20/04/22 at: www.legislation.gov.uk/anaw/2014/4/contents/enacted

Mental Capacity (Amendment) Act (2019), accessed 18/04/22 at: www.legislation.gov.uk/ukpga/2019/18/enacted

Health and Care Act (2022), accessed 03/06/22 at: www.legislation.gov.uk/ukpga/2022/31/contents/enacted

Draft LPS Regulations

When the revised MCA Code and LPS is implemented, use the final versions that will have been ratified by Parliament.

Mental Capacity (Deprivation of Liberty: Assessments, Determinations and Pre-Authorisation Reviews) (England) Regulations 202X, accessed 28/06/22 at https://assets.publishing.service.gov.uk/government/uploads/system/uploads/attachment_data/file/1060136/draft-LPS-regulations-assessment-determinations-and-pre-authorisation-reviews.pdf

Mental Capacity (Deprivation of Liberty: Training and Approval as an Approved Mental Capacity Professional) (England) Regulations 202X, Draft Statutory Instrument, accessed 22/04/22 at https://assets.publishing.service.gov.uk/government/uploads/system/uploads/attachment_data/file/1060139/draft-LPS-regulations-approved-mental-capacity-professionals.pdf

The Mental Capacity (Deprivation of Liberty: Training and Criteria for Approval as an Approved Mental Capacity Professional) (Wales) Regulations 2022, Draft Statutory Instrument, accessed 22/04/22 at https://gov.wales/sites/default/files/consultations/2022-03/the-mental-capacity-deprivation-of-liberty-training-and-criteria-for-approval-as-an-approved-mental-capacity-professional-regulations-2022.pdf

Case law

We have arranged **case law** (or common law) alphabetically by theme to assist readers to find cases relevant to any queries they may have. Some are relevant to more than one subject area, so may appear under more than one heading.

Within the themes, the cases are then organised by date, with the most recent appearing first. For example, the Supreme Court's decision in the *P v Cheshire West and Chester Council* and *P and Q (MIG and MEG) v Surrey County Council* cases, which is binding on all subsequent deprivation of liberty cases in England and Wales, appears first. Then it is followed by the Court of Appeal, Court of Protection and so on judgments in the relevant cases.

16- and 17-years-olds

Re D [2019] UKSC 41, accessed 22/04/22 at: www.supremecourt.uk/cases/docs/uksc-2018-0064-judgment.pdf

D (A Child) [2017] EWCA Civ 1695, accessed 22/04/22 at: www.bailii.org/ew/cases/EWCA/Civ/2017/1695.html

Birmingham City Council v D [2016] EWCOP 8, accessed 22/04/22 at: www.bailii.org/ew/cases/EWCOP/2016/8.html

Trust A v X and A Local Authority [2015] EWHC 922 (Fam), accessed 22/04/22 at: www.bailii.org/ew/cases/EWHC/Fam/2015/922.html

Age assessment

B (R on the application of) v Mayor and Burgesses of the London Borough of Merton [2003] EWHC 1689, accessed 20/04/22 at: www.asylumlawdatabase.eu/sites/default/files/aldfiles/UK_060%20Judgment.pdf

Best interests decision-making, including medical treatment, deprivation of liberty, available options and COVID-19 decisions

Cornwall Council v NP and BKP [2020] EWCOP 44, accessed 20/04/22 at: www.bailii.org/ew/cases/EWCOP/2020/44.html

BP v Surrey County Council and Anor [2020] EWCOP 22, accessed 16/04/22 at: www.bailii.org/ew/cases/EWCOP/2020/22.html

N v ACCG and Ors [2017] UKSC 22, accessed 20/04/22 at: www.bailii.org/uk/cases/UKSC/2017/22.html

A Local Authority v X [2016] EWCOP 44, accessed 20/04/22 at: www.bailii.org/ew/cases/EWCOP/2016/44.html

North Yorkshire County Council and A Clinical Commissioning Group v MAG and GC [2016] appeal EWCOP 5, accessed 20/04/22 at: www.bailii.org/ew/cases/EWCOP/2016/5.html

Re MN (Adult) [2015] EWCA Civ 411, accessed 20/04/22 at: www.bailii.org/ew/cases/EWCA/Civ/2015/411.html

King's College Hospital NHS Foundation Trust v C and V [2015] EWCOP 80, accessed 20/04/22 at: www.bailii.org/ew/cases/EWCOP/2015/80.html

Wye Valley NHS Trust v B [2015] EWCOP 60, accessed 20/04/22 at: www.bailii.org/ew/cases/EWCOP/2015/60.html

Westminster City Council v Manuela Sykes [2014] COP1238388T, accessed 20/04/22 at: www.bailii.org/ew/cases/EWHC/COP/2014/B9.html

Re M (Best Interests: Deprivation of Liberty) [2013] EWCOP 3456, accessed 20/04/22 at: www.bailii.org/ew/cases/EWCOP/2013/3456.html

Aintree University Hospitals NHS Foundation Trust v James and others [2013] UKSC 67, accessed 20/04/22 at: www.supremecourt.uk/cases/docs/uksc-2013-0134-judgment.pdf

Re A (Male Sterilisation) [2000] 1 FLR 549, accessed 18/04/22 at: www.cirp.org/library/legal/Re_A2000

Defensible decision-making

Montgomery v Lanarkshire Health Board [2015] UKSC 11, accessed 20/04/22 at: www.bailii.org/uk/cases/UKSC/2015/11.html

Bolitho v City and Hackney Health Authority [1997] 3 WLR 1151 HL, accessed 20/04/22 at: www.bailii.org/uk/cases/UKHL/1997/46.html

Bolam v Friern Hospital Management Committee [1957] 1 WLR 582, summary of judgment accessed 20/04/22 at: www.lawteacher.net/cases/bolam-v-friern-hospital-management.php

Deprivation of liberty

R (Ferriera) v HM Senior Coroner for Inner South London and others [2017] EWCA Civ 31, accessed 18/04/22 at: www.bailii.org/ew/cases/EWCA/Civ/2017/31.html

Liverpool City Council & Anor, R (On the Application Of) v The Secretary of State for Health [2017] EWHC 986, accessed 20/04/22 at: www.bailii.org/ew/cases/EWHC/Admin/2017/986.html

Re NRA and Ors [2015] EWCOP 59, accessed 20/04/22 at: www.bailii.org/ew/cases/EWCOP/2015/59.html

P v Cheshire West and Chester Council and Another and *P and Q v Surrey County Council* [2014] UKSC 19, accessed 20/04/22 at: www.bailii.org/uk/cases/UKSC/2014/19.html

Cheshire West and Chester Council v P [2011] EWCA Civ 1257, accessed 20/04/22 at: www.bailii.org/ew/cases/EWCA/Civ/2011/1257.html

Cheshire West and Chester Council v P [2011] EWHC 1330 (COP), accessed 20/04/22 at: www.bailii.org/ew/cases/EWCOP/2011/1330.html

Re P and Q, P and Q v Surrey County Council, sub nom Re MIG and MEG [2011] EWCA Civ 190, accessed 20/04/22 at: www.bailii.org/ew/cases/EWCA/Civ/2011/190.html

Re MIG and MEG [2010] EWHC 785 (Fam), accessed 20/04/22 at: www.bailii.org/ew/cases/EWHC/Fam/2010/785.html

Storck v Germany 61603/00 [2005] ECHR 406, accessed 20/04/22 at: www.bailii.org/eu/cases/ECHR/2005/406.html

HL v The United Kingdom 45508/99 [2004] ECHR 471, accessed 20/04/22 at: www.bailii.org/eu/cases/ECHR/2004/471.html

Guzzardi v Italy 7367/76 [1980] ECHR 5, accessed 20/04/22 at: www.bailii.org/eu/cases/ECHR/1980/5.html

Doctrine of necessity

R v Quayle and Others [2005] EWCA Crim 1415, accessed 20/04/22 at: www.bailii.org/ew/cases/EWCA/Crim/2005/1415.html

HL v UK 45508/99 [2004] ECHR 471, accessed 20/04/22 at: www.bailii.org/eu/cases/ECHR/2004/471.html

R v Dudley & Stephens [1884] 14 QBD 273 DC, summary accessed 20/04/22 at: www.lawteacher.net/cases/r-v-dudley-and-stephens.php

Imputability to the state

LB Haringey v R and Ors [2016] EWCOP 33, accessed 20/04/22 at: www.bailii.org/ew/cases/EWCOP/2016/33.html

Staffordshire County Council v SRK [2016] EWCOP 27, accessed 20/04/22 at: www.bailii.org/ew/cases/EWCOP/2016/27.html

Lasting Power of Attorneys, deputyships and deprivation of liberty

Mrs P v Rochdale Borough Council and Others [2016] EWCOP B1, accessed 20/04/22 at: www.bailii.org/ew/cases/EWCOP/2016/B1.html

Length of Deprivation of Liberty Safeguards authorisation including covert medication

Re AG [2016] EWCOP 37, accessed 20/04/22 at: www.bailii.org/ew/cases/EWCOP/2016/37.html

P v Surrey County Council and Surrey Downs Clinical Commissioning Group [2015] EWCOP 54, accessed 20/04/22 at: www.bailii.org/ew/cases/EWCOP/2015/54.html

Mental capacity assessment, including causative nexus, salient points and residence

QJ v A Local Authority [2020] EWCOP 7, accessed 19/04/22 at: www.bailii.org/ew/cases/EWCOP/2020/7.html

London Borough of Tower Hamlets v A and KF [2020] EWCOP 21, accessed 18/04/22 at: www.bailii.org/ew/cases/EWCOP/2020/21.html

Royal Borough of Greenwich v CDM [2019] EWCOP 32, accessed 18/04/22 at: www.bailii.org/ew/cases/EWCOP/2019/32.html

NCC v PB and TB [2014] EWCOP 14, accessed 12/04/22 at: www.bailii.org/ew/cases/EWCOP/2014/14.html

Derbyshire County Council v AC, EC and LC [2014] EWCOP 38, accessed 20/04/22 at: www.bailii.org/ew/cases/EWCOP/2014/38.html

PC v City of York Council [2013] EWCA Civ 478, accessed 20/04/22 at: www.bailii.org/ew/cases/EWCA/Civ/2013/478.html

LBX v K, L and M [2013] EWHC 3230 (Fam), accessed 20/04/22 at: www.bailii.org/ew/cases/EWHC/Fam/2013/3230.html

CC v KK and STCC [2012] EWCOP 2136, accessed 20/04/22 at: www.bailii.org/ew/cases/EWCOP/2012/2136.html

Mental Health Act/Deprivation of Liberty Safeguards interface

Welsh Ministers v PJ [2018] UKSC 66, accessed 18/04/22 at: www.supremecourt.uk/cases/docs/uksc-2018-0037-judgment.pdf

Secretary of State for Justice v MM, Welsh Ministers v PJ [2017] EWCA Civ 194, accessed 18/04/22 at: www.bailii.org/ew/cases/EWCA/Civ/2017/194.html

AM v South London and Maudsley NHS Foundation Trust and Anor [2013] UKUT 365, accessed 20/04/22 at: www.bailii.org/uk/cases/UKUT/AAC/2013/365.html

GJ v The Foundation Trust [2009] EWHC 2972 (Fam), accessed 20/04/22 at: www.bailii.org/ew/cases/EWHC/Fam/2009/2972.html

Objection

RD & Ors (Duties and Powers of Relevant Person's Representatives and Section 39D IMCAs) [2016] EWCOP 49, accessed 20/04/22 at: www.bailii.org/ew/cases/EWCOP/2016/49.html

Re AJ (DoLS) [2015] EWCOP 5, accessed 20/04/22 at: www.bailii.org/ew/cases/EWCOP/2015/5.html

Role of the Relevant Person's Representative and Independent Mental Capacity Advocate

RD & Ors (Duties and Powers of Relevant Person's Representatives and Section 39D IMCAs) [2016] EWCOP 49, accessed 20/04/22 at: www.bailii.org/ew/cases/EWCOP/2016/49.html

Re AJ (DoLS) [2015] EWCOP 5, accessed 20/04/22 at: www.bailii.org/ew/cases/EWCOP/2015/5.html

London Borough of Hillingdon v Steven Neary and Others [2011] EWCOP 1377, accessed 20/04/22 at: www.bailii.org/ew/cases/EWCOP/2011/1377.html

Safeguarding, including Article 8 right to privacy and family life

Essex County Council v RF and Ors [2015] EWCOP 1, accessed 20/04/22 at: www.bailii.org/ew/cases/EWCOP/2015/1.html

Somerset County Council v MK and Others [2014] EWCOP B25, accessed 20/04/22 at: www.bailii.org/ew/cases/EWCOP/2014/B25.html

Milton Keynes Council v RR and Others [2014] EWCOP B19, accessed 23/04/22 at: www.bailii.org/ew/cases/EWCOP/2014/B19.html

London Borough of Hillingdon v Steven Neary and Others [2011] EWCOP 1377, accessed 20/04/22 at: www.bailii.org/ew/cases/EWCOP/2011/1377.html

Local Authority X v MM and Another [2007] EWHC 2003 (Fam), accessed 20/04/22 at: www.bailii.org/ew/cases/EWHC/Fam/2007/2003.html

Index

Printed and bound by CPI Group (UK) Ltd, Croydon, CR0 4YY

25/03/2025

14647338-0001